YOU CAN Grow
African Violets

YOU CAN Grow African Violets

◆

The Official Guide Authorized by the African Violet Society of America, Inc.

Kent and Joyce Stork

iUniverse, Inc.
New York Lincoln Shanghai

YOU CAN Grow African Violets
The Official Guide Authorized by the African Violet Society of America, Inc.

Copyright © 2007, 2008 by African Violet Society of America Inc.

All rights reserved. No part of this book may be used or reproduced by any means, graphic, electronic, or mechanical, including photocopying, recording, taping or by any information storage retrieval system without the written permission of the publisher except in the case of brief quotations embodied in critical articles and reviews.

iUniverse books may be ordered through booksellers or by contacting:

iUniverse
2021 Pine Lake Road, Suite 100
Lincoln, NE 68512
www.iuniverse.com
1-800-Authors (1-800-288-4677)

Because of the dynamic nature of the Internet, any Web addresses or links contained in this book may have changed since publication and may no longer be valid.

The views expressed in this work are solely those of the author and do not necessarily reflect the views of the publisher, and the publisher hereby disclaims any responsibility for them.

Based on the "For Beginners" columns written for the *African Violet Magazine* by Kent and Joyce Stork

ISBN: 978-0-595-44344-4 (pbk)
ISBN: 978-0-595-88674-6 (ebk)

Printed in the United States of America

Dedicated to the members of the Lincoln AVS and the Omaha AVGS and to our many violet friends around the world.

Special thanks for help with editing must go to the members of the AVSA Publications Committee, Barbara Pershing, chairman, as well as to Ellen Frilseth and Chris Leppard.

Contents

Introduction xiii

Section One—The Basics of Growing African Violets

CHAPTER 1	Light: It Makes a Shining Difference 3	
CHAPTER 2	Water: the Essential Growing Factor 13	
CHAPTER 3	Choosing the Ideal Violet Pot 21	
CHAPTER 4	The Scoop on Dirt: Choosing the Correct Potting Medium 26	
CHAPTER 5	The Art of Fertilizing. . . . Just Enough 34	
CHAPTER 6	Air and Temperature—the Invisible Growing Factors. 40	
CHAPTER 7	How to Use Good Advice 45	

Section Two—Special Techniques

CHAPTER 8	Propagating by Leaf Cuttings 51	
CHAPTER 9	Maintaining a Single Crown and Dealing with Suckers 59	
CHAPTER 10	Repotting Violets. 66	
CHAPTER 11	Secrets to Blooming Success 76	
CHAPTER 12	Getting a Violet to Bloom on Schedule 81	

Chapter 13	Big and Beautiful: Growing Huge African Violets	86
Chapter 14	Different Kinds of Violets	91
Chapter 15	Life on the Edge: Growing Variegated Violets	96

Section Three—Beyond the Fundamentals

Chapter 16	A Beginner's Guide to Judging	105
Chapter 17	Good Grooming for Violets	112
Chapter 18	African Violet Diseases	115
Chapter 19	What You Need to Know about Pests and Pesticides	124
Chapter 20	Good Housekeeping	134
Chapter 21	Keeping Cultural Practices in Balance	139
Chapter 22	Can This Violet Be Saved?	144
Chapter 23	Where Do Violets Come From?	150
Chapter 24	Beginner's Guide to Hybridizing	158
Chapter 25	The Sporting World of African Violets	164
Chapter 26	Introducing the Relatives: The Gesneriad Family	169
Chapter 27	Using Violets in Design	174
Chapter 28	Good Investments—Buying Violets by Mail Order	180
Chapter 29	Survival Techniques for Violets When the Owner must be Away	184

Section Four—Just For Fun

Chapter 30	Violet Quirks	191

Chapter 31	African Violets Myths and the Real Truth	195
Chapter 32	What Kind of Grower Are You?	199
Chapter 33	Test Your Violet I.Q.	207
Index		213

Introduction

The African Violet Society of America (AVSA) welcomes you to the wonderful world of growing and enjoying America's favorite houseplant, the African violet. We believe that "anyone can grow African violets." All that is needed is some good advice and information, and this book is designed to do just that.

Before you read this book, we would like for you to get to know the association and the authors who are imparting their expertise just for you. A brief overview of the chapters will give you an idea of the content and organization of this book as you proceed on your journey to successful African violet growing.

The African Violet Society of America was organized in 1946 as an association of persons interested in the African violet. Stated purposes of the association are to stimulate interest in the propagation and culture of the African violet (saintpaulia); promote distribution of cultivars and species; and publish reliable, practical information of interest to members. AVSA is a clearinghouse of information about African violets. The Society maintains a web site <www.avsa.org> where information is available on membership, affiliate clubs, shows, conventions and much more. The FAQ—frequently asked questions—on the web site is a very popular source of information.

The first issue of the *African Violet Magazine*, the official publication of AVSA, was published in 1947. An index of issues from 1947 to the current year is available on the web site and an annual index is published for the previous year's magazines. Membership in AVSA includes a subscription to the magazine.

AVSA maintains a Master List of Species and Cultivars, commonly referred to as the African Violet Master List (AVML), and is the official registration authority on African violet cultivars. In addition to the printed AVML available through the AVSA office, a computer database, FirstClass, is also available for purchase. This database lists nearly fifteen thousand named cultivars, over nine thousand of which are registered with AVSA. The database includes approximately three thousand photos and it is possible to search by name, hybridizer, photos, size, type, color of blossom and more.

AVSA also sells publications including Insect and Mite Pests of African Violets by Dr. Charles Cole, Growing to Show by Pauline Bartholomew and The AVSA Handbook for Growers, Exhibitors, and Judges.

AVSA holds a national convention each spring. In addition, local and regional affiliates hold annual shows and sales. For information on an affiliate or affiliate show near you, go to the AVSA web site

Anyone interested in African violets is eligible for membership in this society. In addition to members and affiliates in every state, AVSA has a large international membership with affiliates and members on all but one continent.

The AVSA Office is at 2375 North Street, Beaumont, TX 77702. Phone 409-839-4725.

Kent and Joyce Stork have written over sixty "For Beginners" columns for the *African Violet Magazine* over a period of ten years. These columns have contained information that is far more than just for "beginners." The AVSA realized these columns contained a gold mine of valuable information that should be available to anyone who wants to know just about all there is to know about African violets, from the very basic culture (light, water, soil, and fertilizer), to the finer points of growing prize-winning show plants and hybridizing for new varieties. This book, *YOU CAN Grow African Violets,* is an outgrowth of bringing these columns together in an updated and organized book.

Kent and Joyce Stork bring to this endeavor a wealth of knowledge and experience that makes them authorities in all areas of growing, hybridizing, showing, and judging African violets. They are leaders in this organization and have served local, regional and the national organization in many capacities. Both Kent and Joyce are senior judges, have served on the AVSA Board of Directors, chaired many committees and have held numerous offices.

Kent and Joyce started their journey to becoming master violet growers in 1973 with the gift of their first African violet, "Rhapsodie Gigi." Joyce says, "My mother had violets in our southeast kitchen window as we grew up and they always seemed effortless." Unfortunately their first violet died. Kent went to the library and found a book on growing violets; they attended a violet exhibition by a local club, searched out named varieties, and joined AVSA. Kent began making hybrid crosses and they were soon selling violets out of their home. Not long after, they opened their flower shop which specialized in growing African violets. They own and operate Kent's Flowers in Fremont, Nebraska.

Kent has received many national awards for his hybrids, his commercial display tables, and best in show and best collections for both amateur and commercial exhibits at AVSA standard shows. Joyce has also won awards in horticulture and design, and has received recognition for her hybridizing work in petrocosmea, a relative of African violets.

Let's take a brief "walk-through" of this book. As you leaf through the pages, you may be overwhelmed with all of the information and wonder if this is a book that you must read from front to back in order to get the most of its content. While this might be a useful way to go, perhaps you have some pressing concerns or problems with your plants. You might go to the chapter that is most likely to help you at the moment and then go back and read other chapters.

If you are just beginning your adventure in growing African violets, start with the first section. Follow along through the next chapters of Section I and learn about the basic growing factors of light, water, soil and potting, fertilizing, and air. You may be amazed at how these factors influence your plants. Chapter 7 cautions you on how advice must be adapted to your personal situation.

Once you get beyond these basics, there is so much more to learn. Section II of this book goes beyond the basics and gives techniques to achieve perfection in your plants. Learn the techniques for starting new plants from leaves, what to do with suckers and necks, how to grow large standards and how to grow the small miniatures and semi-miniatures.

Repotting is a necessary and time-consuming task but it is very important. Learning about soil mixes and potting techniques can help make this task less stressful. Everyone wants their plants to bloom, and if they are going to show plants they want them to bloom on schedule.

Violets with variegated leaves can be a bit tricky to grow, but the tips in the chapter on variegates will get you on the right track. Trailers are lots of fun. Tips on training them as well as learning about species are included in Chapter 14.

Keeping a jump ahead of problems is a very important concept in maintaining a collection of African violets. Section III goes beyond the fundamentals and explains many things you can and should do to improve the appearance and health of your violets. The chapter on grooming gives you many tips and suggestions on keeping your plants looking their best and the chapter on good housekeeping will help you keep your growing environment in tip-top condition. Hopefully, you won't need the information in the chapters on fungus and insects and pests. But just about everyone who grows African violets encounters powdery mildew, mites, thrips, or mealy bugs of one type or another at some time or another. Learn to be proactive and be able to identify troubles before they get out of control. These chapters will tell you what to do if you aren't so lucky and find yourself with one or another of these problems in your collection.

Ever wonder where African violets came from? Africa of course; but learn about the discovery and history of the African violet, the species plants that grew and still grow in Africa, and how we have come to have the thousands of cultivars, many registered with AVSA, that are listed in the current African Violet Master List. The African violet has come a long way since it was discovered late in the nineteenth century and made the journey through Germany to America. From the small blue/purple blossoms on most of the species plants, we now have many colors and shapes, edges, fantasies, chimeras, thumb-prints, and more through sporting and hybridizing. You will find the chapters on sporting and hybridizing fascinating reading even if you aren't interested in hybridizing; but if you are, you will find this information very helpful.

Design sections are included in AVSA standard shows. The chapter on using violets in design will give you information on the various ways that African violets plants and blossoms are used.

African violets are members of the gesneriad family. You could say that African violets are cousins to the "other" members of the gesneriad family. Many people grow some of the "other gesneriads" as houseplants, such as streptocarpus, episcias, kohlerias and others and are unaware that they are a part of this family. Chapter 26 gives an introduction to several of these "cousins."

Section IV, Just for Fun, is more than just fun—the chapters in this section provide good information in another way. For example, how much do you know about growing African violets? Try the Violet IQ quiz. You may be surprised at how much you already know or don't know! There are many myths that have been passed around and down from "grandma." Things change as we learn more about the needs of violets and many of the so-called myths just aren't helpful; some are just downright trouble. Learn the real truth. And, while you are reading this section, determine what kind of grower you are. Do any of the scenarios fit you?

Now that you have an idea of what to expect in the following pages of this book we wish you good reading and good growing. YOU CAN grow African violets!

Barbara Pershing
Chairman, AVSA Publications Committee

Section One—The Basics of Growing African Violets

1

Light: It Makes a Shining Difference

It all begins with light. Light is essential for plant growth. It is one of the most important factors involved in the successful cultivation of African violets. Lack of adequate light often results in poor, asymmetrical growth and the absence of bloom. Finding the right light can turn a novice into a skilled grower!

Variety Makes a Difference

Before we can talk about light, we have to point out an important fact: African violet varieties do not all perform the same way in the same conditions. Some bloom more frequently and/or more abundantly than others. Some plants grow with more open spaces between the leaves, while others grow with overlapping foliage. Some varieties grow large, while others remain small. These are genetic differences that are built into the individual varieties. Similarly, different cultivars (the term commonly used to refer to cultivated hybrids) of African violets also have different genetic light requirements.

As a general rule, plants with darker foliage tend to need more intense light than plants with lighter foliage. However, there are exceptions to that rule. Growers need to watch the violets in their collections for signs of too much or too little light. Violets receiving too little light will bloom sparsely. Foliage will develop long petioles (leaf stems) and stretch upward, reaching for light. Leaves will become thin and weak.

Plants receiving too much light may display distorted tight growth, or may show definite signs of bleaching. Light green foliage will bleach to a pale yellow-green or near-white color. Dark green foliage will bleach to a coppery brown tone. Leaf stems may become brittle. Flowers are often smaller than expected. Some varieties may begin to grow with leaves hugging the pot, pulling down and away from the light source.

Plants receiving ideal light will bloom regularly and (all other conditions being right) frequently. The foliage will retain a healthy green color. Leaves will grow out evenly and horizontally, creating a flat-wheel effect.

Plants growing side-by-side may exhibit the symptoms of too much or of too little light, while others in the group may appear to be perfectly happy. This would be due to genetic differences in the cultivars.

The Choices

There are two main choices of light for most growers: natural or artificial. Each has its advantages and disadvantages.

The best source of natural light is usually a nice bright window. It is homey and pleasant, but quite changeable as seasons pass. Window light is perfect for the casual grower. Some prefer to use greenhouses for large collections; but while they can be excellent for growing many types of plants, temperature variations and humidity must be strictly controlled to avoid major problems with growing African violets.

For those who prefer to provide artificial light, the best choice at this time is fluorescent light. This allows precise control of light without too much heat and is relatively inexpensive. Most serious growers with larger collections choose this means.

Fluorescent Lighting

A poll of the membership was done in 1993 by the African Violet Society of America (AVSA). One of the surprising results of that poll was that 82% of those responding used fluorescent lights to grow their violets, 44% grew at the window (obviously some were using multiple methods), and 4% had greenhouses. If you are a beginning grower who only uses natural window light, you can quickly see that a large proportion of serious growers believe in the value of adding artificial light.

What has that 82% found worthwhile about fluorescent light? Probably the most satisfying benefit is the additional blooming! When violets are grown in natural light, they have to depend on a constantly changing length of daylight. In the spring, as the daylight lengthens to twelve hours or more, plants at the window respond with the heaviest blooming period of the year. In the dead of winter, when the day lengths are much shorter (or even nonexistent for those near the polar regions), violets pout about the lack of light and seldom bloom. There are also the dangerous times of year when the sun may be at just the right angle to burn leaves, or when snow cover may reflect light too intensely causing bleaching of foliage.

Weather patterns can also reduce light, especially when there are long extended periods of cloudy skies. However, if a regular and constant amount of adequate light is provided daily, African violets respond with blossoms throughout the year.

A second benefit that comes from using artificial light is more compact growth. It is often easy to recognize African violets grown in windows by their long, leggy leaves and upward growth pattern. When quality light is provided, new leaves will grow with shorter petioles (stems), and the growth will tend to be flatter. Artificial light helps plants to grow with fewer gaps between leaves. It also slows the development of a neck underneath the leaves, since rows of leaves grow in closer-fitting ranks.

A third benefit of artificial light is more symmetrical growth. Since the light comes from directly overhead, it reaches all sides of the foliage fairly evenly. There is not as much need to turn plants to avoid lopsided growth.

A fourth benefit is less temperature variation which can lead to an unevenness of growth. Plants often take on a sturdier look when they are not exposed to the constantly changing temperatures resulting from natural sunlight.

Finally, artificial light allows growers to use space that would otherwise be unfit for growing plants. Basements, interior rooms, and walls away from windows will all produce beautiful blooming plants with the addition of fluorescent lights. That also means that you can have more plants!

Why is Fluorescent Light Best?

Fluorescent light is produced with vacuum tubes that are lined with phosphors, chemical substances that can be energized to emit light. Phosphors do not all produce the same light spectrum. The color spectrum is divided into three primary groups: the red rays, the yellow/green rays, and the blue rays. By mixing various phosphors, it is possible to achieve the exact color spectrum desired. It is not possible to do this with incandescent light bulbs. Because most incandescent light produces very little of the blue rays and produce more heat than is desirable, these bulbs are usually not satisfactory for growing plants.

Plants do not need all of the light waves that are available in the spectrum. The blue and especially the red rays are the most influential in plant growth and flowering. The yellow/green rays provide the brightness of the light, but are ineffective in stimulating plant growth. Infrared, which is invisible, is actually harmful to plants. Being able to control exactly which rays are used allows growers to maximize their results.

Fluorescent light should not be confused with ultraviolet light tubes. They are quite different and only the former will produce the desired result.

Setting Up a Fluorescent Light Unit

The first fluorescent light system that African violet growers choose will often depend on the budget. The most economical are the shop light units that are usually very affordable at discount stores. These can be hung from the underside of cupboards, tables, or shelves. Primitive light unit structures can be made using sheets of plywood and cement blocks, as we did back in our poorer-than-church-mice days (one of our plywood sheets was actually an old used signboard!). These low-cost systems work fine and are fairly fast to set up.

A second alternative is to build shelves that fit a particular space. The methods of building custom light units vary greatly. We used lumber, but others have used aluminum or PVC pipe. It often depends on the material your in-house builder prefers! Shop lights may be the fixture choice, but higher quality fluorescent light fixtures can be found at a somewhat higher cost.

Obviously growers may also choose to use the pre-built units offered by vendors who cater to indoor plant hobbyists. These are usually a more expensive choice, but they are well-designed, sturdy, and suitable for using in rooms where you live and work and sometimes have company.

Along with the light setup, a timer is useful for turning the lights on and off, controlling the light time. Inexpensive timers can be found in any hardware department. These often wear out in a year or two. Heavy-duty timers (sometimes called "air conditioner timers") are more expensive but will last longer and are probably safer. Newer digital electronic timers, with no moving parts, also seem to last well while offering the advantage of lower cost.

Finally, the whole rig must be plugged into an electrical outlet. One simple shop light will not overtax most household circuits, but when you begin to add multiple units—be careful! Each tube uses up to forty watts of electricity; the ballast uses about eight watts, and the timer will use about two watts. Add these numbers up and compare it to the number of watts that the electrical wiring is able to provide. A simple test is to feel the cords; if they are warm, there is a need to boost the wiring capacity or to increase the number of circuits being used. (This is the point when your loved ones, who do not share your passion, will begin to panic.) As much as possible, plug units directly into the wall and avoid the excessive use of extension cords, for safety's sake. Aside from the damage to your home, consider how many violets you could lose in an electrical fire! Don't take chances with this.

Rules for Growing Under Lights

There are two critical factors that must be considered when setting up to grow under fluorescent light: the length of light time and the distance from the light tube to the foliage surface. These are both factors affecting the foot-candles of light.

For most African violet collections, operating the lights about ten to twelve hours a day and positioning the light tubes about ten to twelve inches from the leaf surface will produce good results. That is a useful general rule, but good growers have learned how to adjust. If it is necessary or desirable to grow the violets closer to the tubes, the hours per day should be shortened. If violets must be further away, then lengthen the day, up to eighteen hours maximum.

Old fluorescent tubes produce less light than new ones. Very new tubes produce extremely intense light for a short period of time then gradually decrease until the tube end blackens, at which point the light intensity decreases rapidly. This means that if a light unit has two brand-new tubes, it may be best to operate the light unit for only eight hours a day at first, and gradually increase the light time by one hour a week until twelve hours is reached. A simpler solution is to replace only one tube at a time. Older light tubes may need to be operated for longer periods of time each day to compensate for the loss of intensity. Blackened tubes are not very efficient, and it is probably less expensive just to replace them.

Certain violets will need more light than others. More light can be provided by extending the hours of light time or by moving the light tubes and plants closer together. Plants demonstrate a need for more light by reaching up toward the light. Miniatures often seem to need more light and do well six to eight inches from the lights. To grow well, heavily variegated plants will probably need to be set directly under the center of fluorescent tubes where the light is the most intense, although those with a greater percentage of green seem to function well without special treatment.

Of course, in all of this, you must also consider a practical matter of space. If plants seem to need more light, you can move them closer to the light, but if the plant and the light tube are too close together, it will be difficult to pick up plants or to move them. It may be more workable to extend the length of light time to give yourself room to move.

If certain plants indicate that they need less light by bleaching or developing tight center growth, it is best to move those to the edge of the light shelf or to the end of the light tubes. The light is far less intense in those areas. They will need to be turned regularly to offset the tendency of leaning into the light.

When using fluorescent lights in a room that has lots of natural light, it is probably not necessary to run the lights quite as long. In rooms that are entirely void of outside illumination, the lights may need to run for longer hours.

Remember, violets also need sleep! It is during the dark hours that many important plant functions take place. Twenty-four-hour-a-day light is very hard on plants. Be sure the plants are in the dark for at least six hours a day.

Watching your plants react to light is a remarkable thing. They will truly tell you how they feel in the light that they are receiving. Pay attention, and every plant will soon be placed exactly where it belongs.

How Much Does All of This Electricity Cost?

We have to thank a fellow African violet grower, Chuck Cromer, of Lincoln, Nebraska, for developing a simple guideline for figuring the cost of running fluorescent light units. He figures that for each light unit (with two forty-watt tubes) operating eleven hours a day, approximately one-kilowatt hour (KWH) of electricity will consumed. If you are using a longer light time, you will be underestimating your power usage.

Now, count the number of light units that you have, multiply by one KWH (this is not very hard), and then multiply that times the cost of a KWH on your electricity bill. This gives you the cost per day of running your lights. If that doesn't seem bad, multiply it times thirty to find the monthly cost. If it seems a little too extravagant, go see how beautiful your plants look under the lights!

Because some areas of the country have extremely high electricity costs, especially during summer, violet growers often deliberately cut back on plants under lights during summer months. This can be done by temporarily moving plants to windows, by removing outside rows of leaves from plants to allow more violets to fit under fewer lights, or by selling or disposing of the extras.

The Issue of Light Tube Cost, Efficiency, and Cosmetic Value

What is the best light tube for you to use? There are three considerations—cost, efficiency, and cosmetics.

Cost is a necessarily important consideration since some fluorescent tubes can cost ten times as much as others! The cheapest tubes, usually called shop lights, produce less light and do not last as long. Slightly higher in cost are the cool white tubes. The warm whites are a bit higher yet, and the specialized-growing tubes, sold under the brand names of Gro-lux and Gro-lux WS (wide spectrum), will be even more.

Efficiency factors are good for all except the low-end shop light. All have good lasting quality (if you are using a reputable brand). The light spectrum is somewhat better for growing and flowering in the Gro-Lux tube, but is not bad even in the cool white tubes. The standard Gro-Lux has a lower light intensity. The Gro-Lux WS is considered by many to be the best for growing at this time.

Cosmetic values also come into consideration. Cool white tubes have a bluing effect on all surfaces—your skin, your interiors, and your violets. Blue violets look beautiful under cool whites, but reds and pinks on the other hand are dulled. Warm white and Gro-Lux tubes enhance the pink tones, and the standard Gro-Lux can actually make burgundy look like brilliant red. It is all cosmetic; colors have not actually changed at all. You will like the additional cosmetic effect of the pinker lights if the light unit is near your make-up mirror (or in a room decorated in pinkish tones).

We have long believed that a combination of one cool white and one Gro-Lux WS make violet colors look as much as possible as they would in natural light—that's the cosmetic consideration. Considering the cost of the Gro-Lux, we also like the economy that comes with that combination. If cost is critical and cosmetics are minor, cool white tubes alone will produce beautiful violets.

This has actually been a short summary of the vast amount of information available about fluorescent light growing. Additional information is available from light dealers and manufacturers. Be careful, though; they seldom recommend the inexpensive (but satisfactory) cool whites.

The good news is that for a fairly small investment of time and money, you can join the crowd of folks who love to grow African violets under lights. It's a brilliant idea!

A Different Art—Growing Violets in a Window

When AVSA did the research study of the membership, it was discovered that 44% grow violets at the window. Because 86% grew African violets under fluorescent lights, it seems to indicate that even those who use artificial light also often enjoy having violets on their window sills.

Top competitive growers insist on using fluorescent light to achieve the perfection of growth and flowering required to win shows. Nonetheless, there is a special charm in seeing violets growing on a windowsill. How often has artwork included a window sill violet? It gives a sense of home, of innocence, and of freshness. The plant may not be perfect enough to win a prize, but it makes us feel good. Window-grown violets deserve their place in our hearts and homes!

Choosing a Window

The real secret to successful daylight growing is the window itself. Violets prefer to have twelve hours of relatively bright light each day followed by a period of relative darkness. Not all windows offer this.

A good growing window needs to be relatively large, allowing lots of light to enter the room. African violets usually need to be within one or two feet of the window so that they receive plenty of bright light. This will encourage them to grow and bloom well.

Even though bright light is desirable, direct sunlight is usually not preferred. Violets will tolerate only some direct light during the day. In the wilds of Africa, the species of saintpaulia (the botanical name of African violets) grew under a dense canopy of overhanging trees which filtered the light. Many window growers find that sheer curtains do wonders in subtly limiting the light during the sunniest hours without blocking it.

Also, consider the temperature at the window. Ideally, it should be near 72º F (20º C). Even with modern air conditioning and heating, it is possible for the temperature near the window to be more than ten degrees different from the rest of the room. Steps must be taken to correct situations in which a cold draft seeps in during colder months or where late afternoon sun beats in during the summer.

If possible, the window selected should not be one that is often opened to outside air. Several insect enemies of violets are able to travel into a home on an air current. Window screens offer little protection because the insects are so small. No amount of chemical treatment will protect violets if new populations of bugs can enter the room with every breeze. Furthermore, violets could be blown over by a strong gust of wind and seriously damaged.

Look also for the location of heating and air conditioning ducts. Outlets that allow dry air to blow across violets will cause flower buds to wither and die as they are forming, causing your plants to remain out of bloom. Nearby registers (those that are directly above or below the window or within a foot or two) should either be closed or modified with a cover to direct the air away from your plants.

Be sure your window is convenient for use as a growing area. A spot with well-placed shelves or old-fashioned broad windowsills usually works well. Avoid placing a plant on top of a television or appliance that will produce too much heat and could be damaged by spilled water. High traffic areas, be they for humans or pets, may not be as safe for plants.

While these guidelines will help you find the best window, don't give up the hobby if no perfect window is present. Most windows offer at least somewhat brighter light than is usually available in interior spaces. That brighter light is the key to getting violets to flower. Plants may thrive at one window in particular but will probably survive (with proper care) in any window that is available.

Fine Tuning the Location

Once a good window is chosen, it becomes important to watch how individual violets react in the location. Some hybrids (often those with light green foliage or with very little red in the underside of leaves) may exhibit symptoms of bleaching when grown in very bright windows. This happens because the plentiful light accelerates photosynthesis in the leaves causing the chlorophyll to be depleted. Usually the supply is refreshed during the nighttime hours when photosynthesis slows. If severe depletion occurs, however, the leaves will lose the vivid green color and perpetually look bleached or faded. These plants need to be set a little farther away from the window or off to the side somewhat.

Some hybrids will react to too much light by hugging lower leaves to the sides of the pot. This is not the same as wilting. In this case, leaves will be quite turgid but will stubbornly grow downward. Ideally, leaves should develop in a flat wheel that extends out horizontally from the center crown. Move these umbrella-shaped plants to a slightly dimmer area, where leaves should relax upward. (Please note that some varieties have this habit as a genetic trait. If dimmer light doesn't improve the shape, accept the shape as inevitable.) Sometimes older leaves on the outside rows never recover and should be removed to allow newer leaves to grow out horizontally.

Some violets will "reach up" in window light, especially if the light is not quite bright enough. When mature leaves begin to stretch upward, it is an indication that violets want more light than is available. Some varieties are more light-hungry than others! Move these plants as near the window as possible, in the very brightest spot.

Most violets will begin to tip or lean toward the glass even in the best windows. Plants are quite good at positioning themselves to receive the maximum light available. As time passes, however, the leaning may become so exaggerated that the plants are apt to tip over easily. To avoid this, consistently turn the plants to expose all sides to the brighter light. We know one grower who would begin each day by turning every plant in his office window a quarter turn. Other growers with less time might choose to turn plants with each watering.

Repotting

The downside of window growing is that your violets will need to be repotted more frequently if you want a well-groomed look. As a violet matures, outside leaves age and sag, needing to be removed. The result of grooming off old leaves is the appearance of an unattractive "neck" or stem under the bottom row of leaves. This happens to all violets, but it seems to happen faster in the window where temperatures tend to be less consistent and, as a consequence, the plant tissue isn't as sturdy. This means that leaves tend to have softer stems and tend to age fairly quickly. It also happens because leaves usually do not grow as compactly in window light because there is more space between leaf axils.

Some Violets Prefer Windows

While many violets seem to bloom and grow more consistently under fluorescent lights, there are some that seem to prefer natural light. They grow quickly and bloom freely there.

Many of the species, the original plants that were discovered in Africa, thrive in windows and even bloom better because of temperature variations. The foliage of species plants is more likely to maintain a rich green color in the window, without the bleaching out that is often seen when these plants are grown under lights. Species also tend to have a less perfect form or pattern of growth no matter where they grow, so the irregularities of growth at the window are less noticeable or annoying.

Some trailing varieties thrive in natural sunlight and are very attractive in hanging containers near a window. Even those varieties of trailers that do best under lights will normally grow acceptably well in windows, especially if they are rotated regularly to expose all sides to the brightest light. Window-grown trailers often develop less perfectly than those grown under lights, but they are particularly charming in windows.

There Are Lots of Reasons to Grow at the Window

If 45% of the membership of AVSA is growing at the window, imagine how many in the general public are using that method. Violets grown this way will seldom win prizes at major shows, but they are a delight nevertheless. A violet in your kitchen window may make it worth the effort to wash dishes. A violet in your living area gives a wonderfully homey look. Violets thriving in bay windows make long winters seem bearable. Surely violets became such a popular houseplant because they grow and bloom in windows!

2

Water: the Essential Growing Factor

We can't live without it and neither can our African violets. It seems so elemental and abundant. But bad water and poor watering techniques can probably be blamed for most violet mortalities.

In Aristotle's Nicomachean Ethics he refers to a "golden mean" in which man finds a balance between two extremes. When it comes to growing violets, the "golden mean" is finding the point at which plants are damp enough without being too wet. It is also finding water that is pure enough without being too pure. It is finding a system that provides adequate humidity without encouraging disease. The "golden mean" also must be affordable and easy, effective and attractive. Aristotle said it was difficult and rare for a man to find that point of moderation, and it is a constant challenge for violet growers as well.

Wet Enough But Not Too Damp

We killed our first African violet. We think it probably suffered from being first too wet and then too dry. It may have had the misfortune to be left standing in water a couple of times. That little "Rhapsodie Gigi" never really had a chance.

A common error of casual African violet growers is to water as we did—whenever they think about it or when it looks dry with sagging limp leaves. They unfortunately give it a thorough watering in an attempt to rescue it. Roots that were first allowed to dry and shrivel now are overwhelmed with more water than can be absorbed, to the point that all air is forced out of the soil. Violets may tolerate this as a rare occasion,; but if it is routine, the root system will be damaged and vulnerable to rot diseases.

Top watering (pouring water into the top of the pot, under the leaves) or bottom watering (filling the saucer, allowing the pot to soak up the water) are both common methods used to water African violets. Both are effective if water is offered on a regular schedule before the soil is bone dry and the plant is wilting. It is imperative that you check the saucer a half an hour or so after watering to empty out water that was not soaked up in that time.

Plants must receive enough water to keep cells well hydrated throughout the plant structure. Turgid leaves are a good indication that a plant is receiving adequate moisture.

Top watering has an advantage in that it leaches the excess salts from the soil into the run-off water. Many growers who use other watering systems still water from the top occasionally for just this reason.

Those who choose to top water should pay close attention to the water temperature. Roots will be damaged if the water is more than ten degrees different (either colder or hotter) than the soil temperature (which is often also the room temperature). Brief root shock caused by too cold or too hot water can result in irregular patches on leaves that are lighter green and often veined. More severe damage to the roots will likely result in premature leaf failure.

Many African violet hobbyists use systems that provide an even supply of water, generally referred to as "constant water systems." These vary greatly in design, but all provide water on a regular basis without allowing too much. Most growers use fertilizer in their water so that the system is also a constant fertilizer method. In such a case, weak solutions of fertilizer are used (often one-fourth teaspoon or less of water-soluble granular fertilizer per gallon of water).

Wick Watering

Wick watering is fairly inexpensive to set up and highly effective. A wick, made of nylon, acrylic, or other man-made materials, is inserted into the pot so that one end dangles into a source of water while the other end is in the soil. It works on the principle of capillary action. Water molecules attract one another and can pull each other along. When the wick is saturated, a chain of water molecules is formed. As the roots absorb water, which is pulled into the plant, the molecules are pulled along the chain. As long as there is a continuing source of new molecules, the chain will keep moving water up the wick and into the root system.

There are several keys to successful wick watering. First, the potting mix must be very light and porous to avoid over-saturation. This is true with almost all of the constant water methods! If in doubt, experiment with a few violets before committing your entire collection to a new watering system.

Second, the water source must be below the pot so that the root system is entirely above the water line, with air space in between. In large growing areas, this water source might be open trays of water that are topped with open wire screening or plastic grating. The plants sit on the wire or grating with the wicks hanging down into the water. A simple version can be done with a plastic food tub, which has a nickel-sized hole cut into the lid. The plant sits on the lid with its wick dropped through the hole into the tub (reservoir) full of water. It is also possible to purchase pots and saucers, as well as big trays specifically designed for wick watering, from indoor gardening suppliers.

Finally, the wick must offer an unimpeded route for the water to travel. If the wick is pinched so that it does not go straight down into the water, or if it becomes clogged with root growth or mineral build-up, the water molecules may be blocked. Similarly, if the water source goes dry, or if the wick does not quite reach the water, there is no continuous source of water molecules. As a result, the water can no longer follow other molecules along the route, and the wick must be restarted. Usually setting the pot in an inch of lukewarm water for thirty minutes will start the capillary action working again, but in the case of overgrown roots or mineral buildup, it's probably best to repot or at least re-wick.

Some materials used for wick-watering, such as yarn, may be treated with chemicals to make it water-repellant. We find that soaking the wicks in soapy water (before inserting them) usually breaks down the chemical and improves water take-up.

How to get the wick in there? Different growers have different methods.

We use a stiff #20 florist wire to make a tool by bending one end into a "U" shape similar to a crochet hook. We catch one end of a wet eight-inch length of wicking material (we prefer acrylic yarn) in the hooked end and then push the straight end of the hook into a hole in the bottom of the pot. The wick is pulled through the root system and up to the top of the soil. It is necessary to guess where the wire will come through and move leaves to avoid puncturing. The wick should then be tugged down a bit so that the end is just below the soil level. The wicking will start more successfully if the pot stands in an inch of water for several minutes before moving it to the grating or individual reservoir.

Other growers choose to hang a damp piece of wicking material over the rim of an empty pot with the other end dangling through a hole in the bottom of the pot and then to repot with the wick in place. Yet another method involves winding the wick in a circle on the bottom of an empty pot before repotting.

Capillary Matting

A second system for providing constant water is capillary matting. In this method, the potted plants sit on a spongy pad or matting, which is saturated with water. The mat provides good contact with the bottom of the pot but keeps the water level below the roots. Some growers like to put wicks in the pots to guarantee that the water moves up and through the soil.

The capillary matting may be made from any soft, man-made material that will retain water and will not rot. Homemade systems using batting, foam carpet padding, or acrylic blanket fabric all work fairly well. Indoor light gardening vendors offer commercially made matting with one surface coated with ventilated plastic.

Regardless of the type of matting chosen, it must be cut to size and placed in a sturdy tray that will hold water. Some growers like to make a wick that hangs from the tray and down to a source of water so that the matting remains constantly wet. We personally prefer to allow the matting to become moderately dry before pouring additional water into our trays.

Again, it is extremely important that the potting mix is very light and porous to avoid absorbing more water than the roots can tolerate.

Texas-Style Potting

A third system for constant water is called "Texas-style potting." This was invented in Texas by some talented growers who had great success with it. It was soon copied in many other states.

Texas potting uses pots with holes strategically placed along the sides near the bottom of the pot. A layer of perlite is placed in the bottom of the pot to cover these holes, and the violet is then planted in a light potting mix above the perlite level. The pots are set in a tray of water which is deep enough just to cover the holes, allowing water to seep into the soil at a predictable rate. It is an effective system, as are the others that have already been described.

Decorative, Self-Watering Pots

A number of specially designed African violet pots are offered in retail outlets. Usually they will be composed of two parts, one to hold the water and one to hold the plant. Each pot is designed so that a small amount of water can reach the soil at all times. Many innovative styles are offered which are made of plastic or ceramic materials. These are oftentimes quite decorative and allow growers to keep beautiful plants in living areas.

Beware of pots that do not provide for drainage. Without drainage holes, salts from fertilizers are trapped in the potting mix. They can be used, but it is wise to repot at least once per year to change the potting mix.

Always remember—it is very important to be sure the potting mix is porous and provides plenty of air for roots. Otherwise, the soil will absorb too much water and the plant will not thrive.

Problems and Cures

Both wicking and capillary matting can result in a few problems for growers. One of the most common is a buildup of alga, a green slimy plant that thrives in stagnant water that is exposed to light. Algae spores are generally found in water and grow quickly when conditions are favorable. Growers may choose to change water frequently, washing trays with bleach before refilling, or they may wish to use an algaecide such as one called Physan 20, which discourages the growth of algae in water.

Minerals in water will also begin to build up on the surface and sides of the trays, especially in areas with hard water. This can be removed occasionally with a vinegar or mild acid solution.

In low humidity there may be extensive evaporation from open trays of water. If this is your situation, it is wise to decrease the amount of the fertilizer added to the water to avoid concentrations of nutrients that could result in fertilizer burn. If the fertilizer is usually mixed at a rate of one-fourth teaspoon to a gallon of water, decrease it to one-eighth teaspoon to a gallon.

It is still necessary to water plants from the top occasionally in order to leach salts out of the potting mix. Fertilizers contain chemical salts which build up and damage plants. When doing this, use plenty of tepid water so that it runs out the bottom drainage holes. Plants are adequately leached when the drain-off water is clear with no yellow discoloration. Discard this drainage water.

Because wicking and capillary matting often use common sources of water for several plants, there is increased opportunity for insects and fungus to travel between plants. At the same time, because it is so much easier to fill one tray every week or so, a grower may be inclined to look only casually at individual plants. If the grower isn't seeing a problem, and the problem has a convenient travel route between plants, that problem may get out of control! It requires real discipline to examine plants faithfully when growing with the ease of a constant water system.

Whenever trying a new system of watering, remember to experiment on only a few plants at first. Once you know the system is working, you can safely switch an entire collection.

Water Quality

Water can vary dramatically from one locale to the next. Mineral content (like iron or sulfur, for example), system additives, salt levels, wetness and the pH level can greatly affect how plants grow.

If your water is very high in mineral content you may have to adjust fertilizer levels. Agricultural regions, in particular, may have high nitrate levels in water which can cause fertilizer burn markings on outermost leaves. Certain minerals may be present in excess and block the absorption of other nutrients.

As a rule, the three macronutrients of nitrogen, phosphorus and potassium affect the outside older leaves when excessive amounts are in the water (especially in combination with an added fertilizer). The micronutrients (such as copper, iron, and manganese) which are needed only in minute quantities will tend to affect the inner newest leaves when in excess. Toxic levels of the micronutrients are most likely to occur when both the water supply and the fertilizer contain the same element.

Water is often monitored by local government. When contamination problems are detected, chemicals may be added to keep the water supply safe. Some of those chemicals are not good for plants. Chlorine has been a common additive for some time, and as long as it was allowed to evaporate before watering plants, it caused no problems. Chloramines are now being added instead for their stability and because they do not evaporate. Many growers are finding that aquarium suppliers are the best source of information and materials to compensate for the addition of chloramines.

Some areas of the United States have to deal with especially high salt content in their water. Similarly, many individuals have softened water in their homes which also has a high salt content. Such water cannot be used successfully for long periods of time to water African violets or many other plants. The salt actually draws water out of the cells and mars leaf margins. Sometimes the salt will accumulate in the center of the crown creating a sort of crust. Older leaves fail more rapidly than necessary and ultimately the plant may die. It is crucial that an alternative source of water be found.

Water wetness can also vary. If water is slightly soapy, for example, it is wetter and more likely to stick to the potting mix. This can lead to oversaturated soil. It may be necessary to add more perlite (or other soil lighteners) to the mix to allow for more air.

Water's pH level can also greatly affect a plant's ability to use nutrients. Arid regions tend to have more alkaline (high pH) water, while rainy regions tend to be more acid (low pH.) Soil can be mixed to compensate for these factors (usually adding dolomite lime to buffer the pH), or plants can be repotted more frequently into fresh potting mix.

There is a delicate chemical balance between the water, the soil, and the fertilizer. It may take considerable experimenting to achieve perfection. Local agricultural extension agents may be able to assist in analyzing water if you believe you have a problem.

Often growers will look for another water source when they suspect that their water is of poor quality. One option is to purchase jugs of water processed in a reverse osmosis system that removes harmful materials. It is possible to install a reverse osmosis system into most home situations and the resulting water seems to be quite good for violet growing.

Collecting rainwater may be another option, but use caution. Rainwater, which runs off a roof and through drain spouts before being collected, may include insect eggs, fungus and bacterial spores. It is necessary to allow the rain to rush over the surface for a period of time to wash contaminants away before collection begins, thus removing most of the impurities and making the water much safer for your plants.

Distilled water is pure water, and easily available if you use a dehumidifier, but it is not perfect either. When used over a long period of time, this water can actually draw minerals out of the plant cells. Because it lacks buffering, distilled water is also prone to quick pH changes (from adding fertilizer for example). It is a satisfactory short-term solution if your regular water source is poor, but exercise caution if using only distilled water for long periods of time.

Humidity and Pesky Fungus

Since many of the constant water systems involve open sources of water, there is a natural increase in the level of the humidity around the plants. This humidity can be a real positive, encouraging flower bud development and extending the life of blossoms. But it can also be a real problem because of fungus disease. Many fungi need high humidity to thrive. Mildew and botrytis, two very damaging fungi that attack African violets, can be almost uncontrollable if humidity levels reach 80%. That level of humidity may also damage your home or growing area structurally, especially if you live in an area with cold seasons.

There are several solutions. One is to limit the amount of open water that can evaporate. Some growers cover trays with plastic or use plastic-coated matting that has many tiny holes to allow seepage without evaporation. Using individual water reservoirs for each plant in sealed containers also reduces humidity. Ventilation systems can also help.

Another solution is to use matting and allow it to go dry before rewetting. We have used this method without any noticeable loss in the quality of plant growth. A side benefit has been a decrease in the population of pesky fungus gnats and shore flies.

Cost Effective, Practical, and Attractive

Whatever system of watering is chosen, it must fit the lifestyle of the grower. It must be affordable, be easy enough to guarantee that watering gets done on time, and be attractive enough to satisfy the aesthetic tastes of the grower.

Individual self-watering decorative pots are great for hobbyists who have a small collection of African violets in their home. Those with extensive collections often choose to use larger community trays to water violets in non-decorative pots.

Regardless of how you choose to water your violets, remember to water them. Water them well, with fertilizer, using the best quality water you can manage. Be sure to provide good drainage and watch the humidity.

3

Choosing the Ideal Violet Pot

Pots are an important element in the growing of African violets, but pots are not a part of nature. In nature, violets species grew in small pockets of compost found between rocks and on the moss that topped the rock. It is probable that the method of growing in pots actually produces stronger plants, but only when the pot reproduces the conditions that nature originated. Those conditions in nature restricted root growth, allowed for drainage of excess moisture, and supported leaves as they grew. So, considering this, what is the best pot?

Clay or Plastic?

Pots are either porous or nonporous. Clay pots are porous—that is, they allow water and air to move through the side walls. Plastic, glazed ceramic and decorative brass pots are nonporous. This discussion will be confined to clay and plastic pots, which are those most commonly used by African violet fanciers.

Clay pots can be a good growing choice, especially for beginners who may be tempted to over-water their plants. The clay pot will allow excess water to evaporate more quickly from the potting medium. This is especially helpful when growing in hot regions or in greenhouses; the evaporation will cool the pot significantly and keep the roots more comfortable. The clay also allows air to enter the pot, and violet roots love to have air.

Clay pots can cause a few problems, too. The salts in the water, soil, and fertilizer tend to accumulate in the clay walls and particularly to collect on the rims. When violet leaf stems (petioles) touch the salty clay, the cells begin to dry at that point and soon the entire leaf may be lost. Growers solve this problem by covering the top edge of the pot with foil, plastic, or even melted paraffin wax (although mold will sometimes grow under the wax seal). Clay pots also tend to be cumbersome, which is a problem if plants are often moved. Because of their weight and shipping costs involved they tend to be relatively expensive, especially for those who grow a lot of violets.

Even with a less porous potting mix, it is necessary to water plants grown in clay more frequently than those grown in plastic, which can be a great disadvantage to busy people. Unfortunately, clay does not lend itself to wicking or capillary mat watering because moisture tends to evaporate out faster than it can be drawn up from below. Plants must be individually watered, usually every four to five days.

And clay pots do need to be thoroughly cleaned before they can be reused. The pots will often develop crusts of mineral around the outside of the pot, and occasionally molds will also grow. It is wise first to scrub the pot, then to soak it for several hours in a bleach solution to kill mold and bacteria.

Plastic pots are frequently the choice of advanced growers because they can wick- or mat-water large collections of plants easily. For those who water plants individually, once-a-week watering works well. Plastic does not absorb salts as the clay does, so it is not necessary to cover the pot edge. Plastic pots are quite easy to clean for reuse. Plastic is also easier to find, lighter weight, and less expensive. And plastic pots are great for those who prefer to write the plant name on the side of the pot.

Since plastic pots are nonporous, it is especially important to use a potting mixture that has a loose texture with many larger bits of material such as perlite or vermiculite. This allows for the incorporation of more air into the soil surrounding the roots and will thus promote healthier roots.

Plastic pots should be chosen carefully. Inferior pots are available with sharp top edges. This type rim may injure the leaves as soon as any pressure is applied. The violet grower should find pots with "rolled" or blunted rims, which will protect the leaf from such injury. African violet vendors do a great job of finding these special pots. If it should happen that rolled rim pots are unavailable, it is possible to slice clear polyvinyl tubing down one side and then to fit it over the sharp rim.

Whether growers choose clay or plastic, there are several other considerations in selecting a good pot.

Adequate Drainage

In east central Africa nature provided a run-off system so that, as the species received water from rain and mist from streams, the natural compost would not become saturated and roots were never left to stand in pooled water. In our homes today, violets rarely survive for long periods in pots that do not provide sufficient drainage.

Clay pots usually have only one hole in the center of the bottom. The porous material breathes off enough excess moisture that this is adequate. Plastic pots will usually have three, four or more holes. When multiple drainage holes are combined with an indented bottom, excess moisture will drain very effectively.

When watering each plant individually, a saucer is needed below the plant to catch the run-off. Nature didn't need to worry about ruining the furniture! The saucer may or may not be attached to the pot. In either case, it is important that the water level in the saucer remains below the bottom of the pot most of the time.

Correct Size

Violet roots will generally not go deeper than 4 inches into the soil. For this reason, violet pots are often more shallow or squatty than pots designed for the more upright-growing plants which have deeper root systems. Some growers have had good success growing in pan pots which are only two or three inches deep.

The root system of an African violet usually grows to be about one-third the span of the leaves. If a violet is twelve inches in diameter, the root ball will probably be only about four inches across. For this reason, the *Handbook for African Violet Growers, Exhibitors, and Judges* recommends that the plants be grown in pots that are one-third the diameter of the leaf span.

Violets do tend to bloom best in pots that are tight for the roots. It seems that when the roots are limited, the survival-of-the-species instinct is set off, causing the violet to bloom (in hopes of making seed).

A pot that is too wide or deep will leave space for excess soil around the root ball. Since no roots are in this excess soil, the water here is not utilized and acts as a kind of shield to prevent air from entering the root ball. Furthermore, the water is an excellent environment for fungus and molds which can kill the plant. Unless the plant is likely to grow quickly into the pot space, it is wise to avoid using oversize containers.

It is possible to use a pot that is too small for a violet without causing any real harm. A violet will tend to grow only to a size that is three times the diameter of its pot. In fact, the tiniest violets sold in thumb-sized pots are actually being grown in pots which are too small for the variety. Because the root system is so confined, the plant's growth is inhibited to only two or three inches. This same principle can be applied to larger African violet varieties (which may tend to outgrow available shelf space) by keeping these plants in three- to four-inch pots. Remember that small pots hold less water; it may be necessary to water plants that are under-potted more often.

Beginning growers often make a mistake in believing that a violet must be put into a larger pot every time it is repotted. Every violet has a maximum mature size. Once the outside leaves and the root ball reach this point, the overall size of the plant will never increase. Younger leaves will grow from the center of the crown, each growing out to the maximum size, but no further. When the outside leaves reach a certain age or are not receiving the proper culture needed to keep them strong, they fail and die. This process eventually results in a plant with a long stem or neck, and repotting is required. The neck must be buried, but since the plant is already fully grown, the new root system will not need a deeper or wider pot than before. The problem is solved by cutting away enough roots to bury the neck in the same size pot. (Hint: This is much easier to do if the neck is not allowed to develop more than an inch before repotting.)

Pot Color

Here is a point for discussion. Certain colors of plastic pots look better with the violet plants, but does the color matter for the health of the plant? Some say it does.

Dark-color pots do not allow light to reach the roots. Since nature intended for roots to be in the dark, there are those that strongly believe that the root systems grow best in green or black pots. Light-color pots offer an advantage to growers who like to write the plant name on the side of the pot, making it clearly visible.

When using plastic pots, some static electricity is likely to cause particles of potting mix to cling to the outside of the pot. Some growers prefer darker pots because the dirt is less visible. Others prefer white pots so that they can see the mess and clean it up!

Most violet growers would agree that whichever color is chosen, it is best to be consistent. It is much prettier to view a collection of plants grown in pots of a uniform color. And if you wish to exhibit violets in competition, you may find that the show schedule requires a specific pot color.

Novelty Pots

"Build a better mousetrap and the world will beat a path to your door." Violet growers seem to look at pots with the same attitude. There are a number of unusual and effective violet pots available for growers to use. Many of these pots have decorative value and at the same time provide a system for watering. These allow growers to bring violets into the living quarters in an especially beautiful way. Since they do tend to be more expensive than ordinary pots, they are often used only for special plants or settings.

When trying an interesting pot recommended for violets, follow the directions carefully and experiment with one plant at first. Sometimes it takes a little fine-tuning before one may safely choose to put an entire collection into the same new containers.

The Best Pot

The best pot for a violet depends partly on the violet grower. Clay pots may be perfect if the collection is small and the grower tends to kill plants by over-watering. If the collection is large and the grower wishes to spend less time watering, plastic pots are often better. If the plants are intended as decoration, novelty pots can enhance the violet's beauty.

The ideal pot is one that holds an African violet!

4

The Scoop on Dirt: Choosing the Correct Potting Medium

If there were one truly great secret to growing violets that bloom and thrive, we would have to pick potting medium. Once violets are in the right "dirt," they become much easier to grow successfully. Here's the scoop!

What's the Problem?

Probably the greatest challenge for beginning African violet growers is finding a potting mix that really works. It is not because the potting mix recipe is such a secret. The problem lies in the fact that the proper medium is not generally sold to the public.

There are lots of bags of "African Violet Potting Mix" sold at retail stores all over the country. Because potting mix is very rarely regulated by states, many of the commercially sold mixes are not consistently the same and do not meet the standards of African violet hobbyists reliably. In order to keep costs low these mixes may use inferior peat and not enough lighteners. Most of these "violet mixes" are too heavy for good long-term growing.

Violets purchased in stores rarely are growing in a medium that is truly correct for violets. Many of the greenhouses who produce violets for the discounts and grocery markets must keep costs at an absolute minimum if they are going to make a profit. Putting mass-market violets in premium potting mix is cost-prohibitive. The correct mix also tends to be so loose that it would spill in the process of being shipped to stores.

Inexperienced growers can hardly be blamed when such newly-purchased violets die, all too often having been produced in soil that was too dense for home growing. It is easy to conclude that you "can't grow violets." This is truly an unfair assumption!

What is the solution? We suggest that potting mix ingredients be purchased and mixed by the grower. As an alternative, potting mix may be purchased from a nearby African violet club or from an African violet specialist.

What Did Nature Use?

It is always wise to try to duplicate the natural environment of a plant if it is to be grown successfully. In the wilds of eastern Africa, violets are not found with their roots growing down into heavy earth. Their roots sometimes grow into the narrowest of cracks in rocks where there is natural leaf mulch or just a little air space. Other times, the roots spread out, fully exposed, across damp, moss-covered rock.

It would appear that nature provided a tremendous amount of air to violet roots and at the same time kept those roots moist. This is the goal of any quality potting mix: Keep violet roots moist while providing ample air circulation.

A Little History

When violets were first cultivated in greenhouses in the twentieth century, growers commonly potted violets in clay pots using organic soil (garden loam). This combination worked because the clay allowed air to move around the outside of the root ball, even though the soil was too heavy. The clay also provided necessary evaporative cooling in greenhouses where temperatures could soar. The early violets rarely achieved the perfection that top growers expect today, however.

When the African Violet Society of America (AVSA) was formed in the late 1940s, more research was shared by growers regarding their successes and their problems. One of the biggest problems of the time was the battle with nematodes, which infested violet root systems. It was soon recognized that violets grown in mixes that used garden loam had the greatest potential of nematode infestation, while those grown in soilless potting medium did not. By the 1960s there were few hobbyist violets being grown in dirt.

Pots also changed during this time period. Plastic became more available. Unlike clay pots' natural ability to breathe, with plastic pots it was necessary to use a lighter potting mix that would include room for lots of air, while at the same time retaining moisture.

A recipe that growers came to trust was called the "one-one-one" formula. It consists of one part of milled sphagnum peat moss, one part vermiculite, and one part perlite. Growers have learned how to adapt this to their own water conditions with a number of additives, but the basic one-one-one has produced fine results for several decades for all levels of African violet growers.

The Need for Porosity

When the roots of an African violet thrive the rest of the plant thrives, and blooming is far more frequent and abundant. In order to promote the growth of a violet's fine fibrous roots, it is critical that the soil have excellent porosity, with plenty of air incorporated into the potting mix.

What does that mean really? Imagine a bucket filled with large rocks. While it might appear to be full, it would be relatively easy to pour a significant amount of gravel into the bucket. The gravel would fall into the spaces between the rocks. Now the bucket looks really full. As full as that might appear to be, water can still be added to fill in the air space left by the gravel. With each addition, the porosity in the bucket decreases.

The suggested porosity ideal for African violet potting mix is 33% air, which is quite high compared to that needed by many other plants. This means that the components must be fairly chunky and large so that the air spaces are not compressed.

Regardless of what is used to mix together the perfect potting mix, it is always extremely important that African violet growers never pack the soil down into the pot. The looser and more aerated the soil, the healthier the root structure is likely to be.

The Basic Soil Components

Sphagnum peat moss is one of the key ingredients to modern African violet potting mixes. It is naturally sterile with a soft texture that is perfect for delicate roots. It has an innate ability to suppress fungal diseases that cause root rot. And not just any peat will do. In North America the best sphagnum peat is said to be found in Canadian peat bogs. Packaging for this superior peat moss will generally have a statement that it is a "product of Canada" somewhere on the bag. Peat moss labeled from New Zealand is also excellent. Sphagnum peat is preferred because of its longer fibers and because of its brown color (the lighter the better) which indicates that it is not totally decomposed. The peat must be milled (either before packaging, or by the consumer) to break up the fibers into looser and more useable particles.

An inferior peat that is common in the marketplace but is undesirable comes from sedge peat bogs. It has very short fibers and tends to be black and smeary when rubbed between fingers. It compacts very tightly around roots, retaining entirely too much water, and is often highly acidic. Sedge peat is not favored by commercial greenhouse operations and seems to be marketed primarily to the uneducated public. The best use of sedge peat is for conditioning soils in the garden, but it consistently shows up in household potting mixes. Discount potting mixes often label themselves with the word "black," which probably should be read to mean that they contain sedge peat.

Sphagnum peat has a good ability to retain moisture evenly, but it is often reluctant to absorb moisture when it has been allowed to become totally dry. It is not uncommon for producers to dry peat completely in order to reduce the weight and cost of shipping. When using dry peat, it is best to stir in hot water to rehydrate the fibers and then to knead or stir until the water is fully absorbed. Wait several hours or overnight before using to allow it to cool to room temperature.

Peat moss tends to be somewhat acid, becoming more so in time as it decomposes. Many growers choose to add dolomite lime to the mix to buffer this acidity (more on this later). Areas that have extremely high pH in the water supply may find that the lime is not required. Others find that simply repotting into fresh medium on a regular basis keeps pH at a good level.

Vermiculite, another key component in the mix, is a natural mineral that has a flaky texture. It is produced using a mineral called hydrated laminar magnesium-aluminum-iron silicate. The mineral comes from mines in several parts of the world, including South Africa, China, Brazil, and the United States. When this material is heated, it expands like an accordion into chunks that are broken up into smaller particles.

Vermiculite is a sterile product with a pH that can vary between 6 and 9.5, according to the Vermiculite Association. It has excellent water absorption capabilities, especially when larger (usually called "coarse") particles are used. These same coarse bits are excellent for increasing the porosity of potting mix.

In the late 1980s a vermiculite mine in Libby, Montana, was found to be contaminated with asbestos. That mine ceased production amid media attention. Even though other mines have not been found to be contaminated, the resulting publicity created a scare that has made some retailers reluctant to sell any vermiculite products. It seems unfortunate that this valuable resource has become scarce in the marketplace when the supplies are ample and safe and the quality is generally good.

Perlite is the third basic component. It is added primarily because it increases porosity, especially when coarser grades are used. It will absorb some water, but this quality tends to decrease as particles increase in size.

Perlite is sterile and has a neutral pH. The one concern voiced about the use of perlite comes from a report in the 1970s that identified fluoride toxicity in a group of plants, not including African violets. Perlite is notably high in fluoride. Does that mean it should be abandoned? Absolutely not. Researchers have established that the addition of dolomite lime will fix the fluoride so that it is not absorbed into the plant tissue. Since dolomite lime is commonly added to buffer the acidity of sphagnum peat moss, the issue of fluoride has not been a concern for African violet growers.

Other Potting Mix Additives

Besides the basic three, growers often add several other materials to perfect their potting mix. We've already mentioned dolomite lime in connection with buffering the acidity of sphagnum peat moss and in fixing fluoride. It is important that only dolomite lime be used. Dolomite lime has about equal levels of magnesium carbonate and calcium carbonate, both of which have a good buffering action. When available, the coarser grind of dolomite lime is superior to the powdered grade because it releases over a longer period of time.

A second common additive is horticultural charcoal. This is not the same as "activated charcoal" or barbecue charcoal. It may be added and mixed through the soil to increase porosity. Many claims are made for the value of adding charcoal. Considering how little is often incorporated into the soil, it may actually have very little effect. Certainly it does no harm. Some growers prefer to layer it in the bottom of the pot, rather than mixing it throughout the medium.

Wetting agents, also called surfactants, reduce the surface tension of water. It makes it easier for water to be absorbed by dry peat moss. Some growers swear by these, while others find them unnecessary. Too much surfactant may cause excess saturation and resultant rotting of roots. Surfactants can be depleted over a period of time. When this happens, growers may find plants will stop taking up water without warning. We find that if the peat is a good quality, is hydrated with hot water, and is kept moist thereafter, it is not necessary to add a wetting agent.

Fertilizer charges (slow release fertilizer pellets) are commonly added to commercial mixes. These are convenient for repotting plants that will stay in the pot for only two to three months (such as bedding plants), but it is a problem when the plant will remain in the same pot for up to a year. It is hard to predict when the fertilizer charge has been completely used, and when it is safe and necessary to begin using plant food on a regular basis. It is best to avoid built-in fertilizer when mixing violet potting medium.

Meals, such as blood meal or cottonseed meal, are a type of organic fertilizer that some growers like to add to potting mix. They are primarily a source of nitrogen. When opting to use one of these, it is necessary to proceed with caution since an excess can possibly burn roots. Just as with slow-release pellets, it is difficult to know when they have been depleted.

Some growers like to add fungicides or insecticides to their potting mix as a preventative measure. We hesitate to encourage this for several reasons. First of all, violet growers tend to have their hands in the potting mix, and these chemicals can be readily absorbed through the skin. Secondly, fungicides and insecticides are targeted for specific pathogens and pests. They are not general-purpose cure-alls. In our opinion, it is far better to treat for the disease or pest that is actually present than to waste money treating for possible problems.

Two other ingredients, sand and bark, sometimes added to potting mix are probably not desirable. Sand tends to be abrasive for delicate roots even though it may increase porosity. Bark adds porosity but also tends to increase acidity. Neither is really appropriate for African violet potting mix.

Some New Components

There always seems to be something new that can be used instead of the basic peat moss, vermiculite, and perlite. The one-one-one mix has proven to be quite dependable, but for those who love to experiment, it can be interesting to try some of these.

Styrofoam beads are commonly used instead of perlite or vermiculite in many greenhouse operations, primarily to add porosity. They are sterile and pH neutral. Greenhouses like them because they are very inexpensive, but they tend to float to the top of the pot over time. Some people with environmental concerns object to Styrofoam because it is not biodegradable.

Another new material that is showing promise is coconut coir as a suggested substitute for peat moss. It is made of ground coconut husk, commonly imported from Sri Lanka as well as other tropical areas. It has good water absorption capabilities, it breaks down very slowly, it is inexpensive, and it has a slightly acid pH. The primary difficulty here is that it not 100% predictable. It must be processed correctly with the proper amount of fresh water in order to be safe for use. If coconut coir is to be used on a regular basis, it would be wise to find a reputable source and use that brand exclusively.

Rock wool is yet another pH neutral, sterile material that has been suggested for use as potting medium. It is a curious material with very fibrous texture. It is often formed into growing cubes so that a plant can be plugged into the center opening. While some violet growers have experimented with the material, it seems thus far to be more useful for growing some other types of plants, including orchids.

Maintaining Soil pH

Keeping the pH of the soil properly balanced in a range of 6.5 to 7 can be fairly challenging. Peat moss is notorious for becoming progressively more acid as time passes, and vermiculite can vary in pH. Local water can also vary on a daily basis. The problem can make even the most talented grower feel helpless.

If pH is suspected to be causing problems, it should be checked. There are many meters, gadgets, and testing kits offered for sale. One simple and inexpensive method of testing pH is with litmus paper and a color chart. The trial plant must have been moist for several days before testing. To check pH, add water to the top of the pot and collect the initial run-off water. Dip the litmus paper into the run-off and compare the color of the paper to the color chart.

As time passes, the pH is likely to become more acid (because of the decomposition of peat). Aquarium suppliers sell products that are effective in raising or lowering pH but these will be of short-term help if the potting mix is the source of the problem. Truly the best solution, usually, is to repot into fresh medium.

What About Pasteurizing the Mix?

Commonly, violet growers recommend pasteurizing potting mix to destroy pathogens and some of the dangerous bacteria, fungi, and pests in the soil. We do not do this in our collection and generally don't encourage others to do it. Before we explain why, let's examine what pasteurizing is.

Pasteurization is a process of raising the soil temperature to 180° F and holding it at that temperature for thirty minutes. It is not sterilization, since the purpose is not to eliminate all bacteria, but only those that cause disease.

If one were adding some organic soil (garden loam) to the mix, then pasteurization is a wise course. Organic soil may contain pathogens, nematodes, and microorganisms that can wreak havoc in a violet collection. Pasteurize this one ingredient only.

When growers use inorganic potting mix with sterile ingredients such as sphagnum peat, vermiculite, and perlite, pasteurization is not needed unless the mix has been contaminated by diseased plant tissue, insects or fungus. In fact, studies have found that pasteurizing sphagnum peat moss actually reduced its ability to resist the presence of pythium root rot disease.

When using the recommended one-one-one formula for potting mix, pasteurizing is generally not required. However, if organic soil is added, it probably does become necessary.

Don't Ignore the Potting Mix

The potting mix is often the one "secret" that separates novice growers from the top competitors. It is tempting to hope for the best, but it isn't easy for a violet to survive when its roots are in cement-hard or waterlogged soil. Growers who make the effort to find a better potting mix will be rewarded with healthier violets and more flowers.

5

The Art of Fertilizing....
Just Enough

Want to start an active discussion or maybe even a fight? Find a group of African violet growers and ask, "What is the best way to fertilize?" Everyone has a different opinion! Some growers use one brand all the time. Others love to rotate different brands and formulations. Some like to boost their plants with extra fertilizer just before shows. There are lots of opinions!

What should beginning violet growers believe about fertilizing? First, know that African violets do best when given fertilizer regularly. Often, beginning hobbyists have not been feeding their plants at all or only sporadically. Secondly, realize that fertilizer can be overused. Once they learn that African violets bloom and grow more vigorously when they receive nutrients, any grower may be tempted to go overboard. Even the most experienced of growers have been known to overdo it with fertilizer.

First—The Basics

Plants actually produce about 95% of the nutrients needed for growth in the process of photosynthesis. Fertilizers aid and supplement this production. That is why it generally takes such a tiny amount of fertilizer to satisfy plant needs.

There are many reasonably good African violet fertilizers out there. This discussion will be limited to the inorganic fertilizers, since that is the type that is most predictable and most commonly used by most indoor growers (organic fertilizers often smell bad!). Most of them work well under the right circumstances (we'll talk about that later). Most violet growers favor fertilizers that recommend a "constant use." Package labels generally suggest a measurement that is appropriate for use once a week when watering. Growers who use a constant-water system (like wicking, matting, or with special pots) either keep that proportion of fertilizer or use a reduced amount, often half-strength, in their water every time they replenish the supply.

The numbers used on American fertilizers represent the percentage of the mix containing each of the three primary nutrients (e.g., 15% nitrogen, 30% phosphorus, 15% potassium in a 15-30-15 formulation.) The remaining percentage is made up of other nutrients and inert carriers.

Fertilizers recommended for African violets vary. They may be balanced blends of nitrogen, phosphorus, and potassium (like a 20-20-20 mix), or they may be heavy to the phosphorus (like a 15-30-15 formulation). One company has had success marketing a fertilizer that is lower in phosphorus (14-12-14). Yet another company offers a special formulation for variegated violets that has very little nitrogen but huge amounts of phosphorus (5-50-17). African violets need more than just the three basic nutrients, so most of the fertilizers have additional trace elements. Some will list them, but many do not. If plants are doing well with a fertilizer, it is probably safe to assume that they are not seriously deficient of any of the necessary nutrients.

It does get more complicated than that, however. Fertilizers are produced from several different sources. Many of the less expensive fertilizers use urea, ammonium phosphate, and/or ammoniacal nitrogen as the origin. Fertilizers that use a nitrate base are more expensive and tend to be harder to find. These sources are generally listed on the label.

Finally, there are also the slow-release fertilizers. These are coated with a resin so that they dissolve slowly in the soil. The formulation, wetness of the soil, and the soil temperature affect the rate of the release. These can be very convenient to novice growers because it is a one-time-then-forget-it system. Be aware that wetter or warmer-than-average conditions will cause this fertilizer to break down more quickly, while dryer or cooler-than-average temperatures will result in a slower breakdown. It can be difficult to guess when it is time to repeat the application.

Next—The Fine Points

Water plays a key role chemically in the conversion of fertilizer into a nitrate form. Roots can only take in nitrates dissolved in water. Nitrate-based fertilizers are already in a usable form and are taken up readily by violets. Urea-based nitrogen depends on soil bacteria to convert it to a nitrate so that roots can absorb it.

Soil bacteria are a group of beneficial microorganisms living in the soil. Some of the bacteria are able to break down ammonium forms of nitrogen into nitrates, which the roots can absorb. Bacteria, generally present in all soilless mixes and just about everywhere else, can be destroyed by excessive heating. When potting mixes are pasteurized, it is important that they not be heated beyond the recommended level of 180° F.

Soil bacteria are relatively active in the soil when the soil pH is between 6 and 7.5. Their activity is also affected by soil temperature. They can be quite inactive at cooler temperatures, but at 70° or above, soil bacteria can break down ammonium-based materials quite efficiently.

The activity of soil bacteria in warm or cool conditions partially accounts for the changes in growth patterns of African violets at different temperatures. Foliage variegation patterns are particularly sensitive to the availability of nitrogen at warmer temperatures. Nitrogen is a key element in the production of chlorophyll—the chemical that makes leaves green. Variegated hybrids grown in changing conditions will have more green in the foliage produced during the warmer time and less green in the foliage produced during the cooler time.

If It Isn't Broken, Don't Fix It

All of this information can seem pretty intimidating. It is actually quite simple to fertilize African violets correctly. Use a good quality African violet fertilizer and follow the directions. As long as the violets are growing and blooming well, there is probably no cause to worry.

Determining the best brand to use continues to be a great source of discussion among growers. If a violet friend in your area is having good success with a particular brand, it will probably work for you too.

Symptoms of Fertilizing Problems

Inadequately fertilized violets may show varied symptoms according to the nutrient that is not available. For example, plants that have a faded green color (chlorosis) across the entire plant may have an inadequate supply of nitrogen available to the roots. It may be that there is an inadequate amount of nitrogen being offered, or it may instead be because soil pH or temperatures have made it unavailable. Magnesium shortages may also be reflected by a chlorosis, but this time it would only appear on the lower leaves and primarily between the veins.

Diagnosing deficiencies is a very tedious, confusing process! Furthermore, if you are using a good fertilizer at the recommended rate under normal conditions, it is extremely unlikely that the plants are lacking nutrients.

What is probably more likely? Overfertilizing!

Excessive amounts of fertilizer may result in changed growth in the foliage (varying from very tight centers to leggy, open-leaf patterns). Sometimes excessive phosphorus can trigger extraordinary amounts of flowers, but there is a penalty to pay in burned foliage in the outer, more mature rows of leaves.

Micronutrients (those trace elements that are often added to the major three in fertilizer) can wreak havoc when a trace element is also available from another source resulting in a toxic level. One example of this might be when water moves through copper pipes (absorbing some of the copper as it travels) and then is combined with a fertilizer that also supplies copper. The two may combine to create a toxic level in the plant tissue. This toxicity will commonly show itself by stunting the growth of the crown. Very tiny center leaves, especially narrow and pointed ones, may give the appearance that the violet is mutating to a miniature size.

One of the biggest problems with overfertilizing is a buildup of a variety of fertilizer salts. This salt deposit can sometimes be seen on the hairs in the very center of a violet crown. It can also form a gritty deposit on the top of the soil. It can be leached out by pouring clear water (an amount equal to at least the volume of the pot) through the soil ball, allowing the waste water to drain through. If any color is noted in the run-off water, continue leaching until the water comes out clear.

In some cases, overfertilizing results in a toxic condition in which there is more ammonia in the soil than the soil bacteria can process. Urea-based fertilizers form ammonia (think about the smell of a wet diaper). When these fertilizers are over-applied, or when the soil bacteria is underactive, the result will be ammonium toxicity.

Hungry and Not So Hungry

Some violets need lots of fertilizer to prosper, while other varieties seem to manage with none at all. It probably ties into the plant metabolism and how efficiently some violet varieties produce enough nutrients for their own needs. Plants that are being grown for show seem to benefit from the boost of a little extra fertilizer. Many dark foliage hybrids also seem to need a steady diet. Nitrogen seems to be the key nutrient that sometimes can be supplemented in greater quantities. Leaves that bleach or turn a lighter-than-normal green color in bright light are indicating a need for more nitrogen.

Extra nitrogen can be supplied to hungry plants by additional root feeding, especially with the use of a good organic fertilizer such as fish emulsion. On the other hand, many advanced growers prefer to supply an extra helping of nitrogen to hungry plants using foliar feeding. This is a process of misting the leaf surface with a fertilizer mix. Theoretically, a very high percentage of this nitrogen is drawn into the plant in about thirty minutes, making it very effective. If you wish to do this, we recommend using about one-sixteenth of a teaspoon of fish emulsion plus a drop of pure dishwashing solution (or a good wetting agent) in a pint spray bottle that is filled with warmish water. The foliage should be spray-misted thoroughly, and wet plants should be kept out of direct light. After an hour, any excess beads of water can be blotted off of the leaves, and plants may be returned to their original position.

A few African violet varieties consistently develop a halo of lighter color around the outside of nearly all leaves. This may be because that variety needs very little support from fertilizer or because they are extremely sensitive to toxic buildups.

Wise growers know that each plant has a little different "personality." When you can match the conditions to your plant's special needs, you will see improvement.

Fat and Not Happy

Being overfed is never comfortable. It seems like a harmless thing to do, but plants can't tell you to stop! It really is better to err a bit on the short side than to risk the serious damage that overfertilizing can cause.

Fertilizer isn't the magic solution to growing perfect plants. It's just one of the elements of growing that good growers have to master.

When you get plants that are growing well, you may be sure that your fertilizing program is working. It may not be the same as what works for someone else.

Ammonium Toxicity in Plants

Ammonium toxicity is a condition linked to the use of urea- or ammonium-based fertilizers. The condition has been studied in florists' gloxinias, and we thank Dr. Paul Nelson of North Carolina State University for sharing the results of his studies. He believes that ammonium toxicity does affect African violets as well.

In florists' gloxinias, ammonium toxicity causes lower leaves to curl downward stiffly. The lower leaves will exhibit irregular and highly unpredictable patterns of chlorosis (lighter green patches). The leaf margins of the most mature leaves will be burned, and as the toxicity becomes more pronounced, leaf burning shows up on younger and younger leaves until it affects the crown itself. The plant may die completely. The root structure will be reduced in size and will have an orange-brown tone that is distinctly different from normal root color, which is off-white to pale tan.

Dr. Nelson stated that other plants which have been studied show similar patterns. Ammonium toxicity can have a phantom-like quality. Symptoms may come and go, appearing and disappearing. The extent of the problem can vary in different hybrid strains of one plant type. Since many African violet growers have several hybrids in their collection, it would be expected that the pattern of symptoms would vary from plant to plant.

Ammonium toxicity is generally linked to the use of urea- or ammonium-based fertilizers along with the absence or ineffectiveness of soil bacteria. Active soil bacteria can break ammonia down into a usable nitrate form as long as the soil temperature stays above 70° and as long as the soil pH is 6.0 or above. When soil temperatures cool to below 70° or the pH drops into a more acid range, soil bacteria becomes progressively less active and less able to process ammonia thoroughly. This results in a build-up to a toxic level.

How to Control Ammonium Toxicity

If violets are in an area with well-regulated room temperatures that remain in the 70s, and if they do not have an acid water supply, there will probably be no problem. There is certainly no reason to panic if no symptoms are present.

Growers who have seasonally cool temperatures must be aware of how it may affect violets. Do not use the lowest shelves in the growing area during the cool months since the coolest air is always closest to the floor. It may be wise to use less fertilizer since the soil bacteria will be less efficient at processing the ammonia. If possible, warm the room or the tray so that soil temperature does not sink below 65 degrees Fahrenheit. Avoid using cold water to water plants or refill reservoirs. (Hot water is also not acceptable. Do not use water warmer or cooler than ten degrees from the air temperature.)

If there is persistent acid pH in the soil or water that cannot be otherwise controlled, it would be wise to consider using one of the nitrate-based fertilizer products. Read the ingredients on the label. Look for a brand that lists at least one of its sources of nitrogen using the word "nitrate." These brands will not add the excess ammonia to the soil, and their nitrates are not so dependent upon soil bacteria for breakdown.

All that having been said, if ammonium toxicity is suspected, you should first try leaching the soil. Once recognized, ammonium toxicity should be easy to control and avoid. Best of all, the treatment is inexpensive and safe.

6

Air and Temperature—the Invisible Growing Factors

Since we don't see air, we often forget the critical role that it plays in the growing of our African violets. It appears to be the cheapest part of the hobby, until you consider the money spent heating, cooling, cleaning, and moving it to make our plants grow beautifully. Don't underestimate its importance, just because it's invisible!

Carbon Dioxide

Plant tissue needs air, and specifically carbon dioxide, to function. During the process of photosynthesis, the cells in the leaves use chlorophyll and light energy to combine water and carbon dioxide into usable energy. Carbon dioxide makes up a very minute percentage (one third of 1%) of the total air. It is most dense close to the earth and to our plants. As a by-product of photosynthesis, oxygen is released by plants into the air for us to breathe.

Some recent horticultural experiments have demonstrated that injecting additional carbon dioxide into the air around greenhouse plants has increased plant growth rate. To our knowledge, no formal experiments have been performed on African violets along these lines. Several years ago, however, an article appeared in the *African Violet Magazine* describing an exhibitor who burned candles in the growing area to increase the supply of carbon dioxide for violets going to show. Unattended burning candles are clearly a hazard so we can't recommend this practice!

In any case, it is clear that African violets, and all plants, cannot perform photosynthesis efficiently without an adequate supply of carbon dioxide. It really is better for you to spend time near your violets, exhaling a regular supply of carbon dioxide for them to use.

Humidity

Air also holds the humidity in which our violets thrive. Violets seem to grow best in relative humidity levels of 40-60%. Relative humidity is the amount of water that the air can hold at a given temperature. As temperatures decrease, relative humidity increases. As the humidity drops to levels of 40% and below, violet buds may not develop and/or blossoms will fade rapidly. If the air is damper than 60%, transpiration (giving off of moisture through the leaf surface) is lessened, and the leaves will not pull as much water (and fertilizer) up through the roots. This results in weaker, ill-fed growth.

Humans seem to be most comfortable in the 40% or lower range. In cold areas it can be hard to maintain even 20% interior humidity without experiencing damaging condensation on windows and walls. Keeping humidity high enough for horticultural perfection is a constant challenge. One solution is to provide some source of evaporating water quite near the plants to increase the moisture in the immediate area without making the home uncomfortably damp. This may be in the form of a constant-water method like wicking or capillary matting. Open dishes of water, or plants set on wet pebbles or sand will also work. Humidifiers can also help but tend to make the entire air space too muggy in some climates.

Temperature

Along with humidity factors, the actual air temperature is important to the growth rate of plants. Violets grow best in moderate temperatures of 65° to 75°F. Cooler temperatures will cause slower growth, curled foliage, and altered (usually deeper) blossom tones. Warmer temperatures will at first increase growth, but as the mercury rises above 90°, cells collapse, and older leaves may become suddenly water-soaked and glassy-looking. Variegated foliage will often develop more extensive variegation in consistently cooler air and may become entirely green when grown in warmer temperatures.

Blasts of dry air also cause problems. Leaf curl is a common response to any cold air draft. Violets grown close to the floor (where cold drafts most frequently occur) may develop irregular streaks or patches on leaves that are lighter green and veined as a result of chilled roots. Drafts of hot air (commonly caused by indoor heating systems) can cause buds to fail or blossoms to fade unusually early. This is because air can hold more moisture when it is warm. As hot air passes over, it absorbs moisture from the plant, which is then carried away with the draft. Buds and blossoms are the most sensitive to this drying effect.

Extreme variations in air temperature over a twenty-four hour period seem to cause weaker growth. Leaves will be less sturdy, have a duller appearance, and be smaller than their genetic potential. Blossoms will not be held up as well or be as long lasting. Seed pods (desired by hybridizers) often fail. Keeping temperatures nearer a constant median temperature of 70° will result in far superior plants.

The Role of Air Movement

It is important for air to move around violets to encourage the process of transpiration and to reduce the problems associated with excessively high humidity. In the process of photosynthesis, plants release water molecules into the air through the stomata on the leaf surface.

Ideally the water molecules are absorbed into the air that is moving across the plant. If the air is not moving, however, or if the air is excessively humid, the water molecules remain on the surface of the leaves. Moist leaves are an open invitation for the growth of fungus.

The easiest way to keep air moving around your plants is to use a fan twenty-four hours a day, seven days a week. Ceiling fans help, as do oscillating fans. Watch for pockets of dead air by dangling a bit of tissue in corners or other suspicious locations. Small fans (sometimes called "personal fans") can help eliminate dead air if they are carefully positioned and regulated to a very low speed so that they are blowing gently, just to keep the air moving slightly. Fast moving air can actually damage newly forming leaves and buds.

Roots Need Air Too

Roots also need air space. Violets have delicate fibrous roots with even more delicate root hairs. Unlike woody plants, violets are not able to force roots into seemingly solid rock or even into firmly packed soil. Researchers have suggested that the perfect environment for violet roots should be one-third air! The roots need the air space to grow into.

The best proof is evident in the common pattern of substantial root growth all around the outside of the soil ball, next to the pot, but negligible root development in the center of the pot. This is most commonly found when potting mixes are too heavy. Peat combined with other soil lighteners like vermiculite and perlite help to keep plenty of air around the roots, resulting in more even distribution of roots in the pot.

So what if violets don't have lots of root growth all through the pot? Simply stated, they will grow smaller and bloom less. Note that we do not recommend a bigger pot to get more air. Pots that are oversized actually can keep air from reaching the roots because of the volume of unused water in the excess soil. Pots that are in good proportion to the actual size of the plant will maximize air flow to the roots.

Airborne Problems

Just as air is necessary and beneficial for plants, it also creates a pathway for some undesirable visitors. Certain insects, fungi, and other pathogens reach our plants through the air.

Some insects have a life stage in which they are able to fly, while others are so tiny that they can be carried by strong air currents. Thrips, the tiny insects that feed on pollen sacs, are able to fly through most window screens, and can be very difficult to eliminate because of constant reinfestation. Other pests, like soil mealy bug and spider mites, can fall undetected from one plant to another when plants are being moved about. It is wise to consider this when removing an infested plant and carefully bag a suspect plant before discarding it outside the growing area.

Fungal disease is one of the most common airborne problems. Powdery mildew, which appears as a white flour-like substance growing on plant surfaces, is a chief offender. Remember that violets appreciate humidity up to about 60%. Fungal diseases like powdery mildew and botrytis multiply at a dramatic rate at 80% humidity. When a growing area has a high relative humidity during the warm part of the day, it will increase further as cooler night time temperatures come on. Remember, warm air holds more moisture than cool air. Therefore a growing area of 60% relative humidity during the daytime can become a perfect fungus breeding ground during the night.

Pollution

Plants are definitely affected by bad air. Some plants are effective air cleaners of certain pollutants (dieffenbachia is efficient at cleaning formaldehyde, for example), but no test results that we know of have ever named African violets in this group. Rather than cleaning the air they are far more likely to indicate the presence of the pollution in their growth patterns.

If a violet has been affected by pollution, it may show signs of retarded growth, browning at the edges and tips of the leaves, or speckling or splotching on leaf surfaces. Some gases used in cooking or heating can cause plants to cease blooming and to develop stunted crowns with only tiny unburned amounts present in the air. A number of years ago, we had one shelf of violets growing near a natural gas connection. We noticed that the violets there were beginning to grow with very tight centers. At first, we thought the problem was an infestation of cyclamen mites, but treatment was not effective. Suspecting a gas leak, we urged the gas company to inspect. It took several checks before a tiny leak was finally detected. Persistence paid off.

If you know that your city or region has air pollution, air filters in both heating and cooling systems might be a wise investment. If you suspect unburned gas seepage, the *AVSA Handbook for African Violet Growers, Exhibitors and Judges* has the practical suggestion of placing a young tomato plant in the growing area. Tomatoes are very sensitive and will bend their leaves down after even a few hours of exposure. With that evidence, your gas company can be contacted to check the area for leaks.

It is likely that violets became popular because they are comfortable sharing our air and people-perfect temperatures. They love space and light breezes and pure clean air. Giving them good air keeps us healthy too. You can't see it, but you know it's doing all of us, plants and people alike, a lot of good.

7

How to Use Good Advice

Finding good advice when growing your first African violets can be tough. The *African Violet Magazine* is a great source of information, but sometimes the advice there may not work in certain situations. Why is that? It is because the advice is often related to a specific region and climate. Many experienced violet growers have moved into new locations only to find they "can't grow African violets there!"

The growing environment is unique for each of us. We have tried to listen closely to growers across the United States as well as those in other parts of the world, but the fact is, our advice is based on our personal experience.

What are the variables of growing violets that make each grower's horticulture unique?

Light and Latitude

Most beginning growers use windows as their source of light. But this light varies a great deal according to the season, to the grower's distance from the equator, and to the distance from the window glass. In Nebraska, which sits in the very center of the United States, we recommend that the grower place a violet within twelve inches of an east window. The light will be bright there, and the temperature will rarely climb above 85° F, at which point heat damage will generally begin to occur. North windows are often too dim, and western and southern windows are often too hot, particularly late spring through early fall.

For growers living in the southern states, and especially for those international African violet growers living nearer the equator, the temperature may often climb above 85 ° at any window. The solution then is to find the brightest location that also provides some relief from the heat. Placing the plant directly in the window does not usually work well there. Some of the Central American growers who are at higher altitudes tell us that they can successfully grow violets out of doors in the shade.

Canadians and Alaskans do not usually have to contend with as much heat, but the amount and intensity of daylight is reduced between September and March. Many of the northern growers resort to artificial light to bring the plants into bloom during winter months.

Average Temperatures

The average temperature in the grower's region will govern where the plants may be placed for light, but it also affects the choice of plants in a collection as well as the amount of artificial heat or air-conditioning needed.

Some varieties of African violets react quite differently to cooler or hotter climates. Southern U.S. growers find that plants grow more rapidly but with smaller flowers and less intense color in the blossoms. Northern growers may have beautiful, deep, rich colors on large blossoms, but find that their plants grow more slowly.

Temperature difference may also produce plants that have a softer growth in warm climates or a hard brittleness in colder areas. The softer growth often results in longer leaf stems (petioles) and longer blossom stems (peduncles). The plants grown at temperatures below 70º F will be just the opposite, with tightly overlapping leaves, and blossoms that may grow under the foliage.

African violets with variegated foliage are notorious for reacting differently to climatic variations. The leaves of many variegates will not display their characteristic white, cream or pink markings in warm climates. On the other hand, in very cold growing conditions, the leaves may become so heavily variegated that there is insufficient chlorophyll for the plants to continue growing or blooming.

Climate also determines the type of mechanical cooling or heating devices available to the grower. In Nebraska with our hot summers and cold winters, central air cooling and heating systems are quite common. At any time during the year, we can warm or cool our growing area to 72º F. In the winter we often warm the building in the morning, and then cool it in the afternoon when all of our fluorescent lights begin to produce too much heat.

In warm southern regions of the United States, people are more concerned with cooling their homes, and so they often do not build in a powerful heating system. A sudden and surprising drop in temperature can spell disaster for violet growers. The heat pump systems usually available in homes to take the chill off of a room may not keep up with a severe temperature drop. Greenhouse growers in these areas are especially vulnerable to damage from a severe cold snap.

Northern U.S. growers have an opposite problem. If they do not have air conditioners, a sudden spring heat wave can ruin the blossom count on violets grown and groomed for competitive shows

Humidity Factors

African violets prefer fairly high humidity levels of 40-60%. The blossom stems are especially vulnerable to air that is too dry. If they lose moisture too quickly to dry air, especially when the buds are first forming, plants will not bloom well, as the buds blast and dry up.

In dry areas, especially desert regions, growers find that it is very important to use a system of watering which adds moisture to the air and provides a constant source of water. Arizona growers often rely on wicking and capillary matting to water their plants.

In very damp areas, the humidity may be well above the 60% recommended for violets. In this situation, plants may not transpire water into the air and thus are unable to draw up nutrients into their root system. The potential problems with powdery mildew as well as other fungus diseases are also greatly increased with high humidity, especially if there is not good air circulation.

Humidity also has an effect on the propagation of African violets by leaf cuttings. Tiny plantlets are quite vulnerable to withering dry air. If indeed the air is dry, it is wise to provide a sealed environment around the 'expectant' leaf. A terrarium, a sealed clear plastic bag, or clear fast food boxes all work well for this. This, of course, is not a necessary step in very humid climates.

Water

It would seem that water is water is water. But, in fact, water supplies vary a great deal in pH levels, in salt content, and in levels of other additives. Violets tend to thrive best at a pH level of 6.8. Growers in regions with acid or alkaline water will probably need to compensate by correcting the pH, often with aquarium products. Some growers have water that is naturally or artificially "softened." The water contains varying amounts of salts, which can build up in the soil and in plant tissues. This is potentially quite toxic to the plant.

Many city water systems add chlorine or chloramine as well as other chemicals. Chlorine should be removed by letting water stand for a few hours. The chlorine gas will evaporate and the water can then be used on plants. If the water supply contains chloramine instead, this cannot be removed by evaporation and must be chemically neutralized, as with detoxifiers used by aquarium enthusiasts.

Other Problems

Other regional factors affect the way one is able to use violet-growing advice. Specific commercial soil mixes are often not consistently available in an area of the country, so it may be impossible for a New York grower to use a soil recipe recommended by a California grower.

The cost of utilities greatly influences the decision to use heating or cooling. Certain communities have far more expensive electricity than others, so growers may have to run fluorescent lights at night in order to avoid brownouts, heat buildup, and huge electric bills.

The physical housing of an African violet collection can also affect plant growth. For some growers, basement or cellar growing is possible, but can result in problems with mildew and with too-cool temperatures. For others, housing space may be at a premium, and these growers are forced to learn how to "stack" their plants if they wish to have large collections. Growers who depend on natural light will find that the width of the windowsill and the design of the windows can make a difference in how easily violets can be grown.

Adapting Advice

Every bit of advice offered is intended to be helpful. No one wants to send a beginning grower astray. It is important to remember that all advice (even ours) must be adapted to one's own specific situation. It is wise to seek the advice of someone in your area who is having success growing African violets.

We are very conscious that many readers do not have the conditions we enjoy in our area. Every grower has to experiment for themselves until they get it right. Read our advice; use it if it seems helpful. Most of all—enjoy growing your violets.

Section Two—Special Techniques

8

Propagating by Leaf Cuttings

One of the great achievements for those beginning to grow African violets is learning to propagate them from leaf cuttings. Whether you start a leaf from a violet you already have, or start one from a friend or a purchase, leaf propagation is fun and allows you to expand your collection without spending much money.

What Violets can be Propagated?

Most violets produced from leaf cuttings will bloom true. This means that the plantlets that grow from a leaf cutting will produce flowers and foliage that will be the same as the violet from which the leaf was taken. They will, in fact, be clones of the parent.

Some violet types will not bloom true. Chimeras, which have a characteristic stripe of color down the center of each petal lobe, will rarely produce offspring with the same color pattern. Chimeras have a unique genetic structure that can only be propagated through side shoots, called suckers, or from rooting blossom stems which is probably best left to advanced growers.

Similarly some violets are unreliable in propagation because they have an unstable genetic structure. Fantasies, violets that have speckles or blotches such as purple markings on a pink background, or multicolored violets will often produce a percentage of offspring that are not true to the parent. Some of the offspring may instead have solid-color flowers.

Some violet hybrids are legally protected by copyright laws. These violets will usually be sold with a plastic stake that identifies the copyright restrictions on that hybrid. Many of these violets are sold by mass marketers, such as grocery and home stores. It is not legal to propagate leaf cuttings of these hybrids, except to replace the original plant (because of a bug or health problem, for example), and then only for personal use, not for sale.

A Few Tips

The process of propagation begins with a good leaf cutting. The mother leaf should be a mature and very healthy leaf whenever possible. Look for excellent green color and no bruises. Don't be tempted to use older leaves with fading vigor, as these are prone to take much longer before new growth appears and to have fewer offspring, assuming they don't rot away in the first few weeks. Small young leaves near the crown do tend to root quickly and produce plantlets sooner; however, more mature leaves generally produce more and stronger plantlets.

Some varieties of African violets are easier to propagate than others. Solid green foliages are usually the easiest to start for the beginner. Violets with variegated foliage are often a little touchier. In our experience, it can often take one to two months longer for variegates to produce plantlets compared to green-foliaged cultivars. Cool winter months can make this process even longer for variegates. To increase success with variegated varieties, choose healthy leaves showing as much green as possible. The babies will carry the same genetic potential for variegation that the mother plant had regardless of the amount of variegation on the selected parent leaf.

If the cultivar you wish to propagate is a fantasy (with spots or streaks in the blossom color), the offspring may not always show the markings exhibited on the parent plant (this is called "sporting"). These varieties are somewhat unstable genetically and occasionally revert to solid-color blossoms. And these plants can also produce the fantasy blossoms on one half of the plant and solid-color blossoms on the other. Be careful to choose mother leaves that are growing next to or beneath blossom stems showing the correct coloration.

Be patient. It will take about a month for a healthy leaf to produce some roots. Once that is done, the leaf will begin to produce tiny plants at the base of the cut stem. It takes a month or so for those plants to grow to the surface of the soil and several additional months for the plants to reach a large enough size to be separated. If the leaf is older, variegated, or stressed, it may take longer yet.

Use a process that works well in your environment. We will suggest several methods later. It may take a bit of experimentation to find the method that works best for you. If you have poor results using one method, try another.

Keep the name of the parent plant with the leaf. Violet hobbyists value the names of their plants. Down the road, an unnamed violet has little value to true collectors and cannot be exhibited in shows. There are literally thousands of named African violet cultivars and many are similar, so once a name is lost it can be nearly impossible to identify it correctly.

How Does Propagation Work?

Each cut cell of plant tissue is inclined to produce offspring. Usually, only one plant will grow from each cut cell when traditional methods of propagating are used. The injury to the cell triggers nature's "survival of the species" reaction. When plant tissue is threatened, the plant uses any method available to guarantee that it does not die. This effort to survive is evident during many phases of the plant's growth but especially evident when a leaf is cut away from the parent plant for propagation.

Violet babies can occur naturally in some less-predictable places. Occasionally, growers will find a tiny plant forming on a crack in a leaf that is still attached to the plant or at the very edge of a leaf that had a slight injury.

The Water Method of Starting Leaves

The traditional way of propagating violet leaves is to place the stem into water until roots begin to grow. In most cases, it is wise to move the leaf into potting mix once the roots have begun to form and allow the babies to grow in the mix. However, some growers prefer to allow the plantlet to develop while the stem remains in water.

Using this method, select a healthy leaf and remove it from the plant by moving it from side to side until it pulls free. Avoid pinching or bruising the leaf as this may lead to rotting. Make an angled cut across the bottom of the leaf stem, about two inches from where the stem meets the leaf. It is best to do this so that the angle of the cut section of the stem is facing the same direction as the hairy surface of the leaf. This positions the future plantlets to grow straight up and in front of the leaf. An extra large crop of babies can be produced by slicing up the stem about one fourth inch (so that the base of the stem is split).

Choosing the container of water is one of the most discussed elements of the water method of starting leaves. Whatever container is used must hold the leaf safely above while the stem extends down into a water source. A long-time violet grower once suggested that a dark, long-necked beer bottle filled with water works well for this. The darkness inside the bottle is good for developing roots and prevents algae growth. Many choose a juice glass filled with water and covered with plastic wrap, foil, or waxed paper (often secured with a rubber band). A hole is poked in the center of the cover so that the stem can be inserted through to the water below. Regardless of container, be sure to label the leaf with its hybrid name.

The water in the container should be relatively pure without softening agents or fertilizer. If water quality is an issue in your area, it might be wise to use bottled water. Check the water occasionally to be sure that it is still clear and not clouded by bacteria or algae. If necessary, change the water.

Watch the bottom of the stem for the development of tiny roots which will be slightly thick and white. While you may wait for plantlets to develop, we would recommend that you move the leaf into potting mix as soon as the roots are one-fourth inch long. Choose a small pot of very loose potting mix that contains a high percentage of perlite or vermiculite. Water it in, and then set it in a bright location. The leaf may be covered with a plastic bag or placed inside a covered transparent container (more on that later) while the babies begin to develop and grow.

The Soil Method

In the soil method, leaves are placed directly into the potting medium and allowed to stay there until the babies are mature enough to be separated from the parent leaf. It requires fewer steps than the water method and also produces excellent results.

Again, remove a healthy leaf from a violet, avoiding any bruising. Make the same angled cut as before, leaving a stem that is one to two inches in length. As an alternative, the stem can be removed and the bottom fourth of the leaf cut away in a wedge shape. Some growers recommend applying salicylic acid or allowing the cut surface of the stem to dry before proceeding as a method of preventing infectious diseases.

Prepare a small pot with loose potting mix. Since violets have rather tender fibrous roots, they always require a fairly light growing medium. Violet leaf cuttings are going to form the most fragile of new roots and need an especially light soil mix. The roots need to be able to grow into tiny air pockets in the soil, but they also need even moisture surrounding them. For this reason, we personally use a rooting medium that has some regular African violet potting mix, combined half and half with coarse vermiculite. Some growers prefer vermiculite alone, and still others like mixes with lots of perlite. Be sure that whatever you choose is very light and porous. Ideally, this mix will be lightly moistened before starting.

Insert the leaf, leaning it slightly backward so that the hairy surface of the leaf is facing up. For best results, do not set the leaf into the soil very deeply, no more than an inch. The tiny plants form at the cut end of the leaf and must grow the distance to the top of the potting mix in order to reach light. They will be stronger if the distance is short. If you are opting to use the leaf with no stem, the cut edge should be set into the soil just enough to support the leaf upright. Do not pack the soil down around the leaf! Add water and allow the excess moisture to drain away. Be sure the leaf is labeled in some fashion with its hybrid name.

Next, place the potted leaf into a clear plastic bag or container. We find that zippered plastic bags or fast food salad containers work well for this. Close it tightly. If using the bag, blow into the bag to puff it up with air. The added carbon dioxide in exhaled breath is good for plant growth, and the sides of the bag will be in less contact with the leaf. The leaf will rarely need additional water when enclosed in this manner.

Packaging the leaf may be omitted successfully in areas that already have high natural humidity (50% to 60%) and warm temperatures. In this case, it is necessary to water regularly.

Set the leaf in a moderately lit area, away from direct sunlight or intense fluorescent light. Rooting leaves do not need as much light as mature plants. The leaf will root much more quickly at 75° to 78° F. If the room temperature is cooler than 72°, try setting the rooting leaf up on a high shelf where the air is a bit warmer. Heating trays are available which warm the soil from underneath to compensate for cool temperatures.

If temperatures are warmer than 85°, there may be a greater chance of leaf failure. Try setting the rooting leaf on a shelf near the floor where the air is cooler and avoid direct sunlight.

There will be no need to move the leaf or to change conditions until the babies are large enough to be separated from the parent leaf.

What about Rooting Hormones?

We personally find that it is not necessary to treat violet leaves with rooting hormone before putting them down. Following the package directions may result in a glob of the hormone on the stem. This excessive amount is more likely to burn away the new roots, and it may take longer to get results. If you wish to use it, dip a small paintbrush into the powder and lightly brush an inconspicuous amount onto the cut edge of the leaf.

Patience

The most trying part of leaf propagation is waiting for the "babies" to appear. After the leaves have been put down, they often wilt to a certain degree, and the first sign that anything is happening is that the mother leaves will become crisp again as roots begin to form and draw up moisture from the rooting mix. Once this happens, it is safe, although not necessary, to start watering with a mild fertilizer solution. Some varieties, in some climates, will be rooted in just a few weeks and begin to show tiny plantlets in a month to six weeks. In many cases, it will take three or four months before new growth is visible. In cool climates, particularly during the winter season, it is not unusual to wait six months. Be patient! If the mother leaf is crisp, babies will usually come along eventually.

If six months have passed, and there is no sign of plantlets, there are a couple of tricks which may help. Try cutting about an inch off the top of the mother leaf. Mother leaves usually continue to grow during propagation. Trimming the tip will often cause the leaf to cease growing larger and to get down to the business of making babies. We routinely trim the tops of the leaves that are rooting close together to increase the amount of light that reaches the soil (and the plantlets) below. Also, some growers maintain that giving a slight tug to the mother leaf will disturb the roots enough to stimulate the growth of new plantlets.

Separating a Clump

After a period of months, there should be a clump of small plants growing at the base of the leaf. While it is possible to transplant even the tiniest of plants, it is generally best to allow the plants to grow until the leaves are at least the size of a dime before separating the clump. It will be easier for a novice to handle larger plantlets and easier to solve the puzzle of where the individual plants are among the tangled leaves. Some leaf cuttings may produce only one or two plantlets, while others may produce a mass of fifteen or more. Murphy's Law seems to dictate that when you desire more plants, fewer plants will be produced. However, oftentimes in smaller clumps the individual plantlets will be sturdier and stronger.

Begin by slipping the entire clump and soil ball out of the pot and laying it sideways on a work surface. Gently begin working away the potting mix so that the stem of the parent leaf is exposed. Sort the small plants apart from one another. This is challenging to the beginner! The plants are reasonably sturdy, so one can be fairly courageous about pulling them apart. A few torn roots will not impede their later growth. It may help to look for a distinctive neck that connects the rosette of leaves to the root system of each plantlet. Besides your own nimble fingers, a sharpened pencil makes a useful tool for separating plantlets.

There are two common mistakes made at this point. Some will believe that each tiny leaf is a plant and literally pull a plantlet apart. This is a fatal error. The other mistake is to fail to separate the plantlets adequately, allowing two or more to be potted together as a single plant. This error can be corrected later when it becomes apparent that there are two crowns competing for space by separating the two or by destroying one of them.

The next step is to prepare the pots into which the little plants will go. Since the plantlets are still small, a two-inch pot is usually a proper size. Fill the pot with pre-moistened loose, high-quality violet potting mix, and do not pack it down! Use the tip of a pencil to make a small indentation into which the plantlet is set. It should be in the very center of the pot, and the stems and leaves should be above the soil with just the roots and the neck (if there was one) below soil level.

Water each pot and allow the excess moisture to drain away. We do not use fertilizer at this stage because we have observed that young plants are especially vulnerable to a build-up of fertilizer in the center leaves. This has a golden, crystal-like appearance, and it often kills or distorts the crown.

Be sure the violet hybrid name is transferred to the new pots. Don't even let the thought enter your mind that you won't forget. Many violets become permanently nameless because of carelessness at this stage.

Return the individual plantlets to a terrarium-like environment at this time. We put trays of young plants inside large clear plastic bags and use stakes to prop up the plastic. Zippered plastic bags or clear plastic food containers will work for just a few plants. Again, watch the temperatures, as you did for the leaf cuttings. Keep the plantlets in this warm humid condition for a month or so. By that time, the little plants will have begun to show more mature growth and strength. They will be ready for the "real" world.

When the time comes to open the container, do so slowly over a period of several days. This will allow the plants to adjust gradually to the change in humidity. Remember that those little roots will have to pull a lot more water once the humidity decreases and it takes a little time for them to adjust. If some leaves dry around the edges, don't worry—new leaves should soon appear after which the damaged leaves can be removed.

Now, begin to water the plant on a regular basis, using a good-quality commercial fertilizer at a quarter-strength. We have found that foliar-feeding these young starter plants (lightly misting them with a solution of a few drops of fish emulsion to a quart of warm water) seems to gives them an extra boost. The plants tend to absorb nutrients more efficiently in this manner than they can through their young root systems. This is particularly effective when dealing with heavily variegated young plants. The high nitrogen boost may help "green-up" the plant. If you do not care to use fish emulsion (the smell is not especially pleasant), remember that placing the small plants in a warmer location may also be of help.

A young plant should take off and grow rather quickly. As the leaves grow larger and the diameter of the plant increases, it may need a larger pot. Typically, a plant should be mature enough to bloom in six to nine months.

First Bloom

On the average, it takes us about a year from when the leaf is put down to when the plant is in nice bloom in a four-inch pot. This can happen much faster (or slower!) with some varieties and conditions than with others.

The first blossoms are often smaller and less sturdy than the later ones will be, so don't panic if it isn't as pretty at first as the mother plant was. Generally, more mature plants will produce blossoms that are larger and richer in color. With "fantasy" varieties that have speckles and streaks of color, the first bloom will tell you if the plant is going to bloom true. If the first blossom shows no sign of the characteristic markings, at least part of the crown has sported to a less desirable color. This will keep it from ever being a good plant for competition, but it may still find a place in your affection. If it (or any violet) fails to bloom true, the plant name should be changed to read (Variety name) Sport. We'd rather that you discarded these altogether, hoping for better results with other plantlets from the clump.

Go Ahead and Propagate

African violets have gained tremendous popularity since they were first discovered in 1892. Propagation of African violets by leaf cuttings is one of the most satisfying aspects of growing. Aside from the parental feelings evoked, it opens the door to a new world of sharing varieties of plants with others by the exchanging of leaves.

Furthermore, it gives the opportunity to produce more plants of favorite varieties which you can keep for yourself, share with friends, or even sell to help support your hobby. If you have the patience, it is also much less expensive to buy a leaf cutting when purchasing new varieties at a show or by mail order. Some violet growers even believe that the plants they get from leaf cuttings are stronger and more adapted to their own growing conditions than are purchased plants.

One of our customers likes to buy leaves "because my husband doesn't notice them coming into the house!" For whatever reason, put down a leaf and make some babies.

9

Maintaining a Single Crown and Dealing with Suckers

If you asked the average man on the street to explain a violet "crown" he would probably describe something to wear on your head. If you asked about a violet "sucker" he might come up with some joke. Ask an African violet grower, and you will get a far different answer! For those who are halfway between being an average person and an accomplished violet grower, the terms can be quite confusing!

What is a Crown?

In an African violet, the crown is the center of growth. All new leaves begin here as tiny shoots which mature into larger leaves. The result should be a beautiful rosette of leaves, all of which radiate from the center.

The *AVSA Handbook for African Violet Growers, Exhibitors and Judges* describes the crown as a single, thick stem with a rosette of foliage attached. This may seem confusing because the stem is so well hidden by leaves. Think of the crown as a growing point where every leaf in the rosette originates forming multiple rows of leaves all of which are connected to a center stem (whether you can see it or not!).

African violet crowns produce leaves in a sort of triangular pattern. Close study of a mature violet will reveal that as each new leaf came in, it developed about 120 degrees to the side of the previous leaf. Rather than pairs of leaves, there are triplets of leaves that form the rows of the crown.

Single- or Multi-Crowned

Most African violet varieties are single-crowned. That means that these hybrids should be grown with only one crown; all other side crowns (often called suckers) that develop need to be pruned away. Single-crowned plants need to be alone in a pot of their own! If growers do not prune out suckers, a violet will develop a bushy, confused, and distorted appearance that is not pretty. As this tight tangle of leaves forms, light is blocked from the main crown, which may be one reason why violets are also less likely to bloom well in this condition. Bloom may also be restricted by a lack of nutrition, since one root system must supply the entire mass of growth.

Trailing African violets are a distinct group of plants that are genetically multi-crowned. These plants thrive with many centers of growth and at the same time will still produce blooms. These are different from single-crowned hybrids. The leaf nodes are spaced slightly further apart as they develop, causing more of a stem to develop. There is more room for leaves from the multiple crowns to intertwine. As a trailer matures and stems lie near the soil surface, roots develop along the stems and grow into the soil to nurture each crown. Trailers are enhanced by the addition of more crowns, since each crown has adequate room and root structure to support itself, while at the same time being connected to all the other crowns.

Crown Troubles

Crowns will often indicate the health of the plant. African violet crowns should have actively growing leaves that have a rich green color but are delicate with only light "peach fuzz" hairiness. Gray tones might indicate a serious infestation of cyclamen mites or the onset of a fungus. A thickened or twisted appearance or a coarse hairiness might also indicate the presence of mites.

Orange crust on the center leaves of the crown results from the presence of too much fertilizer. Leaching the soil with clear water and temporarily discontinuing fertilizer will usually improve the situation.

Stunting is a problem that is usually first evident in the crown. New growth ceases and leaves fail to increase in size. It can be the result of serious problems with the potting mix, usually either in pH level or in lack of aeration. It may also result from pollution, mites, or fungal disease. Stunting is not itself a disease, but rather the symptom of another problem, whether it be cultural, pest-related or fungus-induced.

We frequently repot violets for customers in our flower shop. On occasion we've had people bring in plants with a split crown. These are otherwise healthy plants which have spontaneously formed two crowns in the center of a plant. This can be caused by some sort of physical damage to the plant, but sometimes there just seems to be a defect in the center that causes it to split. In our experience, trying to save crowns from these plants is usually futile, since they will often split again. It appears that it is better to start a new plant from a leaf cutting.

Love Those Crowns

Nature does something very special with African violet crowns. When they are grown well, the resulting symmetry of overlapping rows of leaves, interspersed with lovely flowers, is almost too perfect. Many of the top growers are people who are true perfectionists, and there are few plants which so lend themselves to that level of perfection. African violets are one of nature's crowning achievements.

(Usually) Undesirable Crowns Called Suckers

A sucker is a crown that forms on the main stem of a mature African violet either at the base of the plant or between the leaf nodes. It may be left to grow there, competing with the mother plant for space. Or it may be removed and rooted to start a new plant. This process will be discussed later in this chapter. Suckers can be valuable or a nuisance, depending on the situation.

Isn't There a Nicer Name?

Somehow the word "sucker" seems somewhat rude. It is, however, a name commonly used by horticulturalists in reference to the side-shoots of plants. Once removed, the small plantlets might be called "propagules" instead, if you wish for a loftier term.

Where does the word come from? Perhaps it is derived from the term used to describe infant mammals: suckling. It may also suggest that the side-shoot is drawing nutrients and moisture away from the parent plant.

Recognizing a Sucker

Spotting a sucker early and managing it correctly are keys to keeping your violets growing in lovely form. Please note that top growers expect their violets to have one center crown of growth with a perfectly symmetrical "wheel" of foliage forming around that center. In African Violet Society of America shows, all violets, except trailers and species, must have only one crown. Any suckers or secondary crowns that are present will eliminate a violet from consideration for ribbon placement.

Suckers may show up either at soil level next to the base of the plant, apparently growing from the root area, or in the spaces between leaves. When a violet sucker first develops, it will have an infinitesimally small tuft of two opposite leaves. Newly forming flower buds will have almost the same appearance at this stage. Blossom stems also may sometimes have two opposite leaves, before the bud is apparent, which are called "wing leaves" or bracts. At these early stages, it is best not to assume the extra growth is a sucker, because, by doing so, a bud stem could be accidentally removed instead.

Once a second pair of leaves appears, four leaves total, you may be certain that a sucker is forming. At this point, you should make a decision. Should this sucker be removed to propagate, removed and destroyed, or left to grow? If you delay that decision for a few weeks, your parent violet may begin to change its appearance. But delay it for a few months, and the symmetry will be gone. Your plant will be a bushy tangle of leaves going in all directions. There will be major work repotting and restoring the parent to its former beauty.

This is a good time to mention an oddity in African violets. Very rarely, some varieties form tiny growths with four or more leaves right where the wing leaves normally would develop on the flower stem. These are called "baskets." In effect, they are much like suckers except that they are not tucked down into the leaves, but are held up higher above the foliage and just below the flowers. Not surprisingly, baskets may be used as propagules to grow a new plant, just as any other sucker could be. The truly odd thing is that they will not distort the symmetry of a violet, since they do not increase their size on the flower stem. Baskets are not considered secondary crowns.

Why Keep a Sucker?

There are occasions when suckers are allowed to grow rather than being removed. One such time is when the violet is a trailer, which was just discussed. Trailers in competition should have at least three crowns, but they frequently have more crowns than can be counted. These varieties develop multiple crowns easily and in that process take on a lovely form.

It is also desirable when secondary crowns appear on chimera African violets, because propagation of these is possible only from suckers or from bracts. Chimeras have two sets of genetic material in one plant. They are actually a combination of two violets, growing and blooming as one. In Greek mythology, a chimera was a monster, but in African violets a chimera is something special and certainly is not frightening.

Chimeras are notable for the dramatic center stripe of color on each petal lobe of the blossom, giving them a pinwheel effect. Leaf cuttings will produce offspring that carry only one of the sets of genes, usually resulting in plants with solid-color blossoms. Suckers, however, taken from the original plant will generally bloom true with the pinwheel pattern.

Because chimeras are so unique and beautiful, growers will often force the mother plant to produce secondary crowns. This can be done by paring out the center of the original plant. (This pared-out crown can be re-rooted to form a new plant.) Since the center growth point has been removed, a chimera violet will react to preserve its survival, and secondary crowns will form at various points on the stem. Multiple crowns may also grow where the original crown was pruned.

How to Remove Suckers without Repotting

There are several tools which can be used to remove suckers including dental instruments, nut picks, or "sucker pluckers" (a tool made just for this job). Our favorite is a slightly dull pencil. It is cheap and usually available, and it feels comfortable in your hand as you perform the delicate maneuvers required. Sucker removal can also be done with a firm finger, but it is very easy to break leaves unintentionally.

Closely examine the plant from the side to determine exactly the point from which the sucker is originating. Place the point of your tool just behind the lowest leaf, right at the growth point, and apply a little pressure to the side and/or up. If the tool is properly positioned, the sucker will pop loose intact. This takes a little practice! It is especially difficult if the leaves of your violet are growing in very closely aligned rows (like perfectly grown violets should).

If the sucker breaks apart into several pieces as it is removed, just throw it away. Do go back in and do some housekeeping. Using your tool, prod and poke at the spot from which the sucker came to remove any remaining sucker tissue. It is very important to be sure that none of the growth point remains. Otherwise, the sucker will grow right back.

How to Divide a Violet with Overgrown Suckers

If suckers have been allowed to grow to a size nearly equal to the original crown, it will be necessary to divide the plant. This is best done when the plant is a little bit dry and the foliage is less turgid so that fewer leaves accidentally get broken.

Remove the entire plant from its pot and lay it sideways so that there is a good view. Close observation should reveal the fork(s) where the crowns are joined. Gently cut into the fork between the conjoined crowns until one of them can be pulled free. The leaves will almost certainly be tangled together, so be patient as you work them apart. The detached sucker(s) will probably be left without any roots. The main crown with roots is usually left with a distorted-looking appearance, an exposed stem, and an uneven form. It will need to be repotted and shaped before it can regain its former beauty.

It may seem heartless and destructive to tear a violet apart like this. The true harm is in neglecting your violet until the problem becomes this severe! Imagine a mother who never paid any heed to her child until he was completely wild. True kindness comes in constant attention and training both for children and for violets.

Propagating Suckers

Much of the time, suckers are discarded. If you wish to save a sucker, it needs to be placed into a pot of its own. First, remove any faded or weak leaves. Strip large suckers back to a crown with perhaps six of the healthiest and strongest leaves with a small stem extending below. Weak leaves often do not survive the stress of replanting and would have to be removed soon anyway. This also allows the new plant to develop good symmetry.

Choose a smallish pot and fill it with an excellent quality, very porous potting mix (See Chapter Five) which has been pre-moistened. Set the sucker into the very center of the pot, gently inserting the stem, if there is one, into the mix. If the sucker came with some roots, simply make a small indentation in the top of the soil for the roots to fit into. Handle the same way from this point as plantlets produced from leaf cuttings as described in Chapter Eight. Usually, new roots will begin to develop quickly and the sucker will begin to grow new leaves.

Discouraging Suckers

Some plants seem to sucker almost constantly. If it is supposed to be a trailer, this is good; if not, it is just a nuisance. So how do we stop suckers before they start? First of all, be careful to place plants into the pot with the bottom row of leaves just above the level of the soil. Leaves that meet the main stem under the soil will act like leaves that are being propagated, and they will make suckers.

Immature plants just reaching their first bloom cycle are often more prone to suckering. Many of them will grow out of this as they mature and become established. Nonetheless, growers must keep a close eye on young violets to prevent the development of suckers.

It is also important to avoid injury to the crown or stress to the plant. The law of the survival of the species would indicate that anytime a plant feels threatened it may go into a reproductive mode, in this case by producing suckers.

Discouraging suckers is a special challenge for those who grow plants to show in competition. Disbudding (removing all bud stems) is a technique which allows growers to time the bloom cycle for the show and to encourage additional flowering. Unfortunately, the plant may interpret that disbudding as a threat to its existence, which can result in additional sucker development.

Other stress factors might come from uneven watering, water droplets in the center of the crown, or insect damage. It is wise to examine your growing conditions if suckers are a constant problem.

If suckering continues, with no apparent reason on a plant or two, the variety may be to blame. Some hybrids have a genetic tendency to sucker. The only viable solution is to toss them out. We would only recommend keeping these unruly plants if they had some sentimental value and you were willing to keep up with the constant maintenance of sucker removal and repotting.

Be a Sucker Expert

Growing and grooming your violets with a watchful eye can prevent a lot of problems if you spot them before they get out of hand. This especially applies to pests and disease, but also includes the prompt removal of suckers to keep your plants growing in good form.

When you understand crowns and suckers, you have taken a gigantic step forward in your mastery of African violets. Understanding the form of the plant and maintaining that form will properly become the goal of your hobby. That is quite different from the goal of the true beginner who only seeks to keep violets alive.

10

Repotting Violets

Of all the violet tasks that can be put off until another day, is there any as easy to put off as repotting? It seems like so much work. And it makes such a mess! The plants are still blooming. Maybe it can be done next week when there's more time. The day always comes, however, when it can no longer be delayed. Plants become so ugly that even a few blossoms can't hide their ungainliness. Top-heavy violets are falling over. Company's coming and your reputation is at stake. Either throw them out or repot. It's time to do it!

How Do You Know When to Repot?

Recognizing the need to repot a violet is a basic skill. A good rule is to repot any time an exposed stem, or "neck," becomes visible between the lowest leaves and the soil line. If it has been more than six months since the soil was last changed on a standard-size violet (three months on a miniature), then repotting will usually be beneficial.

Your violets should be kept single-crowned unless you are growing trailing violets that have many crowns (See Chapter Nine). If it appears that you have more than one plant in a pot, they need to be divided and repotted.

Good growers also recognize that African violets need to be in properly-sized pots. If a plant has grown to more than three times the diameter of its container, it may be wise to transplant it into something larger. As a general rule, miniatures and semi-miniatures are never placed into a pot larger than two or three inches in diameter. Standards need shallow pots that are usually anywhere from three to six inches across, depending on how broad their leaf span is. Mature trailers may be grown in almost any size shallow container, as long as there is only a minimal amount of soil visible around the perimeter of the plant.

Repotting may be an emergency effort to save a violet that is in crisis. Overwatered violets may react by developing limp outer leaves as if the soil were too dry. Moving the plant into fresh soil and perhaps even into a smaller pot may divert the onset of crown rot. Similarly, plants whose roots have been damaged by any number of enemies (e.g. temperature extremes, heavy soil, excess fertilizer, insects, chemicals, etc.) will reflect that damage in the foliage. When leaves wilt, spot, or age very rapidly, it might be wise to repot as a first course of action.

If the leaves seem to yellow, in spite of regularly-used fertilizer, the pH of the soil may be out of balance. This also may be remedied by repotting.

One other good rule: if you feel like repotting your violet, do it!

Assembling the Materials Needed

The most important element of successful repotting is the use of a good potting mix. African violets are fibrous-rooted plants. Their root balls are comprised of only fine, hair-like roots. A high-quality porous potting medium is needed to allow plenty of space between soil particles into which the tender roots grow, as well as providing room for air. At the same time, it must maintain a moist environment that keeps roots from drying out.

Several African violet vendors sell potting mixes which work quite well. You may find a local violet club that offers soil for sale at their annual shows. These are especially good because local growers have already adjusted the mix to suit the local conditions. (See also Chapter Four.)

It is also always smart to pre-moisten the potting mix before using it. Roots can be stressed by contacting extremely dry soil which absorbs moisture out of the roots, causing them to wither. Add water to the mix, and stir it well so that it is evenly moist. Peat usually absorbs hot water faster and more effectively. Pre-moistening will also cut down on excessive dust in the air and residue on leaves.

The correct tools will also help make repotting more pleasant. A good knife for trimming roots and separating crowns is essential. A dull pencil or a specialty tool called a "sucker plucker" will be useful for removing secondary crowns. We also like to have a piece of heavy wire bent into a hook so that a watering wick can be pulled through the freshly repotted root ball. It's wise to have a broad working area with a garbage can nearby to catch the worst of the mess. You'll also need a container of water for watering the plants in their new pots and saucers or trays to catch the run-off.

It is helpful to keep shallow pots in several sizes on hand. You will also want marking pens and labels to ensure that the variety name stays with the plant.

One very helpful trick is to place newly repotted plants into a clear plastic bag or some other clear plastic container. This is especially helpful when the roots have been highly stressed. We maintain a quantity of clear bags in several sizes for each stage of repotting and transplanting. Many growers justify buying fast food salads and store-bought cakes to get the clear plastic containers that will hold repotted plants.

If you really want to enjoy all of this, add some pleasant music to the background. Some growers enjoy sharing this adventure with a violet friend, while others love working alone so they can really concentrate. Maybe you shouldn't attempt to eat while you are doing this, but a beverage can usually be protected from flying potting mix. Try to clear your schedule of other tasks when you are repotting, and maybe let the answering machine take any phone calls. Interruptions will make the job much more tedious, and the plants do not enjoy waiting once they are out of their pots.

Repotting African Violets with Necks

"Is it normal to have a neck on a violet, or am I doing something wrong?" That's a question that we have often been asked. It's an interesting question, because a neck is normal but not desirable. Poor growing can speed the development of a neck, but a neck can be one of the easier problems to solve in the process of caring for African violets. It is also the primary reason for repotting mature African violets.

What is a Neck?

A neck is the exposed stem that gradually appears as leaves whither or are removed. It is seen between the lowest row of leaves and the top of the soil. It is fairly thick. On a standard violet the neck would be similar in diameter to one of your fingers or maybe even your thumb. The more slowly the neck develops over time, the thicker it will be.

When violets are growing in excellent light, the neck may become coiled around and around under the foliage and may be almost hidden by sagging outer leaves. When growing in poorer light, especially when the light comes only from one side of the plant, the neck will be more visible as the plant leans toward the light. In a worst-case scenario, the violet's crown will actually hang from an extended neck. We once insisted on repotting a violet that was hanging in a window in a friend's home before we sat down to lunch. The neck was at least twelve inches long, hanging well below the bottom of the pot. The tiny crown was trying desperately to face upward. It had a will to live though, and eventually bloomed about six months after repotting.

The exterior of the neck will have many ridges from where leaves were once attached. When the leaf is removed, the tissue calluses over with a tough, brown surface that protects the neck from pathogens. If leaves were allowed to wither and were not removed, there would be paper-dry membranes still clinging to the neck. Sometimes the neck will have several tiny plants trying to grow along its length. Wherever the neck makes contact with the soil, it may have some root development.

How Does the Neck Happen?

Violet necks occur because of the loss of lower (older) leaves. All new growth comes from the crown of the plant. As new growth occurs, each previous row of leaves continues to mature and age. Once the leaves have aged to a point where they are no longer efficiently producing energy for the plant, they begin to lose green color. They soften and begin to sag. Eventually they die, becoming completely brown and limp. If the leaf were not removed at this point, it would shrivel and dry on the stem.

Advanced growers remove aging leaves at the very first sign of color loss. Allowing a leaf to remain until it has softened and become limp increases the possibility of rot developing. Mostly, however, we remove aging leaves for cosmetic reasons. African violets do not look attractive when there are dead or dying leaves present.

Can a Neck Be Avoided?

Necks are the natural result of an African violet's growth. They are inevitable. But it is possible to slow their development.

When violets are grown under near-perfect cultural conditions, new leaves develop in very close proximity to previous leaves. Show-winning violets often have many rows of leaves extending from a crown that is only an inch or so above the pot. Those leaves can be stripped away to reveal a very thick neck that almost resembles a miniature pineapple.

When violets are grown in poor cultural conditions, especially when the light is inadequate, the neck will become elongated and much thinner. This is because new leaves are developing farther apart from each other. Plants have a tendency to grow toward better light, which causes the leaf nodes to be farther apart. In violets, this results in the quicker development of a neck. It also results in leaves with longer stems (petioles), gaps between leaves, and a tendency to grow upward or toward the light source.

The best way to slow the development of a neck is to provide bright and even light directly over plants. Violets are also far more likely to grow compactly when they are grown in cool conditions. Temperatures in the lower and middle 60s will provide significantly more compact growth, almost to the point of being too compact. A temperature of 72° F is generally considered to be the optimum for African violets.

How to Repot a Neck

Ideally, violets with necks will be repotted as soon as the necks are evident. If you can see a neck, even a short one, it is time to act!

It is best to wait until violets are just a bit dry before attempting to repot. If they are watered weekly, do the repotting just before they would be watered again. If violets are on a constant watering system, take them off of it for several days before repotting. Dry plants are less brittle and leaves will be less likely to snap off unexpectedly.

It is necessary to remove any leaves that are aging. Break away lower leaves that are faded in color, are marred by spots or cuts, or that are wilting. Make sure that a leaf is fully removed from the stalk so that no stub is left. Don't be afraid to remove leaves! Leaves that are aging will fade more quickly during the stress of the transplant. Only strong, healthy leaves endure this process well. Leaving old foliage will mean that you will have to repot again quite soon.

Leaf removal will expose even more of a neck than was present before. The entire neck must be buried in fresh soil. This is not done by using a larger or deeper pot! Ideally the pot should be one-third the diameter of the leaf span and no deeper than about four inches (violet roots do not grow deep). Anticipating that your repotted plant will grow quickly, you can use a pot that is closer to half of the foliage diameter. It is likely that the violet will soon reach the ideal size ratio. If your violet was thriving in the previous pot, use the same size again or just clean it for reuse.

Most of the above can be done before your violet is removed from its original pot. To do the actual repotting, lift the plant out of the old pot. If it is firmly stuck in the pot, tap or squeeze the pot to loosen it. Another effective method is to slip one's fingers (palm down) around the main stem of the plant to secure the soil. Then, turning the pot upside down, tap the edge of the pot on a hard surface, allowing the plant to drop into your hand as it comes loose from the pot.

Next, gently scrape the callused tissue off the exposed neck. Removal of the callus will allow new roots to form more quickly, since they will not have that hard barrier to grow through. We use the dull side of a knife for this task. This is a good point at which to take a break and allow the scraped tissue to dry for a few minutes, creating a barrier against bacterial infection.

Then, cut away from the bottom of the root ball, removing enough to make it possible to set the entire neck down into the pot. The bottom row of leaves should be even with, or slightly below, the top of the pot, and the crown should be centered. Fill in at the top with fresh potting mix. Don't be tempted to pack the potting mix down! Finally, give it a good watering and drain the runoff. You may have to add a little more mix at this point, since water will cause some settling.

What if you have to cut away the entire root ball to bury the neck? It is not a problem! Cut away some stalk too, so that the remaining stem is only about an inch-and-a-half long. Discard the lower section of the plant. Fill your pot with premoistened potting mix and water it just enough that it drains a bit. Then set the plant into the pot with the stem positioned down in the moist soil. Be sure the plant is in the center! Plants that are off-center in the pot will often grow less symmetrically.

When the stem is bent, especially in relation to the foliage, it is best to set the stem straight down into the potting mix with the leaves at an odd angle. The leaves will usually level out into a better position fairly quickly. When it is done the other way, with leaves straight and the stem crooked, the violet will not stay centered and will continue its crooked growth.

Putting the plant inside a clear plastic bag or container (and tightly sealing it) helps increase the humidity and gently increases the air temperature. This comfy atmosphere seems to bring plants through the shock of the transplant. Plants that have gone through radical transplant (amputation of roots) especially need this extra measure. Often a week or two is enough but a month or two is not too long. Usually the plant will not need additional water during that time. Only add water if there is no water condensation inside the container. If you live in an area with high relative humidity, this may not be necessary.

What about the flowers? If your plant has open blossoms, or even buds above the foliage, you might as well remove them. They rarely enjoy the shock of the transplant and usually fade quickly. This will allow the plant to concentrate its energy on producing new roots. New buds usually form within a few weeks.

Necks are Normal, but They Aren't Pretty

It is normal to have a neck develop on violets. Good growers know how to battle the problem. Looking at the positive side, a neck is a great reminder that violets need repotting once a year, just to change the potting mix. Without the reminder, it's easy to forget.

Repotting to Change the Potting Mix

Sometimes violets need to be repotted just to change the medium in which they are growing. Most of the potting mixes that we violet growers use have a fair amount of peat moss as a base ingredient. Over the passage of time, the peat moss begins to break down, and the soil gradually becomes more and more acid. When the pH level of the soil goes awry, nutrients in the soil become locked up chemically. Even with a regular program with fertilizer, plants will starve if the pH is too high or too low. The nutrients might be there, but the plants are not able to utilize them. Periodic repotting of African violets, perhaps once a year for standards and more often for miniatures, is extremely beneficial for the plants in your collection.

Another thing that does tend to happen in time is the settling or compacting of the potting mix around the roots. It will take place even with good light fluffy potting mixes. African violets have very fine and tender roots that cannot readily push through heavy or compacted soil, and when you can't get good healthy root systems under your plants, you probably also will not be seeing good abundant bloom. A way to test soil compaction is to push your finger down into the soil and all the way to the bottom of the pot. If this is not relatively easy, the potting mix is either compacted or too heavy.

Changing the mix without changing to a larger pot can require some finesse. Allow the plant to become mildly dry so that plant tissue is not quite so crisp and the root ball is not wet. This should help eliminate excess damage to the foliage during transplanting. Remove any leaves that are showing age or faded color. Then, after removing the plant from the pot, gently work some of the old potting medium away from the root ball, loosening tight or tangled roots. Set the plant into the pot again and fill in as needed, gently tamping the mix in, but never pressing it down. More mix may need to be added after watering for the first time. If the roots were manipulated or disturbed, it may help to put the plant into a clear plastic bag or container to reduce plant shock.

Inspection

Whenever you have the root ball out of the pot, examine it. Pests might cause damage so that there are fewer roots then expected. Roots encircling the outside of the root ball, but not filling in the middle would indicate that the soil did not have enough air in it. The soil may need additional perlite or other coarse material to add air. A sour smell might indicate over-wet conditions and the onset of rot. Another indication of rot would be a separation of the outer skin of the main stem from the core, or soft, brown desiccated tissue in or on the stem.

How to Repot if Rot is Found

Whenever rot is detected, it is necessary to repot immediately if there is to be any hope for the plant to survive. You must cut above the rot and save only the part of the plant that has not been infected.

The procedure is much the same as when a very long neck is buried. A cut is made through the main stem, amputating the crown, and the lower section is discarded. Examine the cross-section of the main stem. It is normal to find an outer ring of green with an almost full circle of purplish dots around a green core. If darkened tissue or a corky material is found in the core, or if the outside skin on the stem is separating or loose, then rot is present. If detected, your knife should be disinfected, several lower leaves should be removed, and a second, higher, cut across the stem should be made.

Repeat the procedure until no indication of rot is evident. A plant can be saved unless the rot is well established into the very center leaves of its crown. Finish by placing the violet onto a clean pot that is filled with moist fresh potting mix, making sure that there is some contact with the soil. Again it will be necessary to place the violet inside a clear plastic bag or container until new roots have formed.

Repotting or Potting Up?

This is a good time to define "repotting" and "potting up." When repotting, the same size pot will be used. Repotting should occur when a violet is at its mature size and needs to have a neck buried and/or needs to have fresh potting mix. When potting up, a slightly larger pot will be used because it is anticipated that a violet still has a greater potential for overall size or maturity.

Repotting properly will occur throughout a violet's life. Conversely, potting up typically occurs only in the first year or so of life, as a tiny plantlet matures to a blooming plant. Potting up might also occur as a competitive show grower anticipates a larger overall size as the result of show-growing techniques to be discussed later in Chapter Thirteen.

Potting Up Successfully

As violets grow from starter plant size to blooming size, to perhaps large show size, they need repotting occasionally to keep them growing well and looking good in proportion to their pot size.

According to the *AVSA Handbook for African Violet Growers, Exhibitors and Judges*, the ideal pot size for a violet is one-third the diameter of the plant. Therefore, if a plant is approximately twelve inches or so in diameter, the ideal pot size is four inches. Another way to look at it is that a twelve-inch plant will just about fill a shallow four inch pot with roots. This does not need to be followed exactly when growing plants at home, but it is a good guideline. Plants that are planted in too large a pot will generally not perform as well as they should because the roots cannot fill the space provided, inviting problems with potting mix that stays too wet. Plants that are underpotted tend to have their growth retarded and may not grow to their full potential. They also often need more frequent watering and are more likely to fall over.

When starter plants in small two-inch pots reach a diameter of three times the pot size, we personally like to pot them up directly into four-inch pots and keep them there. We are, of course, talking about standard-size plants here! Only those plants that are selected out for growing into larger show plant size might be planted into bigger five- or six-inch pots. There is a slightly longer wait for plants to come into bloom when potted right up to four-inch pots, but it does save the step of moving them up first to three-inch and then to four-inch pots. If you want to see blooms on your plants sooner, then you may choose to pot first into three-inch pots and then on to four-inch pots after they have grown to eight or nine inches in diameter. Keeping the roots confined to a smaller space will usually bring on blooming more quickly. This is something that will depend upon the individual grower's wants and needs.

Miniature and semiminiature plants should never be potted in pots larger than two to three inches if you wish to maintain the small size and health of the plant. A few semiminiatures seem to grow beyond their desired limits of eight-inch diameters when overpotted. Trailers need pots that relate to the overall size of the plant.

An important consideration in determining when a plant should be repotted is whether or not a plant is in an active growth mode. Some varieties do grow faster and with more vigor than other varieties, and it really is best for these plants to be repotted when they are actively growing to avoid holding them back. Watch for vigorous center growth and be sensitive to the overall diameter of the plant. Correctly timing the transplant allows them to continue growing and thriving at the same pace. Sometimes you can see the aftereffects of waiting too long for a transplant. Sometimes a row of leaves appears that is smaller than the leaves above and below. This "break in culture" can be avoided by transplanting at the proper time.

Plants that are large genetically or those that are being grown large in optimum conditions with a show in mind, do need adequate root space and thus a larger pot to support a sizeable leaf structure. Continue to use the rule of a pot one-third the plant diameter when potting up these larger plants. A plant that is twenty-four inches across should have an eight-inch pot. However, as one does repot such plants into larger and larger pots, it is also important to note that violets do not grow deep roots. The broad, shallow pan-type pots are an excellent choice for these.

When potting violets up to the larger pot, first place potting mix into the new pot, making a well in which to fit the root ball. This can be done using the smaller pot to mold a space the exact size of roots. Don't pack the mix tightly however. Do not loosen the roots, and make the least possible disturbance. Doing otherwise can result in a dwarfing of the flowers that are just setting on and distortions on outside leaves.

Sometimes violets will seem to be sitting still and although they are healthy, they aren't thriving. These may be those plants that are just plain better off growing in slightly smaller pots. Give them a chance to do their thing! This probably is more common with those cultivars that are classified as small standards.

Some Tips

Remember to pot without packing the mix and into properly sized pots.

Repotting time always offers a good opportunity to check the soil for pests and insects.

The use of a spoon or soil scoop is helpful to place soil under the leaves and into the pot instead of all over the leaves and everything else.

Never try to repot in a hurry, especially with large, mature African violets.

If using a root growth stimulant (for example, one of the products containing B vitamins), remember to follow directions. More is not better.

Repotting during the winter months will help prepare your plants to look their best during springtime, whether for shows or just for your own enjoyment.

Don't be afraid. In this case, chickening out is the most dangerous decision. Your plants will appreciate that you took the time to correct their problems.

11

Secrets to Blooming Success

There are many reasons why we love African violets, but the fact that they bloom tops the list. Very few other plants in the world can live in our homes and bloom so often with minimum care. Sometimes, however, even violets can pout and not bloom as well as we might like. There are a few "secret" methods that anyone can use to encourage better blooming.

Secret One—Bright Light

It's not much of a secret that an African violet will bloom best in good light. Light is one of the primary factors plants need to produce the energy necessary for the production of blossoms. In our experience, the most common reason why violets are not blooming is because they have not been placed in adequate light. Violets that do not receive enough light will often communicate their needs by reaching their leaves upward or growing toward the light source. Often the petioles (the stems on leaves) will elongate, and new leaves will grow to a smaller adult size.

When violets are to be grown at a window, they need to be placed within twelve to eighteen inches from the glass. If they are farther away, in most situations, the light will be too diffuse. In addition, it helps to place the plant at a large window. Tiny windows or heavily draped windows do not allow much light to enter. Windows that face the morning or midday sun are often the most desirable in areas with moderate temperatures because the plants are not receiving direct sunlight during the hottest part of the day. Be aware that violets love bright light but dislike extreme heat. The best window will be one that properly balances these factors.

If there is no window which can produce enough light, then the grower may wish to consider using fluorescent lights. These can be very inexpensive "shop lights" hung under a cupboard or beautiful and more costly light stands with multiple shelves. But any fluorescent light will produce a light spectrum that will significantly increase the amount of bloom.

As a general rule, fluorescent light should be on ten to twelve hours a day and be ten to twelve inches from the violet plant with adjustments made according to the plant's reaction. If there is too little light, the plant will stretch up toward the light; if there is too much, the plant foliage will show signs of bleaching (loss of green color) or the plants may grow with tight centers. (For more on this, see Chapter One.)

Secret Two—Water

Another secret to getting a plant to bloom and to stay in bloom is to find a system of watering which allows the soil around the roots to stay evenly moist but not drenched. When tiny buds begin to set on the plant, they are extremely fragile, and if the plant should be allowed to become thoroughly dry at that point, the buds will wither and dry off. Furthermore, a violet in full bloom uses significantly more water than one not in bloom. A blooming violet transpires more moisture into the air, so the plant is liable to dry out more, and the blossoms are likely to be the first part of the plant to suffer.

There are many systems for constant watering that work well: wicking, capillary matting, "Texas" potting, and specially designed pots with water reservoirs. Violets can also be hand watered when the soil begins to feel somewhat dry to the touch, but this requires a wary eye since not all the plants will use water at the same rate. (For more on this, see Chapter Two.)

Secret Three—Humidity

Along with having even moisture throughout the root ball, violets will bloom better if there is also sufficient moisture in the air. Again, the tiny buds will die off very easily when humidity is scarce, and open blossoms will fade more quickly if the air is dry. Currents of dry air seem to be especially hard on blossoms and buds.

Growers in the Arizona desert find that it is impossible to bring violets into bloom without a constant water method that also allows water to evaporate into the air around the plant. And, don't forget that desert-like conditions often prevail when heating an interior growing area during the cold winter months. Wicking or capillary matting are both systems which will increase the amount of humidity around the plant as they also provide water to the roots.

Secret Four—Fertilizing

Starving violets lack the energy to bloom. Violets grown indoors, at near-constant temperatures and often (under fluorescent lights) at constant light levels, have a constant hunger for nutrients. The plant functions will only perform at peak levels when the plant is nourished. Therefore, violets need to be fertilized regularly.

There are many excellent violet fertilizers available, but we especially like the ones which give directions for use with every watering. Very few people are good at remembering when they last fertilized if they only do it once per month. These fertilizers are commonly mixed at a rate of one-fourth teaspoon per gallon of water and used with every watering. They can be used in constant water systems also, but if the system allows for evaporation, it is probably advisable to mix the fertilizer at a weaker strength (perhaps one-eighth teaspoon per gallon) to avoid over-concentration. Many growers prefer violet fertilizers that have a high phosphorous level, the middle of the three numbers on a fertilizer package. The phosphorous is said to strengthen roots and thus lead to greater bloom. Healthy roots are critical to blooming! (For more on this, see Chapter Five.)

Secret Five—Potting Mix and Keeping Roots Happy

Healthy violet roots can only grow in potting mixtures that do not inhibit development. Healthy, fully-developed roots are necessary for maximum bloom.

Violet mixes should produce an environment for the roots that is a balance of equal parts of air, water, and potting mix. This requires choosing and mixing a soil that will not absorb too much water and will permit a lot of air to surround the roots at all times. (For more on this, see Chapter Four.)

Temperature extremes, pH levels that deviate from the recommended standard of around 6.8, and over-sized pots can cause roots to deteriorate, often resulting in limited or sickly flowering.

Violet roots prefer to remain within a temperature range of about 65 to 75º F. Colder nighttime temperatures can cause roots to stagnate or actually die back. Higher temperatures will affect plant growth and often cause blossoms to deteriorate as well.

Fertilizers will not help if the soil pH is unbalanced, because the roots can only access or use nutrients within a narrow range of pH. If you have been fertilizing but the plants appear sickly, check the pH.

Over-sized pots can cause real problems for roots, because the violets have an inbred size that determines the size of the roots as well as the size of the foliage growth. When growers place a full grown violet into a pot that is larger than the roots can fill, trouble follows. First of all, the soil without roots tends to remain saturated, limiting air flow and encouraging rot. Secondly, violets tend to react to confined roots with flowering. When the roots fill the pots, plants will bloom freely. This is not possible in a pot that is too large.

Secret Six—No Bugs, No Fungus

There are several insects and fungi which can keep plants from blooming or cause blossoms to fade too quickly.

Thrips live primarily on the blossom, feeding away inside the yellow pollen sacs. They are small, but definitely visible, especially when they skitter across a blossom after being disturbed by a probing finger or a puff of air. When thrips are present, flowers will fade prematurely and often have pollen spilled on petals.

Soil mealy bugs sap the strength of the entire plant as they feed on roots. These pests, because they live in the soil can be tricky to spot. Plants under such attack may bloom, but the flowers will often be sickly-looking.

Cyclamen mites are microscopic and are thus impossible to see with the naked eye, but experienced growers quickly recognize their presence when blossoms become small and distorted along with the stunting of the center foliage. (For more on disease, see Chapter Eighteen.)

Powdery mildew, probably the most common fungus to affect African violet flowers, looks like flour on the surface of the blossoms as well as leaves. Mildew causes flowers to fade much sooner than they should.

A less common fungus is botrytis blossom blight which grows inside the flower petals, dulling or stripping away the color of the blossoms.

All of these require immediate attention, not just to promote blossoms but also to protect the health and very life of an entire African violet collection. In many cases, it is best simply to discard the affected plant immediately. (For more on pests, see Chapter Nineteen.)

Secret Seven—Choose the Right Violets

Some violets don't bloom because it isn't in their genes. Some violets bloom wildly in the worst of situations. The genetic make-up of a violet hybrid has a lot to do with its ability to bloom and the way in which it blooms. Some bloom occasionally; some keep a few blossoms up most of the time; some burst into heavy bloom on regular intervals. Some almost never bloom at all. If everything else is correct, culturally speaking, and your violet refuses to bloom, it may be genetically at fault. We would throw it away.

Choose new plants carefully, and ask questions about plants' ability to bloom. Most violet growers are very willing to suggest plants that bloom especially well. We all love those plants the best.

Secret Eight—Threaten Them!

A gently threatened violet is often a blooming violet. The survival of the species instinct causes plants to increase photosynthesis and to try to make seed when there is a possibility of death. Confining roots in small pots or disbudding for competition (See Chapter Twelve) are two examples of gentle threats that improve flowering. Yet another is a simple trick. Lightly tap the bottom of the pot on a firm surface a few times, just enough to disturb the roots. This minor "earthquake" will do no harm, and it often leads to flowering in a reluctant bloomer.

Happy Violets Don't Keep Secrets

Happy violets will bloom. If conditions around your plants are properly maintained, your violets can be happily blooming most of the time. They brag to anyone who sees them that a really good violet grower owns them.

12

Getting a Violet to Bloom on Schedule

One of the most interesting things about growing African violets is how a change in cultural conditions can affect a plant. Not only can this be a result of circumstances, but also, a grower can do this intentionally. A horticulturalist once described this as the art of "manipulation." It is the mastery of this art, which takes the average violet grower from simply keeping a plant alive and blooming to growing a show winner. Webster's dictionary defines manipulate as "to control or operate with dexterity." As we grow African violets, we need to learn which factors can be controlled as well as developing dexterity in making necessary adjustments.

Those who grow violets for competition are real experts at manipulating their violets. But even a beginner can have fun making a few changes and then watching the results. Probably the most rewarding "manipulation" is timing the African violet into bloom through the process known as "disbudding."

Set a Date

Let us say that a grower has a target date for when a violet should reach full bloom. The violet will have some bloom before this date, and some bloom will continue for weeks afterward, but with a little luck the heaviest bloom will be there that day. For competitors, this day will be the date of the show. For home growers, this date might be a special celebration such as a wedding, a holiday, or some other special occasion. It can be any day the grower chooses, but the target date should be determined months in advance.

This date should be marked on a calendar. Then count backward and mark the following: One week to go, Two weeks to go, Six weeks to go, Eight weeks to go, Ten weeks to go. Make sure this calendar is in a prominent place so these dates do not go by unnoticed!

Choosing the Plant

It is easiest to begin this procedure with a mature African violet that is already blooming or about to bloom. If the plant has a tendency to stay in bloom most of the time it will work especially well.

Do not be tempted to try this process for the first time with a lot of plants. Concentrate on one or two plants. Even advanced growers find that they do best when they concentrate their efforts on a limited number of their African violets.

Growers planning to enter a competition also look for characteristics that would earn points during judging. Among others, this would include a beautiful symmetrical leaf pattern, a tendency to bloom heavily, and a violet that is correct in size and type for the specific variety.

Repot the Plant

The selected plant usually benefits from being repotted. Once disbudding begins, the overall size of both the leaves and the roots can be expected to increase dramatically. It is better to do the repotting early on in the disbudding process, anticipating that a slightly larger pot ultimately will be needed.

Choose the correct size of pot. As a general rule, an African violet at its peak should be growing in a pot that is about one-third of the span of the leaves. Since it is possible to predict that the plant is going to grow during the next few months, choose a pot that is about half the width of the leaf span. A standard violet grown under normal conditions might require a four-inch pot, while the same plant disbudded may need a five- or six-inch pot by the time it is allowed to bloom. Semiminiature and miniature plants generally should never be planted into a pot that is more than three inches in diameter.

Remove any older, tired-looking leaves at this time. Bury any neck or stem that is left under the leaves. It may be necessary to cut off some of the bottom of the root in order to fit the plant into pot comfortably. Add fresh potting mix at the top to come up to just below the bottom row of leaves. Avoid disturbing the roots any more than absolutely necessary.

Choose a Good Light Location

Find a bright location that is not hot. If the plant has been growing and blooming well in a certain location, it may be placed there. If it is possible to use fluorescent lights, set the plants about twelve inches from the tubes, and keep the lights on for twelve to fourteen hours a day. The advantage of using fluorescent light is the control that the grower has over the light, especially compared to natural light which can vary from day to day.

Water the Plant Consistently

Water the plant using the same method for watering as usual. If the current method allows the plants to get quite dry between watering, it may be wise to try one of the constant watering systems such as wicking or capillary matting, as discussed in Chapter Two.

Fertilize

In order for the plant to continue to thrive, it will need regular fertilizer. Plants constantly receiving small doses of needed food will produce more even, healthier growth. (For more on this subject see Chapter Five.)

Occasionally, competitive growers will suggest using a "bloom booster" fertilizer twelve to fifteen weeks before a show. These are generally fertilizers that contain unusually high levels of phosphorus in comparison to other elements. Bloom boosters must be used according to directions, taking care not to burn violet leaves with too much. If used, they should always be a substitute for the regular fertilizer; they should never be used concurrently.

Take Off All of the Bloom

Removing all the blossoms may be a very painful thing for a beginner to do. Each blossom seems so precious! The key to manipulating the plant into bloom at a specific time is to restrict its blooming until approximately eight weeks before you want it to bloom. That means that all blossoms and all buds will be removed regularly, every week, up until the date marked on the calendar as "eight weeks to show." From this date on, the plant will be allowed to come into bloom. It should take the next eight weeks for the new buds to develop and open into full bloom, just in time for the target day.

The blossom stems can be removed by using a small pair of scissors. Trim the stem so that only about one-fourth-inch, or less, is left. As you become more experienced, it may be easier to do this using other methods, but this is a reliable system for the beginner. As new bud stems form, continue to trim each stem back weekly before any blossoms begin to show color or open.

The Last Two Months

The plant will probably grow larger during the time it is not allowed to bloom. More leaves will appear and others will grow larger. If this growth was not anticipated in the initial transplanting, the violet may need to be moved into a larger pot, following the rule that the pot be one-third of the leaf span on the target day. Do so without disturbing the root ball, if possible, taking great care not to break any leaves. If you are doing this for a show, do not repot until the week before the show or blooming may be interrupted since the violet may switch gears and try to grow more roots. If you are doing this for fun and not competition, this repotting can be omitted.

A disbudded violet may be a little more persistent about developing suckers (small secondary plants under the leaves) during this time too. Remove these as soon as it is evident that they are not blossom stems; suckers will have two pairs of leaves, whereas blossom stems will show, at most, one pair.

Many growers try to provide a little additional artificial light to help support the plant's natural urge to bloom in the last few weeks. If fluorescent lights are used, the length of day may be increased by one half hour a week up to sixteen hours total per day.

As it reaches full bloom the plant will need a little more water. Flowers require lots of water to stay fresh. Don't let your violet dry out now. That does not mean that the soil should be any more saturated than usual, only that the plant will have a tendency to dry out more quickly and must be monitored closely.

Heat waves, as well as other factors, can cause the plant to come into bloom a little earlier than planned. If blossoms are already open two weeks after disbudding has ended (this would be the "six-weeks-to-show" date on the calendar), remove those bud stems. Individual blossoms that have opened by three weeks ahead of the target date will probably not last. These individual blossoms may be carefully trimmed off their stems, one by one with a pair of manicure scissors, leaving unopened buds in place. This encourages other buds on the flower stem to develop to full size and eliminates flowers that will not make it to the target day.

What if It Didn't Work?

Occasionally, even the most experienced growers have failures. Try again! There are some African violets that can be more difficult to predict. Many have found that variegated-foliage plants are more reluctant to reach full bloom in eight weeks. It may be wise to allow ten or even twelve weeks for some of these varieties. Green-foliaged cultivars with very double blooms may also take ten to twelve weeks to come into full bloom, while single types will often bloom out in six weeks and sometimes less! This is where the "dexterity" that Webster talked about comes in!

The cultural factors of pot size, soil, water, temperature, light, and fertilizer need to be correctly maintained throughout the disbudding period. Poor culture is tough on violets at any time, but it can especially affect the quality and quantity of bloom on disbudded plants. Temperatures have a pronounced effect on the blossoming, especially in the weeks when the bud stems are finally allowed to grow and open. Heat will bring the flowers up much more quickly, and cold can have the opposite effect. If buds show color four weeks out, try turning the heat down a couple of degrees to slow them down.

Give It a Try

The process of "disbudding" will not injure an African violet plant. It is simply one of those manipulations that man can make upon the plant in order to take advantage of the natural pattern of blooming. Thwarted in its effort to bloom for weeks, a violet that is finally allowed to flower can often produce an outstanding display. Large standard-sized violets are quite capable of one hundred or more open blossoms.

Learning the joy of this manipulation is risky though. It's easy to get hooked. If this happens, join a club and compete with other good growers! If not, you will still have fun timing a violet into bloom for a special occasion. At the very least you can take pride in learning how to make a violet put on a command performance.

13

Big and Beautiful: Growing Huge African Violets

Growing a violet to a huge size requires very similar techniques as growing a violet to bloom on schedule. Here, however, we won't worry too much about when it blooms, however. This time we are going to concentrate on the techniques and conditions to maximize size.

Have you ever seen a masterfully grown giant show plant? Imagine an African violet that is more than twenty inches in diameter, with one hundred or more open blossoms held proudly above perfect rows of overlapping leaves. It is an awesome sight!

African violet shows across the country often place the biggest and most beautiful plants near the entrance of the show room, because they capture and hold the attention of even the most novice plant lover. We love to watch the reaction of an individual who has never seen African violets with such power and size. "What are these? They're not African violets, are they? Are they real? They sure don't look like the ones Mom has! Wow!"

Growing large standard violets is not for everyone. Space limitations often prohibit growing lots of the big plants in any collection. But it is amazing to watch a plant begin to assume massive proportions, and it is equally satisfying to know that you can make a plant grow like that!

Impress your friends and family. Follow a few simple rules and see how big you can grow an African violet.

Choosing a Plant that will Grow Large

Every African violet has a genetic code inside its cells that determines how large it can grow. The code controls the maximum size of the individual leaves and the maximum diameter of the foliage. Usually the two go together, and a variety that has very large broad leaves will also grow to a very broad diameter. Conversely, a variety with small or tiny leaves will tend to grow to a much smaller size.

The smallest of African violets are classified as miniature. Those only slightly larger are described as semiminiature. Even with four or five rows of their tiny leaves, these plants are genetically small and expected not to exceed an eight-inch diameter for a semiminiature or six-inch diameter for a miniature. African violets classified as standards are genetically capable of growing to a larger size with mature leaves that are usually at least two inches wide and long and may be expected to grow to at least ten inches in diameter.

Large standards have the genetic ability to produce leaf blades that may measure six inches wide and long. When a large standard is well grown with several rows of these huge leaves, it can easily achieve an overall diameter of twenty or more inches.

So, if you wish to grow a violet with impressive size, you must first select one of the "large standard" varieties. If you are ordering by mail, look for the descriptions that emphasize large-growing size.

Several varieties we have observed that can grow quite large include "Rebel's Splatter Kake," "Buckeye Love's Caress," "Harbor Blue," "Geronimo" and "Lollipalooza"—all cultivars that have been introduced in recent years. "Picasso" and "Happy Cricket" have both been around for a bit longer and are also known for their size.

Remember, you must start with genetically large varieties, and then you must provide them with optimum conditions to grow them to their maximum size.

Basic Care

The large-growing plants will need the same quality conditions that are recommended for growing good African violets of any size.

Provide adequate and consistent light for a twelve-hour period each day. Be sure the light is intense enough to allow the plant to grow flat without the leaves reaching upward. We would recommend that fluorescent lights on timers be used to guarantee day-to-day consistency and good quality light. This is needed if the large standard is going to continue to grow at a maximum rate.

Provide a consistent water source. You may choose to wick-water, to use capillary matting, or to use any of the self-watering pots or potting systems. Once-a-week watering may allow a rapidly growing violet to become too dry, thus slowing the rate of growth. The constant-water systems provide water on demand as well as raising humidity levels, proven advantages to many expert growers.

Provide good temperature controls. African violets prefer temperatures in the low 70s during the day, with a slightly cooler temperature at night. If a large standard plant is in cooler conditions, it will have a slower growth rate and smaller size. Warmer temperatures will speed up the growth rate, but the plant may lose its compact quality and become leggy. It also may lose some of the sturdy vigor that the largest plants need to sustain outside rows of leaves.

Provide an excellent porous potting mix. All violets benefit from growing in a soil medium that provides adequate air space for developing roots while maintaining adequate moisture. Be sure the soil mixture remains loose around the roots. Avoid packing it down when repotting.

Potting up

Most standard African violets do well in four- or five-inch squatty pots. But large standards that may grow to diameters of more than twenty inches probably need seven- or eight-inch pan pots to accommodate the roots.

There is an interesting twist to this, however. A large standard that is kept in only a four-inch pot usually will not grow to its maximum genetic size. Since the root system has been confined and limited in size, the leaf span also will tend to be limited. It is the same principle that is used in bonsai to produce dwarf-sized plants. This principle is most often used in the growing of miniature African violets. By using exceedingly small containers a miniature can be dwarfed to a remarkably tiny size.

Since the object of our discussion does not involve dwarfing the large standards in any way, but rather achieving maximum size, it is necessary to provide as much pot size as the roots are capable of filling.

Excess pot size could result in saturated soil around the roots. This may retard good healthy root growth or result in root rot due to a lack of air in the soil. Too little space will slow the rate of growth in both the roots and the leaves. Timing the transplanting perfectly is a real art!

A young, non-blooming plant requires a small pot. When the roots begin to fill the pot, becoming dense enough to hold shape when lifted out of the pot, the plant may safely be moved to the next size pot. This can happen fairly quickly with the large-growing hybrids. As a plant grows, it needs to be repotted into a pot that is one inch larger in diameter approximately every two months. Some top growers may be able to push this along faster, and some who are more cautious might wish to allow the plants three months before transplanting.

Fertilizing

It is also important to provide adequate nutrients to push a large standard violet along at its maximum growth rate. Again, it requires some skill neither to under-fertilize nor to over-fertilize. Providing a constant source of African violet fertilizer with the watering system will provide the basic nutrients for everyday needs. As a rule, use from one-half to full strength according to directions on the package, the former being best if wick-watering.

To achieve maximum size in their violets, many growers believe that it is helpful to provide extra support to the leaves with periodic foliar feeding. This is a process of misting a mild fertilizer solution directly onto the leaf surface. While other fertilizers can be used, we prefer to use fish emulsion for this process. Add about one-sixteenth of a teaspoon of fish emulsion to a quart bottle of warm water, and lightly mist the foliage (avoid spraying until the leaves are dripping wet). It is best to do this early in the day, so that the plants will dry off before the usually cooler and more humid nighttime hours. Spraying late in the day could encourage the growth and spread of fungal diseases.

We recommend foliar feeding be done whenever a large standard plant is transplanted, and once or twice a month between transplanting to achieve maximum size. Many skilled show plant growers like to foliar feed as often as once a week during the last few weeks before a show.

Theoretically, foliar feeding provides a quick absorption of nitrogen into the plant cells. The nitrogen is needed to build chlorophyll so that light can be processed into plant energy. When plants are very actively growing, additional nitrogen, provided through the leaf surface, will support the cells and allow them to continue growing at the most efficient rate.

Disbudding to Achieve Size

African violets tend to focus their energy on specific parts of the plant's anatomy at different times. When the plant is small, the focus is first on root development and then leaf development. As the plant matures, the focus is on flower development. If a seed pod were to set, the focus would be on the seed. When a grower prevents the development of buds and flowers, the energy is quite naturally redirected to the roots and the foliage.

This prevention of bud and flower development is done by disbudding. Growers disbud by removing the bud stem when it is quite small, before the flowers have opened. Buds can be gently prodded out with a dull tool or clipped off with tiny scissors. Disbudding for four or five months will allow for a dramatic increase in a plant's size. The leaves will become thicker and sturdier. A plant may, however, develop a coarse appearance if the process goes on for too long. Every violet has a maximum genetic size, and excessive disbudding will not cause the plant to grow beyond its hereditary limitations.

Maximum Size—Peaking at the Right Time

The maximum size of an African violet can be compared to an athlete reaching a conditioning peak just in time for the Olympics. Athletes are conscious that they cannot sustain that peak for very long, so they must pace themselves and take excellent care of themselves especially as they near the competition. An African violet that is grown to its maximum size cannot keep a maximum head of bloom for more than a few weeks. It will begin to slow its growth rate and often the outside row of leaves will lose color and begin to fade. With good care it will maintain some of its size, and it may continue to bloom steadily but not with the overwhelming frenzy that occurs after disbudding has been completed.

Many growers use an ebb-and-flow technique of growing these large standards. They grow them to their maximum size and bloom, then remove outside leaves and the flowers and pot them down for a while. As they recover energy, the plants will again begin a growth spurt and the process begins all over again.

Love a Big Violet

You may be able to tell that we personally love big violets. A massive African violet in full bloom is awe-inspiring to us. We know we are not alone. It is often the big violets that attract attention at African violet shows, and the big violets that cause the public to want to try the hobby themselves. Of course, the big violets take up lots of room. It can easily happen that only two of the large standards will fit under a four-foot fluorescent light fixture. Not many of us have that kind of room to spare. On the other hand, it only takes one big plant in full bloom to earn tremendous praise for your ability to grow magnificent African violets! Where else can you get so much acclaim for something a plant wanted to do anyway?

14

Different Kinds of Violets

The first violet for most people is usually a standard-sized plant. That is the kind of violet most commonly found for sale at grocery and discount stores. But there are a number of other violet types out there, including miniatures and semi-miniatures, trailing types, and species. They have lots in common when it comes to basic culture, but there are some differences.

In Some Ways All Violets are the Same

Regardless of type, all African violets need adequate light. Some types need more and some need less, but the amount of light is closely related to a violet's ability to bloom.

All violets also need evenly moist conditions. Extremely dry conditions will limit the ability to bloom, while extremely wet conditions will almost certainly lead to rot. Any method of watering may be used, regardless of type. This would include top or bottom watering, wick watering, and using any of the specialized self-watering pots.

All violets need light porous potting mix. The mix should provide lots of air circulation around the roots and still retain moisture. Potting mix should never be packed, as this eliminates necessary air. A pH of 6.8 is recommended in order to absorb the nutrients properly. Many growers choose a mix that is similar to a one-one-one mix, which is one part Canadian sphagnum peat moss, one part perlite, and one part vermiculite. The addition of dolomite lime will help to buffer (prevent wide variations in) the pH.

All violets need shallow pots, since their roots do not grow deep. In most cases, all violets will bloom best when their roots completely fill the pot, so using a pot with a small diameter is usually best.

All violets need fertilizer. Nutrients will improve plant growth and the quality and quantity of bloom. The fertilizer should be applied according to directions, usually on a weekly basis. Avoid over-fertilizing, which can lead to burning. Balanced formulations (e.g., 20-20-20) or formulas with higher phosphorous (e.g., 15-30-15) are both commonly used by top growers.

All violets also need some humidity in order to allow tender flower buds to develop without drying out. In most cases, 40 to 60% humidity is optimum.

All violets can be propagated by leaf cuttings or by suckers. All can be pollinated by any type of African violet and will produce seed.

In all violets, new leaves appear in the center of the crown. Older leaves will gradually die and be shed. Over time, this will always result in a neck which is often unsightly. All violets will need maintenance repotting in order to bury the neck and to freshen the potting mix.

Single-crowned Violets

There are three types of violets that are grown as single-crowned plants: miniatures, semiminiatures, and standards. Ideally, these should have a flat shape with all leaves growing in a horizontal rosette from the one central point of growth.

Special Needs of Miniatures

Miniature violets, by definition, must be no larger than six inches in diameter. These little gems have some special needs, most especially the size of the pot. The pot must be no deeper than about two inches and up to two and a half inches in diameter. Growers have discovered that miniatures potted into tiny "thumb pots" may bloom when the plant is only two or three inches.

To avoid drying out in such small pots, miniatures need to be watered more frequently if they are not on a constant water system. They seem to do especially well on capillary matting.

Miniatures also need to be repotted very frequently. Most top growers find miniatures do best when repotted three or four times a year or whenever a neck becomes visible below the bottom row of leaves. Repotting often triggers a showy bloom cycle.

Miniatures do well on bright window shelves with frequent rotating to maintain an even shape. They also do very well under fluorescent lights. When grown in artificial light, they need to be only six to eight inches from the light tube for ten to twelve hours daily.

One common problem: they need to be watched closely for the development of suckers (side shoot growth between the leaves). Suckers should be removed promptly to prevent distortion of symmetry.

Special Needs of Semiminiatures

Semiminiature violets, those no larger than eight inches in diameter, are remarkably similar to the minis, except that they may be grown in slightly larger pots. While many growers put semiminis in the same size pots they use for minis, semi-miniatures can be grown in pots up to three inches in diameter.

Some semiminiature violets have a genetic tendency to grow slightly larger than eight inches. These can be kept smaller by confining them to smaller pots.

Special Needs of Standards

Standards are those that grow larger than eight inches in diameter and may be as large as thirty inches (according to variety) when grown for competition. Here it is recommended that the pot be about one-third the overall size of the foliage. Most standards do well in four or five inch pots that are not deeper than three to four inches. Squatty pots and bulb pans are often chosen.

Standards will grow well on windowsills but often do not fit there as neatly as the miniatures or semiminiatures. They thrive under fluorescent lights but need to be about ten to twelve inches (from foliage to tube) below the light unit with lights on for ten to twelve hours daily.

It is best to transplant standards at least once a year to bury the neck that developed normally as lower leaves were removed. As with miniatures and semi-miniatures, suckers must be removed promptly in order to keep a single crown of growth.

Trailing African Violets

Trailers can be classified as miniature, semiminiature, or standard size according to the size of the individual leaves. The miniature size may actually be microminiature with tiny leaves that are only a quarter-of-an-inch wide and a half-inch long. The overall size of a mature trailer, regardless of its size classification, can be quite large or quite small. For example, it is not difficult to grow a miniature trailer to fill a shallow round 12-inch tray. Similarly, a standard trailer can be fully mature in a four-inch pot.

Trailing violets are expected to have many (at least three) centers of growth so that they form a pretty mound of leaves and flowers. Trailing is an inbred trait and should not be confused with violets that genetically should have only one crown but have been allowed to sucker without discipline. True trailers often have the word "trail" as a part of their name and tend to have more space between leaves on the main stems. This space allows them to have multiple crowns that are not so tightly packed as to be unattractive.

They may be grown either at windows or under fluorescent lights. They are especially charming when grown in natural light and the more open growth that occurs in that situation can actually enhance a trailer's appearance.

Trailers may be grown in two ways. One method keeps a trailing violet in a pot that is approximately one-third the overall diameter of the plant. This allows the plant to grow out over the sides of the pot in an attractive way as the various crowns of the plant develop. In this method, the main stems of the trailing growth are not allowed to come into contact with the potting mix. Growers often pinch out the crowns to encourage secondary growth between leaves so that a pretty form develops. Plants tend to bloom when the foliage has begun to trail well over the edges.

A second method of growing a trailer is to place the plant into a broad shallow pot or tray. As crowns develop, the centers are pinched out and leaves that are closest to the soil are removed to allow the bare stem to touch the potting mix and root. This ultimately results in a mound that extends just to the edge of the pot when it begins to bloom freely. It will often appear to be many violets planted together in the same dish, but all crowns should be connected to the original crown by stems.

With either method, grooming off older, yellowing or damaged leaves is important to keeping the plants attractive. The older leaves will often be a faded green color and sometimes larger in comparison to other leaves on the crown. Leaves that are inside the mound (and not receiving light) may dry up and need to be removed. Since the plant may have hundreds of flowers when it is at peak, grooming off old flowers (sometimes with long tweezers) is important to keep the plant attractive.

Species

The species African violets are the ones that were found in nature. There are over twenty unique African violet species that have been described. Depending on the individual species, they may have a rosette form or a multiple-stemmed trailing form. They may also have a small or larger size. All have single blossoms, often blue.

With so much variety of type in this group of violets, one would expect to have a variety of special growing needs. That is true. Each of the species came from a unique area in Africa and as such has a preference for temperature and light. Anyone who grows these should study the individual species' inclinations. Those who choose to grow species successfully must approach them scientifically.

Generally, species need less light than the hybrids and thrive when grown in or near windows rather than under artificial light. They may need lighter fertilizing. They also need to be allowed to be wild, growing as they please. That means that they might have multiple crowns or long spaces between leaves. They may vary in color, have pale green foliage, or have flowers which hide below the foliage and still be considered well grown.

Species plants also prefer to be grown in relatively small pots, but the rule here is often simply that the pot should be just large enough to avoid tipping over. Growers shouldn't be discouraged if they wish to experiment, attempting to find the perfect growing situation even if it is unconventional by modern standards. Growing species is much like caring for wild animals in the zoo. The goal is always to make the wild creature feel most at home while still in captivity. (For more about species, see Chapter Twenty-three.)

Variety is the Spice of Life

While new growers often begin with standards, it is fun to branch out and grow the other types of African violets. A grower may find that miniatures and semiminiatures fit better into limited space. It may be that trailers will grow well in a situation where single-crowned plants never do. For those who love nature and science, the species offer a challenge that is very satisfying.

We have always loved the drama of the big standards, but we treasure every plant in the African violet family. With a few adjustments and attention to details, they can all successfully live under one roof!

15

Life on the Edge: Growing Variegated Violets

African violets with variegated leaves can be a spectacular sight. There is great beauty in foliage that exhibits colors like cream, pink, yellow, white and lavender in addition to the basic shades of green. Some growers like them because "they are pretty even when they aren't in bloom." On the other hand, growers often experience some problems in getting these plants to thrive, and just enjoying the foliage isn't really that satisfying! There are several extras that variegated violets seem to need to perform as well as their all-green sisters.

Plants of all kinds are green due to the pigment chlorophyll which is found within plant cells. Variegation is the genetic tendency of certain African violets to produce uneven amounts of this green pigment, resulting in foliage that shows other contrasting colors. Any color blossom can be found above variegated foliage, and many hybridizers seek to combine blossom colors with complimentary variegated foliage to create new effects.

Often, the variegated portion of the foliage is found just around the edges of the individual leaves. This is generally termed "Tommie Lou" variegation. For the most part, plants with this type of variegation trace their ancestry back to a violet named "Tommie Lou," which had sported to green-and-white foliage from the green-leafed "White Pride." Infrequently, violet hybrids may have variegation running down the spine of the leaf or scattered across the leaf. "Crown variegation" refers to those varieties which have a lighter greenish pattern in the crown of the plant that disappears as the leaves mature.

Regardless of the type of variegation, the lighter areas do not have as much of the chlorophyll that is found in the green part of the leaf. The variegated cells are genetically less capable of producing chlorophyll. The chlorophyll absorbs light and converts it into chemical energy. This is the basis for the process of photosynthesis.

The Significance of Nitrogen and Bacteria

Nitrogen is needed by green plants to produce chlorophyll. Air is about 79% nitrogen and is one source from which plants can draw this important nutrient. Soils can also contain nitrogen, especially when it is added in the form of fertilizer. This nitrogen cannot enter the plants through the roots in its raw form, however. Plants often depend on the presence of bacteria, which lives in the soil and on the roots, to process the nitrogen into oxygen-nitrogen compounds called "nitrates." Nitrates are in a form which the plant can then absorb through the roots, carry into the cell cytoplasm, and use to manufacture the green pigment called "chlorophyll." Bacteria are very important to plant growth!

This may sound rather complicated, but understanding the value of bacteria and their relationship to nitrogen is very important to understanding how to control variegation in African violets so that the plants can still thrive.

Less Chlorophyll Means Less Energy

The cells with little to no chlorophyll are not able to produce chemical energy for the plant; thus they tend to make the plant less efficient. When an automobile engine is less efficient, it tends to waste fuel, go slower, and eventually die. Violets react the same way. The grower has to "tune up" horticultural skills in order to get the expected performance. All of the basic elements of good growing have to be a little closer to perfect, because variegated plants are more sensitive to poor conditions and have less ability to thrive when a grower makes a mistake.

A lack of energy in an African violet is also going to result in a lack of something else: blossoms! And, face it, no matter how lovely variegated foliage might be, we do expect our violets to produce abundant blooms.

Real mastery comes when you also learn how to control the amount of variegation on the foliage, so that there is always enough chlorophyll in the plant to sustain it, and at the same time enough variegation to please the eye.

Controlling the Basics

We keep coming back to the basic elements of growing. But, even if you're bored, here we go again. The basics are critical to healthy growth which leads, in turn, to blooming.

All violets, and especially variegated ones, need about twelve hours of light daily. This needs to be very bright, but not hot. Variegated violets grown in low light do not have the ability to produce enough energy to bloom. Very often, they will become spindly and lose outside leaves.

All violets need to be watered evenly and need to have humidity in the air around them. Variegated plants use water in the same way as the solid green foliage and there are not many differences here.

All violets need to be grown in light, airy soil. Since the air in the soil is one way that nitrogen contacts the bacteria and becomes useful as a nitrate, it is important to expose roots to air within the soil medium. The airy soil is also useful in allowing fibrous roots to grow without resistance.

All violets need to be fed. This is especially important with variegated violets. The green portions of the leaf must be well supported with nutrients so that they are able to operate as efficiently as possible. If the plant is "starving," there will be less chlorophyll produced and thus less energy produced. Remember, the light portions of the leaf depend on the green sections to sustain them. That's what "life on the edge" is all about.

Don't forget, along with nutrients, the pH factor of the soil must be maintained at or near 6.8 in order to allow the nutrients to be absorbed by the plant most efficiently.

The Critical Factor of Temperature

All violets thrive when grown at moderate temperatures. Variegated violets, however, are especially sensitive to temperature changes. This is at least partly due to the fact that bacteria in the soil are more active in warmer temperatures. Hot bacteria are busy bacteria! (Now, aren't you glad you understand how bacteria make nitrogen into nitrates for plants to use?) When the bacteria are more active, it makes more nitrates available to the plant.

Variegated violets grown in warm temperatures have more active bacteria about them, and thus plenty of nitrates are available. When this happens, even the less-efficient variegated portions of the leaves begin to produce some chlorophyll and they become greener. Plants grown in these conditions may appear to lose their variegation entirely.

When variegated plants are grown in cooler temperatures, the opposite happens. Cold bacteria are lazy bacteria! With less active bacteria, there are fewer nitrates available and thus less chlorophyll is produced. The overall effect is that the plant becomes more variegated, and less green is evident. Ultimately, the plant may lose all of its green color. This beautiful effect often means eventual death. It's sort of like falling off the edge.

Controlling the Amount of Variegation

Ideally, a variegated violet should have enough interesting markings to please the eye, while sustaining enough green to support growth. The trick for the grower is to recognize when a plant has reached that balance and to master the art of encouraging and discouraging variegation to maintain that balance.

One way to control variegation is to control the temperatures at which the plants are grown. Most variegated hybrids will keep a good balance of color when grown at 72° F. Growing them warmer usually produces a greater percentage of green, and growing them cooler produces more variegation. If you live in an area with cold winter temperatures, you will probably need to place variegated plants up on higher shelves where the air tends to be warmer. If you must live with extremely warm summer temperatures, you will probably find that the plants show better variegation when kept on lower shelves where the air is somewhat cooler.

Another way to control variegation is through fertilizing. Some growers prefer to use fertilizers with very little nitrogen (5-50-17 is one formulation that is specifically recommended for variegates). This may be of use in areas where temperatures are so warm that the soil bacteria are able to produce all the nitrates needed just using available air. In cooler areas, this formulation may cause plants to become too variegated and thus weak.

Plants that are showing too much variegation (especially in cool areas) may have bacteria which are too inactive to process nitrogen efficiently. Foliar feeding (a process of spraying nutrients directly onto the foliage) can be used to add nitrogen to the leaf cells. This results in increased production of chlorophyll and greener leaves. Most fertilizers can be applied in this way, but our favorite is to use fish emulsion (at a rate of about one-sixteenth teaspoon to a quart of very warm water. Apply this by misting the surface of the leaves thoroughly. Keep them out of direct sunlight while the leaves are wet. A drop of dishwashing liquid can be added to reduce spotting on the leaves.

Selecting Variegates

Just as with any other violet hybrids, one does need to be somewhat selective in choosing variegated African violets for one's collection, especially for those with limited growing space as well as growers who are still tentatively experimenting.

Different plants will perform in different ways depending upon the growing conditions to which they are exposed.

Individual hybrids will have specific genetic capacities when it comes to degrees of variegation exhibited. Cultivars which may perform wonderfully for those in warm climates may variegate too heavily for those who grow in cool climates. And conversely, cultivars that just variegate nicely for those in cool areas may not show any variegation at all for growers in warm areas.

As a beginner, it might be wise to seek out the advice of other growers in your area for good reliable variegated cultivars. After mastering the care of these plants, it will be more fun to venture forth and experiment with a host of other available variegates.

Propagating Variegated Leaves

Both green and variegated cultivars can be propagated by leaf cuttings. There are a few tricks to getting strong babies from a variegated leaf successfully, especially in cooler climates.

First of all, when choosing a leaf from the variegated plant to put down, avoid heavy variegation. Remember that variegation is a genetic tendency and even if a leaf is showing no variegation, it carries the genes. Mostly green leaves from variegated violets will be much stronger in surviving and producing plantlets.

All leaves seem to root faster and produce clumps faster when the soil is somewhat warmer than average. Variegated leaves will benefit from being placed in an area where the temperatures are slightly above 75°.

When plantlets appear, watch them closely for variegation. If the babies are too white, in spite of your attempts to keep them warm, foliar feeding may help them to survive.

We have found that it is most helpful to foliar feed the plantlets just after separating them from the clump. We then place them inside a closed clear plastic bag for a month or so, until they begin to show more mature growth.

Notice that we are recommending that every effort be made to encourage young plants to grow as green as possible. As they mature, they will develop the characteristic variegation, and at that time they will have the strength to support it.

Beautiful

Although variegated African violets really are weaklings genetically, they can be incredibly beautiful. When all the conditions are met and the balance of variegation is controlled, the plants are capable of lovely blooming habits as well.

Growing variegates may at times seem like living on the edge, having to balance out cultural conditions a little more carefully. But in the end, it is certainly well worth the effort because you can enjoy your variegates for more than just their foliage. Get out there on the edge!

Section Three—Beyond the Fundamentals

16

A Beginner's Guide to Judging

Do you grow blue-ribbon violets? Does that just mean you are pleased with how your violets are looking? No, not unless you are familiar with the standards set by the African Violet Society of America (AVSA). Novice growers often find it hard to realize that a full head of bloom does not equal blue ribbons. There are other factors besides blooming that make a plant a winner.

One of the major activities of AVSA is its supervision of violet shows in which plants are judged for their quality. A primary goal of the society is to educate the public regarding African violets, and it deems shows and merit judging to be excellent tools in the education process.

What if you have no intention or opportunity ever to exhibit a plant for judging? Can these standards help you grow better violets? Yes! When you evaluate your own violets against the standards used for judging show violets, you can work to improve your horticultural shortcomings and grow even better plants. There is very little else in the world that can rival the simple beauty of a well-grown violet.

The Scale of Points

In order to make judging consistent, a scale of points was designed to help judges look at all aspects of each plant. This scale allows the greatest majority of points for the appearance of the plant; it also allows a few points for being true to the variety. The scale of points for judging most African violets is:

Symmetry or leaf pattern—twenty-five points
Condition (cultural perfection)—twenty-five points
Quantity of bloom—twenty-five points
Size and type of blossom, according to the variety—fifteen points
Color, according to the variety—ten points

Presumably, only a perfect violet could ever receive a full one hundred points. The perfect violet is a very rare item! Do notice that there are no points for extreme size. A perfect violet could be less than six inches across; it could be twelve inches across; it could be twenty-four inches across. So, choose your best violet, and let's judge it!

Symmetry

Beautiful foliage patterns greatly enhance the overall appearance of an African violet. The goal here is to grow a plant whose leaves lay in precise, overlapping rows. For perfect symmetry, there must not be any apparent leaves missing, and there should not be spaces between the leaves where the soil or table surface below is visible.

The perfect plant would have a very round shape, and each of the leaves in a row would be exactly the same size as the other leaves in that row. Each succeeding row's leaves would be the same as or slightly larger than the row above it. The petiole (stem) of each leaf would be just long enough to extend beyond the row above but not so far that the resulting pattern shows gaps between the leaves.

Achieving perfect symmetry isn't always easy. First of all, violets are individuals. Each variety has a tendency toward a type of foliage pattern. Some varieties do not consistently form a good over-lapping foliage pattern. Some varieties are very sensitive to warm temperatures and tend to grow long petioles that make the plant look "open" with many peek holes between the leaves. Some varieties need more light than others to grow compact form. Some varieties have ruffled or wavy foliages that resist lying neatly on top of previous rows.

Aside from the differences among cultivars, it is common for there to be differences between plants that are of the same variety. Think of a litter of puppies. There may be one or two pups that are "show quality;" they show all the qualities of the breed to perfection. There are other pups that are very nice, but may have some small fault according to the standards of the breed; these puppies are called "pet quality."

Finding the "show quality" symmetry in a group of plants all of the same variety requires looking at the pattern in which leaves are growing from the crown. Generally, the first three rows will show the plant's tendency. The leaves should form an even and compact rosette.

The plant will do much of the work in growing out symmetrically, but the grower has some responsibility too. Care must be taken to give the plant enough secure space to avoid breaking leaves from crowding, bumping or falling. Maintaining even horticultural practices is also critical. The plant must be regularly fertilized and watered, and the light and temperature must be consistently correct. Overhead light, such as fluorescent tubes, will significantly improve symmetry.

A violet starts with one hundred points. Twenty-five points are allowed for symmetry. To judge the symmetry, deduct up to three points for each gap between leaves, for each change in leaf growth patterns and for each leaf that is obviously missing.

How many points did you get for symmetry? Could you improve that score immediately by removing one leaf or even a row or two of leaves? Remember, there is no penalty for having a smaller-sized plant!

Condition

Condition, or cultural perfection, is the term used to describe the quality of the horticulture. Mistakes in growing are reflected in the appearance of the plant. Some of these are easily remedied in a few minutes.

One of the most easily corrected problems of condition is dust or debris on the leaves. In some cases, brushing with a soft brush (like a makeup brush) will remove cat hair, light dust, and other debris on the leaves. This brushing should be done from the center of the plant outward.

Plants can be washed at the sink under a very gentle flow of tepid water, being very careful to keep water away from the center crown. Very dirty plants benefit from being misted with a soapy solution (a few drops of dish detergent in a quart of water) and then rinsed. Blot the leaf surface, and keep the plant out of direct sunlight until the moisture has evaporated.

Another easily correctable condition fault is the presence of stubs of removed leaves and bud stems. These need to be completely weeded out. Aside from their unsightly appearance, stubs that are left can begin to rot, allowing fungus or bacteria to enter the plant. A dull pencil point, a nut pick, or even a dentist's cleaning tool can be used to prod these away.

Along these same lines, any dead or fading flowers and any flowers with seed pods should be removed. Flowers can be snipped off with small scissors (try not to leave a stub) if other flowers on the same peduncle (stem of flowers and buds) are still developing or fresh looking. If all of the flowers on the peduncle are spent, it should be removed by gently rocking the stem from side to side until it pulls free from the main plant.

Young violets have smaller leaves than mature plants. As the plant ages, the baby leaves do not continue to increase in size. This is why small leaves can often be found growing under larger leaves. These leaves are not necessary to the plant's energy-making system and should be removed. At the same time, remove any leaves that are faded and tired looking.

A violet should be in a pot that is correctly-sized to the span of the foliage. (See Chapter Three for details.)

A neck between the bottom row of leaves and the soil is a sign of horticultural neglect. A neck of one or two inches can be buried by trimming away enough from the bottom of the soil ball to sink the plant lower into the same pot. Unfortunately, disturbing the roots is stressful on the plant and likely to cause flowers to collapse. If the neck needs to be buried so that the plant looks perfect in the very near future, it is better to try to add potting mix at the top of the pot to hide the neck. If you think you need to increase the pot size to bury the neck, avoid disturbing the roots and be sure to keep the pot in the proper relation to the diameter of the foliage.

Some condition problems are irreversible. Cracks, mars, and bruises on the leaves can't be hidden, except to remove the entire leaf. Removing the leaf might ruin the symmetry, although when it is done far enough in advance other leaves may grow in and hide the space. Exhibitors learn to compute which fault will cause a bigger point deduction and act accordingly. Giving plants safe and adequate space where they are not crowded or subject to other injuries, and handling the plants with care when they must be picked up, is critical to avoiding these blemishes.

Of the one hundred total points, there are twenty-five points allowed for condition. To judge, take off a half point for each faded blossom; take off up to one point for each occurrence of dust or debris, for each stub, and for each seed pod; also take off one point for each baby leaf and faded leaf; take off up to three points for over- or under-potting and the same for a neck; take off up to a point for each crack, mar or bruise (little ones count less).

How many points do you score for condition? Could you improve by cleaning, by removing stubs, flowers and leaves, or by repotting?

Quantity of Bloom

The amount of bloom on the violet is very important in judging. One of the most difficult skills for a judge to master is evaluating how many blossoms ought to be open on the plant. Very large plants need to have more and tiny plants fewer. To simplify the problem, the *AVSA Handbook for African Violet Growers, Exhibitors and Judges* suggests that the judge should decide how many blossoms might be expected on any plant that is the size of the one being evaluated and then award points proportionately. For example, a plant that is twelve inches in diameter might be expected to have about twenty-five fresh open flowers.

On an average day, there are very few violets that could stand up to this expectation! The reason that the goal is so high is because it is rather easy to control when the violets bloom. We can time it so that the maximum numbers of blossoms are open exactly at show time. This is done by removing all blossom stems for a period of time, up until approximately eight weeks before the plant should be in full bloom. The recommended time period for disbudding varies among growers, and some varieties need more or less time to come into bloom, but this is a good guideline. (See Chapter Twelve for more on disbudding.)

Many exhibitors who grow for show have learned to expect far more than a mere twenty-five open blooms on the best plants in the show. It is not impossible for some plants to carry over two hundred fresh blossoms. They are incredible!

Of the one hundred total points, there are twenty-five points allowed for blossoms. To judge your plant for quantity of bloom, count the number of fresh, open blooms. If your plant is about twelve inches in diameter, and expected to have twenty-five flowers, you would lose one point for each missing flower.

How many points do you score for bloom? You might try disbudding to see if you could increase this score on another day.

Size and Type of Blossom

Now we get into the points allowed for a plant performing at its genetic potential. Each plant variety has a genetic inclination to produce blossoms of a certain size and type. "Type" refers to the variety's tendency to have single, semi-double, or double layers of petals as well as the shape of the blossom. Violet flowers are either pansy-shaped, with two smaller upper lobes and three larger lower lobes, or star-shaped with five evenly sized lobes. If there are blossoms on the plant which are not correct for the variety, it is a fault and points should be deducted. Remember the puppies? The plants that vary from the variety type are "pet quality" and shouldn't score highly in competition.

It may be obvious to some, but if your plant does not have a variety name attached to it, it is automatically "pet quality." No puppy, without American Kennel Club papers, gets to be entered in a poodle show, regardless of how much it looks like a poodle. No papers, no show! Learn to keep a violet's name with the plant.

To judge for correct size and type of blossom requires lots of experience and a good book or software program. A good judge needs to know how the variety is supposed to grow and bloom. In order to help judges, AVSA is the official registration authority for African violets and publishes a Master Variety List as well as computer program, First Class, which describes many of the varieties currently being cultivated. Either of these provides the information needed to decide if your violet is blooming with the correct size and type of bloom.

In addition, good judges also try to grow many plants to get experience. They also visit shows and speak with other growers about their favorite violet varieties. Unless you are able to compare your plant's blossom with other plants of the same variety, do not deduct points here unless the blossoms are not consistently the same size or type on your one plant.

You should be able to have all fifteen points on size and type of blossom, but if you decide to enter a show, you must verify that the plant is blooming true according to its official description.

Color of Blossom

This is another set of points awarded for blooming true to the variety's genetic code. The blossom color must conform to the variety color description in the Master Variety List. Sometimes, African violets may bloom in colors that are faded or are not the intensity of color expected for those varieties. Improper temperatures and light or poor fertilization are the most common causes.

Sometimes, varieties will show signs of mutation (or sporting) by putting up a blossom stem that is entirely different from the other blossoms on the plant. This is especially true of bicolor plants and fantasies (blossoms that are speckled). This is a fault which costs one-half point per wrong color blossom. Avoid the penalty by snipping away only the miscolored blooms.

Again, you can have the full ten points unless you can see an inconsistency in blossom color or know that it is not blooming with the color that it is supposed to. Learn to shop for plants that are blooming true. Avoid the novelty of a plant, which has blossom stems that carry different colors. It's interesting but it's a "pet."

Unforgivable Show Faults

Before we add up your score, take another look at your plant. If it has evidence of insects or disease, it is not allowed to be judged in a violet show and would be removed. This protects other exhibitors' plants from being exposed to such problems.

Your plant also may not judged if it has suckers or secondary plants growing between the leaves. Except for trailing types, violets that are judged must be single crowned! If suckers are removed by prodding them with a dull pencil point or sucker plucker when only four leaves are evident, they can be easily controlled. (See Chapter Nine for more on suckers.)

You're a Winner

Now, total the score for each of the five areas. If the total score is above ninety points, the plant deserves a blue ribbon. If it scores from eighty to eighty-nine, it would earn a red ribbon; and seventy to seventy-nine points would score a white ribbon. A violet scoring below seventy points earns no award. Violets are judged by merit, and every plant receives the ribbon that matches the point score.

All these numbers may seem intimidating, and you may tend to be overly critical (most novice judges are). AVSA judges work in panels of three at shows, which helps them to make balanced decisions. You might find that it would be helpful to invite a violet friend over so that you could work together evaluating the quality of your plants.

If you followed our suggestions, you probably noticed that as you fixed some of the correctable problems to increase your score, you also got a prettier plant.

There is a real joy in judging your plants against the scale of points. It will raise your expectations of your plants; higher standards will result in higher quality. Maybe this judging primer will even lead you into attending a judging school or entering a violet show. You wouldn't regret it. Don't worry if you don't score high today. Set your goals to improve. Ask questions to find out more and keep reading!

17

Good Grooming for Violets

A specific African violet cultivar can be absolutely gorgeous for one grower, and be absolutely ugly for another. People also look better at some times than others—you should see us early in the morning! What is the difference? Grooming. And it's as important for the violet as it is for people.

Violets do tend to bloom in cycles, so there is no way to maintain the level of beauty often seen in a show. But even when plants are only blooming a little, they do need regular grooming.

Remove Old Blossoms

Every time a good grower looks at his violets, he should absent-mindedly remove blossoms that are old or faded. Fading blossoms will be just a little different in color and often somewhat transparent. Some varieties of violets have blossoms that remain fresh for weeks, some for much less than that. After a blossom has faded in color, it begins to lose its sturdiness and shape, and it sags on the stem. Soon after this, the blossom will begin to dry to a tan color.

When the first flowers on a pedicel (the short stem connecting the flower to the rest of the flower stalk) begin to fade, use a small scissors or sharp fingernails to trim off these aged blossoms trying not to leave a stub.

Once the majority of blossoms on a peduncle (the flower stalk that has multiple buds) have faded, remove the entire stem. This is usually best accomplished by gently moving the peduncle back and forth from side to side until it is released from the main stem of the plant.

Occasionally, a dead blossom will have a swollen "bulb" at its center which is a seed pod. Hybridizers would not remove these pods for many months, but most growers would remove these in the grooming process.

Remove Old Leaves

In the process of generating new leaves in the crown of the violet, older leaves begin to age. As long as these leaves are sturdy, green, and healthy, they add to the beauty of the plant. Once the leaves begin to yellow or show damaged edges, it is better to remove them.

Leaves are removed by gently moving them from side to side until the leaf snaps away from the stalk. Leaving any stem stub can make the plant vulnerable to infectious fungal diseases like botrytis.

As a young plant matures, you may note that the oldest leaves on the plant are noticeably smaller and growing under the larger leaves above them. They are often a less healthy green color and are usually quite smooth. These "baby leaves" should be removed as soon as the newer leaves mature; definitely remove them when the plant is old enough to bloom.

African violets may begin to grow much larger than the space available. In this case, healthy outside leaves may be removed to reduce the plant size. This will not cause serious injury to the plant although it may be necessary to repot to bury an exposed neck more often.

Leaves that have mars on them may be left on the plant, so long as the leaf continues to keep a healthy look. If the mar begins to work its way across the leaf in the form of wilting or drying, the leaf should be removed.

Remove the Suckers

African violet plants are often prone to developing secondary crowns or suckers between rows of leaves. If these are left, the plant will develop a bushy look. The suckers detract from the beauty of the plant and often limit the plant's ability to thrive and bloom. (For more on this subject see Chapter Nine.)

Suckers can be removed as soon as two pairs of leaves are visible in the tiny crown. It is fairly easy to poke them out with a dull pencil point at this stage. Don't get in a hurry. Flower stems often emerge with two leaves, never more. Once four leaves are visible, it is certain that the growth is a sucker.

Clean It Up!

One should remove dead and dying blossoms and leaves on a daily or weekly basis.

But violets do need deeper cleaning occasionally. A cat, nearby cooking, or an excessively dusty area like a woodworking shop may make it necessary to clean the plants even more often.

The simplest cleaning method is to brush the plant with a soft artist's brush or a make-up brush. This is an excellent way to sweep off debris and light coatings of dust. It can also help remove animal hair.

Eventually brushing will not be enough to get the plant clean, especially if the leaves have been subject to the greasy residue left from cooking or any source of smoke. Then it is necessary to wash the leaves with soapy water.

Our favorite method is to put several drops of a mild dish detergent (Ivory Liquid or Palmolive Dish Washing Liquid work well) in a quart spray bottle filled with very warm water. Spray the surface of the leaves, avoiding the center crown, until the leaves are dripping. Let the plant stand for a few minutes to allow the soap to work, then hold the plant at an angle under the tap and rinse the soap and dirt off the outside leaves with a very gentle flow of tepid water. Again avoid getting the crown wet. Lightly blot the leaves dry using a soft cloth, paper tissue, or natural sponge. The leaves will not be totally dry when this process is finished, so set the plant away from any source of sunlight until the leaf surface has completely dried.

Repot and Bury That Neck

As lower leaves die and are removed, the African violet plant will begin to develop a neck or bare stalk between the soil and the lowest row of leaves. As soon as the neck is visible the plant can be repotted in order to bury the neck. It should be done at least once a year, or the neck will become so long that repotting may cause undue stress on the plant. (For more on this subject, see Chapter Ten.)

It's Okay to Talk, but Remember to Listen

Grooming plants on a regular basis is a great way to pay attention to their health and well-being. We once read that talking to your plants is not nearly as important as listening to them. If a grower is grooming the plants regularly, he will be able to "listen." Small changes in health will be noticed. Those small changes may signal the beginning of serious trouble. If it is detected early, the grower can affect a cure. Watch for pests. Watch for a change in the color or texture of the leaves. Watch for changes in growing and blooming patterns. Most of all, just watch—that's where much of the joy of growing African violets lies.

18
African Violet Diseases

Fungus

"Now where did I get that?" is a question often asked by the beginning violet grower after diagnosing the problem with a sick violet. In fact, many violet ills do indeed come in from another place. Bugs, for example, only come from other bugs that somehow find a mode of transportation into your personal collection. But one group of violet illnesses is virtually always present, just waiting for conditions to make it easy for them to cause serious problems. These are the fungal diseases.

What is Fungus?

Fungus is actually a form of plant life that reproduces with spores. The spores germinate and produce one or more branched threads called hyphae. These hyphae are very rapid-growing and quickly mature to a stage that is capable of producing more spores. Their growth literally mushrooms!

Fungi have no leaves, flowers, or chlorophyll. From edible mushrooms to penicillium (the fungus used to produce the medication penicillin), these fungi are everywhere around us in several different shapes, colors, and sizes.

The fungi that favor African violets are pathogens (disease-producing). The damage that they cause comes as the result of the fungi infecting the cells and competing with the plant for nutrients. Some fungi appear to be on the surface of the plant, but have actually entered surface cells and are causing damage. Some groups of fungi can be entirely internal and are among the most damaging and difficult to fight.

Here's How to Make Fungus Thrive

Fungi grow best in high humidity and dampness. Each pathogen has a preferred temperature range, but most flourish in temperatures that fluctuate. This is because warm air can contain more water vapor, and when the air cools the relative humidity increases, often condensing onto surfaces. Since the spores and the resulting hyphae are so delicate and likely to dry, fungi prefer high relative humidity with little to no air movement.

Give a fungus the desired temperature, moist conditions and no movement of the air, and you will have a very healthy fungus!

There are three common fungal diseases that affect African violets: botrytis (in several forms), root/crown rot (pythium or phytophthora), and powdery mildew.

Fungus One—Botrytis

Botrytis is an invasive fungus; that is, it can grow inside the plant structure, as well as on the outside. When it is on the surface of blossoms or buds, it is a gray fuzzy mold. The blossoms react by becoming tan in color and then mushy in texture. This mold can also grow on other plant parts with similar results.

Botrytis can enter the plant through aging leaves or blossom stems with soft, limp, or watery stems that are left on the violet too long. Using a contaminated knife blade to cut leaves for propagation can also spread botrytis. In fact, botrytis will follow any moist pathway produced by a cut, a puncture (such as a mite seeking food), or a break.

When botrytis is inside the plant structure it will appear in two ways. The most common is blighted leaf tissue and wilting. The leaves simply lose their stiffness and fail. This is especially distressing (and common) when propagating leaf cuttings.

A second way botrytis can appear inside the plant is in a form called botrytis blossom blight. In the earliest stage of development, the plants will have healthy foliage and look strong, but inside the blossom petals the botrytis causes the flower color to take on a light gray cast and then dry off prematurely. Perhaps the best description is that it appears that the color has been "sucked out" of the flower. In more advanced stages the foliage will also begin to show signs of graying and stunting.

Controlling Botrytis

First of all, as with any of the problem fungi, control is achieved by reducing humidity and avoiding over-watering. Temperatures must be controlled especially to avoid cool periods, and air movement increased. Ceiling fans can be especially helpful when allowed to run during the day and night. It is also helpful to space plants further apart to allow more air movement.

With traditional botrytis infestations, remove any moldy blossoms or leaves immediately, and then wash hands. Aerosol disinfectant spray (Lysol is one common brand) can be misted into the area, allowing the mist to drift onto the affected plants. The spray is cold coming out of the can so avoid getting too close; the chill could further injure the plant. Please note that this will not cure botrytis that has already invaded plant tissue, but it will slow the spread to other plants by killing spores in the air or on the plant surface.

Once botrytis has occurred in a plant collection, it is wise to take precautions against its reoccurring. Use only sterilized knives (cleaned with chlorine bleach or in the dishwasher) when cutting leaf stems. Use a pastuerized potting mix. Remove fading leaves and blossom stems before stems become watery and limp. Watch for evidence of insects that can spread the fungus.

Fungicides that are specifically designed to control botrytis may be used. Chemicals on the market at this time vary according to effectiveness, application, and systemic ability. Some of the chemicals will leave residue on the foliage. Others will damage flowers. If botrytis is detected, it may take some time to locate the fungicide that is currently the most effective. The African Violet Society of America (which publishes articles on current recommended treatments in the African Violet Magazine), the website www.avsa.org or violet club members are often good places to begin the search.

Fungus Two—The Crown and Root Rot Diseases

It is quite common for beginning growers to overwater their violets and to end up having a fungus fight with one of the several diseases causing crown and root rot. Pythium and phytophthora are the two most common pathogens which result in rot in African violets. It is not usually necessary to identify which one of the two rot diseases is present since most of the fungicides and other controls work on both. Like botrytis blossom blight, they work internally. Neither shows the characteristics of fuzzy mold or other typical fungus form on the plant surface. They are only revealed by the results of its presence inside the plant.

Depending on the species and the strain, the two diseases may present very similar symptoms affecting the crown, the stem and the roots. Underground, the roots become dark brown or blackened, as well as matted and deteriorated. Above ground, the plant will first develop yellow patches on leaves, followed by wilting, and often showing a darkening and withering on the main stalk or at joints with leaf stems. It is common for outside leaves to wilt first, but ultimately the crown dies. This can happen very quickly, but it can also take months. In its final stage, the plant will not be attached to the roots at all and can be lifted off the pot.

The rot is quite obvious when an affected plant is subjected to an autopsy. The inside of the main stem may be darkened and may be somewhat hollow. Sometimes the infected main stem will be filled with brown cork-like tissue. A normal stem will be have light green color inside and be dense and firm. A healthy stem will have a nearly complete circle of purplish dots around the center that should not be confused with symptoms of rot.

Another classic symptom is a darkened spot that forms at the base of the petiole (leaf stem) at the point where it meets the main stem. This almost always happens first with the oldest leaves which are nearest the soil. Soon after the petiole darkens, the tissue shrinks or withers and the leaf will pull away from the stem easily. Often the thick skin (the cortex) around the main stalk of the plant separates from the core of the stalk. The pathogen will progress up the main stalk of the plant until it reaches the crown and the plant is dead.

Both pythium and phytophthora are sometimes called "water molds." This is because the spores are mobile in water; they actually have a sort of swimming foot to propel them. This swimming spore is much more mobile in very wet conditions, and thus rot is most common in plants that have been potted in heavy soils and overwatered.

Controlling Rot

It is possible to eradicate crown and root rot from a specific plant by repotting and cutting away all infected tissue. Usually, this means cutting the crown away from the roots. The stem must be examined for any sign of infection. If it is found, leaves must be removed and another cut must be made higher on the main stem until no sign of rot is evident. Be sure that the knife used is cleaned in bleach before each cut. Also be sure to dispose of all infected plant parts and old soil well away from the growing area. Once the fungus has been cut away, the plant can be set into fresh soil to be rerooted. (See Chapter Ten for more on this technique of repotting.)

To avoid the onset of the disease, it is necessary to steer clear of too moist conditions, especially overwatering. A dry, wilted violet needs water, but it is not wise to allow it to soak for several hours. The extremes seem to invite infection. Water allows the spores to travel quickly, and weakened roots are more vulnerable to infections. Rather, when violets become unusually dry, it is best to add a very small quantity of water to the soil and allow the roots to plump. The next day, additional water can be added, and the plant will slowly re-hydrate without falling victim to rot.

Crown rot can also invade more easily when plants are being overfertilized, which can harm the roots. The roots damaged this way allow the rot to enter the plant structure. Similarly, fungus gnats may injure roots and make the plant more vulnerable to rot. The gnats thrive in the same damp condition that encourages rot.

Because the rot spores are extremely common in water supplies, it is important to use very porous potting mix that allows air to move through the soil. Be sure always to use fresh potting mix and clean pots when repotting, especially if infected plants have been present.

If crown rot has become well established, with many plants infected, it may be necessary to use a fungicide to protect newly repotted plants. These products are often mixed into the potting medium and are quite effective. In healthy collections of violets, however, fungicide is usually not necessary.

To protect the remaining violets, discard sick plants and used potting mix outside the growing area. Cleaning the pots and the growing area with fungicides, disinfectant sprays, or chlorine bleach water will also halt the progress of the fungus. Always wash hands after handling an affected plant and before touching a healthy one.

Fungus Three—Powdery Mildew

Most growers eventually have to deal with powdery mildew. Violets need humidity to bloom at their best, and mildew flourishes in humidity. Air that is too dry to allow mildew growth will probably be too dry to allow violets to thrive.

Powdery mildew appears in the form of a white or light gray powder—similar to talcum or flour—on the surface cells of blossoms, stems and/or leaves. These are the hyphae, which very rapidly produce spores, which find a home and quickly grow into more mature hyphae. As it becomes established, the hyphae begin growing down into the epidermal cells of the plant. As this happens, mildew can become chronic or fatal. Mildew can appear and spread very rapidly when conditions are right.

Mildew thrives in high humidity, at moderate to cool temperatures, in shaded areas away from direct sunlight, and in areas where the air is still. If mildew is not dealt with right away, blossoms will be lost, deformed, or discolored, and ultimately the entire plant could be overwhelmed and lost.

Controlling Powdery Mildew

Of all the fungus spores floating about, it would seem that powdery mildew is among the most common. Violet growing conditions are often ideal for producing good strong stands of mildew.

Mildew will grow in even mildly humid conditions, but it is almost inevitable in high humidity, above 60%. Since violet growers must have some humidity for healthy plants, it is not possible to get rid of mildew by eliminating humid air. Instead, try controlling the other factors, which encourage fungal growths.

Increase air circulation by constantly running fans at low speed. The gently moving air will keep plant surfaces dry and less vulnerable. It is especially important to keep the air moving when temperatures are likely to drop more than 10° F. As the temperatures drop, the relative humidity rises. The mildew is most likely to grow at these cool temperatures when the air is more saturated with water and more likely to condense on plant surfaces. Be aware that during seasons of the year when furnaces and air conditioners are not running, the air is moved less than usual. This is when mildew often develops.

Avoid temperature fluctuations and avoid temperatures that are consistently below 70° F. Again, when outside daytime temperatures are so pleasant that the heating and cooling systems are not in use, it often happens that the nighttime temperatures are quite cool. If the grower is reluctant to warm up the growing area at night, mildew is more likely to grow.

Since it will probably happen that the air will be too humid, too cool, and too still at least occasionally during the year, growers will have to fight mildew. A very light infection can be resolved by removing the affected blossom or by gently washing leaves under running water (pat dry afterward and let the plant dry well before returning it to its usual location). Once mildew becomes established, it will be necessary to resort to the use of a fungicide to control it. There are a number of useful products for the control of powdery mildew.

We have found that Lysol disinfectant spray in the aerosol can is a most effective day-to-day control of spores in the air. When we find powdery mildew, we remove affected blossoms, and mist Lysol over the area. Disinfectant spray may cause some damage to the blossoms, but if handled carefully, will not damage foliage.

It is helpful to clean the growing area including walls, shelves, matting, lights, windows and pots, with either Lysol or chlorine bleach water, if mildew becomes a persistent problem. The spores will settle everywhere in the room, and when they find a surface as comfortable as an African violet, they will multiply quickly.

Some growers have even had their air vents checked and cleaned as a way of eliminating the infection.

Sublimed sulfur (available from drug stores) has also been used to eliminate mildew with good success. Use it at a rate of one-half teaspoon combined with three drops of insecticidal soap and two cups of hot water. It must be kept shaken as it is misted on plants to keep it in suspension.

Other fungicides are available, often at a high cost, and often prone to spotting foliage. One product available to home growers is Phyton 27, which has proven to be effective against powdery mildew without leaving residue on leaves. Neem oil, more commonly used as a deterrent against insects, has also shown itself to be helpful against powdery mildew.

Please note that powdery mildew can only grow on plant surfaces. Sometimes a mold will appear on the top of soil under the leaves, but this is not mildew and shouldn't be a concern.

Winning the Battle

Like most of nature, fungus is very good at protecting itself against extinction. Growers are not likely to eliminate totally the presence of various fungi. The key is to recognize when the growing space is offering unusually fine conditions for the growth and spread of fungus. Act quickly to correct the problems of dampness, fluctuating temperatures, and non-moving air. Also, dispose of plants or blossoms that are already infected and keep the area clean (not just neat!). The fungus among you will keep a low profile.

Erwinia—Bacterial Disease

Bacterial disease is closely related to fungal diseases. It can occur in similar conditions and is similarly controlled.

Erwinia is the primary bacterial disease affecting African violets. It is commonly called bacterial soft rot. There are many types or species of the bacteria but only a few to which violets are susceptible.

When Erwinia is present, violet leaves will develop dark water-soaked patches. Often stems will wilt and rot. When the disease becomes well established, the entire plant may collapse.

To avoid infection, avoid high humidity and maintain temperatures below 80º F. Keep tools clean, because infection spreads quickly through wounds, such as occur with leaf propagation. Fertilizer that supplies nitrogen seems to improve resistance and may explain why many hobbyists (who fertilize faithfully) rarely experience outbreaks.

Once infected, a bactericide will be needed to control the spread. Copper-based bactericides seem to be most effective. All affected plant tissue must be removed from the area and destroyed. Pots may be reused after a thorough cleaning with bleach. Potting mix from contaminated plants should never be reused.

Virus Disease

About five viral diseases have been identified as affecting African violets. Virus disease is passed by fluid to fluid contact rather than through the air. Thrips (an insect that feeds on pollen) and tools that are contaminated are probably the prime method of spreading virus in violets. When there is no vector (carrier), virus will not spread.

The most serious virus currently affecting violets is Impatiens Necrotic Spot Virus (INSV). The classic symptom is a curious circle within a circle spot on the foliage. Unfortunately, many infections have now been reported that do not include the classic symptom, making it much harder to diagnose accurately without a laboratory test.

The best recommendation today is to seek a diagnostic test if there is a general malaise of the plants that is unexplained by more common causes such as poor cultural conditions, fungus disease or insects. INSV often will not kill the affected plant but leaves it struggling to grow properly. Often color and health of the center leaves of the crown are affected. Diagnostic tests may have to be performed several times before a positive identification is made. It appears that the virus advances slowly within plant tissue and is not always discovered on the first test.

There is no cure for virus once it is identified. The only way to manage the disease is to destroy the sick plants. That being the case, it is very important to practice safe growing techniques to avoid infection.

First and foremost, control thrips (see Chapter Nineteen for more about this pest.) Avoid growing violets near open windows, since flying thrips can move through screens very easily. If you have had an outbreak of thrips and your violets now seem unhealthy, consider having them tested.

Secondly, be careful about exchanging leaf cuttings with individuals who may have the virus. With the advent of the internet, it may be tempting to exchange leaves with growers you've never met, but it can be an avenue for virus to enter your space.

No disease is welcome in an African violet collection. It really pays to maintain a quality environment, to watch for signs of disease, and to react quickly when violets are infected. If nothing else, throw away the sick ones and buy some new healthy ones!

19

What You Need to Know about Pests and Pesticides

Pests scare us. The thought of a pest invading and destroying a valuable and beloved violet collection can keep us awake at night. That fear can lead us to overuse chemical controls, putting both grower and plants at risk.

Fortunately, there are only a few insects and mites that are really attracted to African violets. Pests are manageable if we keep a sharp eye out for when they first appear and dispose of affected plants immediately.

Use Chemicals with Care

What should strike fear into the hearts of wise growers is overusing chemicals. Disposal of infested plants should always be the first line of defense. When the use of chemicals becomes necessary, especially when a collection of violets is large and irreplaceable, one must proceed with great caution. When handled properly, the benefits do outweigh the dangers.

We think that it is as important for growers to understand what the chemicals are and how they work, as it is to know which pest to shoot with which spray. It is also important to know how to read the label so you can comply with the way the manufacturer intended for his product to be used. It is not as simple as "take two aspirin and go to bed," but it will make you a happier and healthier grower.

There are many different products which can be used to control pests, including the synthetic insecticides, biological insecticides, botanicals, organic and inorganic products, and soap. None are perfectly safe, but the synthetic insecticides are among the most carelessly used. For that reason, we will focus most of our attention on using those chemicals responsibly.

We often try to add humor, but you will notice that this subject is taken more seriously. We urge you to be serious about the use of pesticides too.

Recognizing the Enemy

Not every type of insecticide works on every moving creature found on violets. The pests vary in the numbers of legs, the presence of wings, and in the chosen method of eating. For example, a population of mites (tiny spiders with eight legs) can be controlled by particular chemicals (chlorinated hydrocarbons) which have little effect on six-legged pests. Some mild and relatively safe-to-use chemicals won't kill the most damaging pests, and some of the most toxic compounds out there won't control some pests that are just irritating. If it won't kill the intended victim, don't expose yourself to the pesticide!

Short of a college entomology class, how does the average grower decide what to use? First of all, it is important to get an accurate diagnosis of what pest has invaded.

A good book on the subject is *Insect and Mite Pests of African Violets* written by Dr. Charles Cole. It is available from the headquarters of the African Violet Society of America in Beaumont, Texas, or online at www.avsa.org.

Another source for identifying the insect is your local agriculture office. The staff there concentrates on the major agricultural crops in your area, so they may not immediately recognize your violet pests. For example, the cyclamen mite is virtually invisible without a microscope and is usually diagnosed by the visual appearance of the African violet plant. If your agent isn't familiar with violets, he may not recognize the source of the problem. If you feel that you are not getting a good answer, you may request that they take your plant to a higher authority (often an agricultural university).

Finally, local greenhouse or garden center managers can be quite helpful in diagnosing insect problems. Note that a department manager will often be far more informed than most other employees. Avoid anyone who suggests that an all-purpose spray will kill just about anything without identifying what pest is present.

The Main Pests

For your convenience, we will list the most common insects here. Other pests may invade, but these are the ones to watch out for.

Thrips in the larvae stage are frequently found feeding on the pollen sacs (the yellow center) of violet blossoms. They are about the size of a printed dash, and vary in color although on a violet blossom they often appear to be a soft white. In the adult flying stage, they enter growing areas easily through the air. One of the best ways to prevent them is to keep outside air from entering the growing area through open windows and doors. Spilled pollen on the petal is a good indication of their presence. Flicking the pollen sac with a fingernail, or blowing on the center of the flower, will often cause them to move out of the sac and onto the petal where they can be seen.

Those who have small collections may find that removing flowers and buds will help reduce the population without the use of chemicals. Since several strains have become resistant to common insecticides, it is wise to seek advice before making any purchase.

Cyclamen mites are rarely seen but easily recognized. The entire mite family has eight legs and several can damage violets. Cyclamen mites, the chief offenders, feed on the tender growth of the violet: the youngest leaves in the crown and tiny buds that are just forming. They nourish themselves by inserting a tube-like mouth part into a cell, extracting juice and leaving a toxin behind that distorts the growth. When they are present in sizable numbers, the crown will become tight and twisted, brittle, and finally gray in the centermost leaves. Sometimes the hairs on leaves become more apparent. Blossom stems that have been affected will twist and may be shorter than usual; flowers may fail to open or be smaller than usual and often misshapen.

Mites can be discouraged by keeping the potting mix evenly moist so that the plants do not wilt. Turgid plant tissue is harder, making it more difficult for mites to feed. Once it is obvious that mites are present, all damaged plants are best destroyed. Traditionally, miticide is recommended to treat healthy plants that have been exposed to cyclamen mites. One could consider alternatives since there has also been considerable progress in the effort to develop effective biological controls.

Broad mites are also very hard to see because of their small size. Young mites will be transparent but as they age they develop a green or golden color and they prefer the underside of the leaves. It is more likely that their presence will be noted because of brittle foliage that tends to curl under at the edge. As the leaves continue to try to grow, cracks and breaks may appear. If the infestation is well established, growth may stop entirely and plants will die.

Control of broad mites is very similar to that of the cyclamen mite although they seem to be easier to kill. Be sure to treat the undersides of the leaves since this is where they are most commonly found. Destroy any plants with obvious damage quickly.

Soil mealy bugs live below the soil surface, feeding on the roots by sucking juices. They are related to, but distinct from the more commonly seen foliar mealy bugs. They are about the size of a piece of perlite, with six legs and a grayish color. They move very slowly, so it is easy to miss them. Many growers find it easier to recognize an infestation by examining the roots for clumps of webbing and residue from the white waxy powder that coats the insect's body, especially around the perimeter of the root ball. Above the ground symptoms include dull-looking foliage, wilted outside leaves, and a general lack of vigor.

Soil mealy bugs may spread rapidly through a collection when an infested plant is passed over other plants, allowing the bugs to drop out the pot's drainage holes. When a grower provides excellent care, the soil mealy bugs may live in the soil for a long time without any visible damage to the above-ground parts of the violet. In this case, the damage to the foliage is only likely to appear when some stress to the plant occurs, such as when a violet is moved to a new location or becomes too dry.

Once soil mealy bugs have been found, it is wise to check all violets by lifting each out of its pots and examining the roots. In small collections it is probably better to cut off the roots, remove several rows of leaves from the remaining crown, and reroot the plant using the techniques described in Chapter Ten. In larger collections it may be feasible to invest in the currently recommended chemicals or try one of the biological approaches.

Foliar mealy bugs live on the foliage, as one might expect. On many green plants, these are controllable, but when they attack African violets it is virtually always a lost cause. The foliar form of the mealy bug is about the size of a sesame seed and has a gray or tan color. The mature bugs lay eggs in web-wrapped sacs that are deposited between the leaf hairs on the surface of violet leaves. The egg sacs may also appear between the stems and the main stalk of the violet. The webs and the bugs both have a waxy coating that resists insecticidal treatment and swabbing with alcohol is very difficult because of the protection that the leaf hair provides. Systemic insecticides may prove effective by making the plant tissue toxic to the sucking pest, but should only be used to prevent the spread into healthy plants. Infested plants should be destroyed immediately.

Fungus gnats are primarily a nuisance. They are a small flying insect that feeds on decayed matter in the potting mix. Very similar to gnats are shore flies. Rarely does either feed on live tissue, so they do little physical harm to the plant, unless they are found in great numbers. They need moist conditions for the eggs to hatch, and are often found where violet growers are using a constant watering method. Sometimes the best control is simply to allow the violets and the water reservoirs to go dry for a while. Both have been suspected of spreading diseases so it would be foolish to ignore their large populations. While insecticides can be used, there are also some biological chemicals now available.

Springtails are another of the nuisance pests. They are usually found moving quickly on water reservoirs. This quick movement is because of a sort of tail that allows them to spring about, especially on the surface of water. These can only survive in very damp conditions, and rarely cause damage to violets. They are just unpleasant to see. Again, allowing plants and reservoirs to dry out for a short period of time is an effective way to control them.

Cockroaches, mice, caterpillars, beetles, slugs and other incidental chewing insects occasionally find African violets as a food source. They don't really favor violets but tend to choose them only because they are available. Evidence of bite marks will be fairly clear, although it may be difficult to identify the source. Sticky traps may help identify nocturnal creatures and eliminate them at the same time. Rather than applying chemicals, it is best to simply handpick these pests off of the plants whenever possible.

Choosing Your Weapon

Once the pest has been accurately identified, you must decide how you want to handle the problem. You might be best off to dispose of the infested plants. You might choose to use one of the predatory insects or some other biological method. You may choose to use chemicals. Whichever you choose, be sure that you understand the rules. For example, one should never use a beneficial insect and an insecticide in combination.

If a pesticide is to be used, the correct chemical can be found by reading the container. There are two items to find. First, the container must list the name of the pest you wish to control. Secondly, the container must list African violets. Using an insecticide on mites will be ineffective, just as using a miticide on insects is foolish. Similarly, certain formulations, especially those with oil, may be toxic to violets. Using products not labeled for violets is very risky.

Many different kinds of growers use chemicals. A chemical intended for use in the garden or an orchard is not appropriate for indoor use. An indoor pesticide will have little effect outside. The chemical companies take great care to test each pesticide formula and to qualify it for a specific use. Because of lawsuits, they are notably careful about what is allowed for indoor and greenhouse use. Certain chemicals will be off limits to home growers. These are often sold in very large quantities with directions for treating large areas. Often these are highly toxic, requiring suiting up during treatment and restricting reentry for a period of time. Home growers should never expose themselves to these products.

The job of finding the right product can be made considerably easier by ordering your violet pesticides from vendors who serve the African violet hobbyist market. They list and sell the most commonly used pesticides as soon as it is legal to do so, and these small-business people will offer expert advice to guarantee your satisfaction.

You've heard it before, but it bears repeating. Follow the directions. Read the label! If you are going to kill the pest, you must use the strength that is recommended and use it as often as recommended. Weaker concentrations will not give you good control and can even result in stronger succeeding generations of pests who can tolerate the pesticide at regular strength. Using a stronger rate than is recommended seldom increases the effectiveness; it just puts the plant and you at a greater risk.

The Pesticide Recipe

Many insecticides contain an "active ingredient" which is the part of the mixture that will do the work. This active ingredient is listed on the label of any pesticide package. We will focus more on specific active ingredients a little later.

Along with the active ingredient there may be several other ingredients. Sometimes the active ingredient may be already water-soluble and have only a carrier added. (The carrier consists of something inert like powdered rock or clay.) In other instances, the active ingredient may need a solvent added which dissolves the active ingredient and/or an emulsifier which allows it to mix with water.

In most of the recipes, the user determines the concentration by adding the appropriate amount of water. This is where growers can make serious trouble for themselves! If the directions use terms like parts-per-million, and you do not know how to do that, choose a different product. Those directions are deliberately written so that only experienced professionals will use them. Most chemicals recommended for home use will use common measuring units that will be clear to the most novice grower.

If it is in a consumer-friendly aerosol can, no mixing is necessary. But insecticides like this contain a propellant to force the chemical into the air. This spray is always quite cold, especially to temperature-sensitive plants like African violets.

Always allow at least eighteen inches of space which will allow the spray to warm before it reaches the plant surface.

Systemic pesticides are a special group. Several systemics come in the form of granules in which the active ingredient coats or has been absorbed by the carrier (often clay or ground corn cobs) and is used dry. The active ingredient is a type which can be absorbed by the plant and distributed through at least a part of the plant structure making it toxic to feeding insects. Systemic insecticides can be limited by the size of the molecule. Large molecules may not be able to move through all parts of the plant. Blossom thrips are often not affected by systemic action because the vascular system narrows in the peduncle (the flower stem). The large molecule of most systemics cannot move through the unyielding tissue to reach the flowers where the thrips will continue to thrive.

How Does the Active Ingredient Work?

The most common type of synthetic insecticides used on African violets is the organophosphates. They include Diazinon, Malathion, and Orthene. The organophosphates all affect the nervous system by inhibiting the enzyme cholinesterase which allows acetylcholine to accumulate. Whoa! If that seems like too many big words, think of it this way: They are nerve poisons. When the nerves stop sending their messages, the body ceases to function. Please note: we didn't specify just the insect's body; it often works the same way on people.

There are also a few botanical insecticides. These are not synthetic; they are derived from plants. Pyrethrum is one of the more popular choices right now. It also affects the nervous system with a fast-acting effect, but without much strength. Resmethrin is a commonly used derivative of pyrethrum.

Yet another is biological products which act on various pests in wide-ranging ways. Among the biological group is an effective miticide called Cinnamite which works against all stages of mites including eggs. Yet another is Avid which works as a stomach poison. Neem oil is a biological that prevents the maturing of many insects to an egg-laying stage.

Soaps are another of the commonly recommended insecticides. These work by breaking down cell membranes in the insects on contact. They may be toxic to plant material if used outside the recommended temperature ranges.

There are also the inorganic pesticides which are made from minerals. Diatomaceous earth is an inorganic pesticide, which cuts or pierces the insect body resulting in dehydration. Its effectiveness is a highly debatable topic. Some think it solves many insect problems with few human health hazards. Others have reportedly been less than successful in achieving insect control with its use. It seems to work well only in dry conditions; moist conditions cause the diatoms to swell, making the edges less sharp.

These are by no means all of the product types which may be effective. Researchers are constantly seeking new ways to battle insects which are safe for both the plants and the users.

How Can Synthetic Insecticide Affect Humans?

Synthetic insecticides are generally taken in either by digestion or by absorption through the skin. The pest may eat plant parts, which are covered by or contain the poison; or it may be poisoned when the spray contacts its body.

This all seems a little gory. Do we really have to think so much about how the poor little pests die? Yes, we do, since it closely resembles how nerve poison can also enter the human system.

When plants are sprayed with a synthetic organic insecticide or treated with a systemic granular form of the insecticide, the plant becomes poisonous to eat. Since African violets aren't for consumption this isn't usually a problem, unless you have children or pets who are inclined to exotic eating habits.

Similarly, the insecticide in the air or on the leaf surface can also be absorbed through the mouth, lungs, and readily through the skin. It is critical to avoid contacting the chemical directly if the person involved does not wish to fall victim to nerve poison. It is also wise to avoid touching the plant surfaces for a period of time, at least until the surface dries, following application.

Human Symptoms of Toxic Dose

If a person receives a toxic dose of the organophosphates, he may experience the following symptoms: headache, giddiness, nervousness, blurred vision, weakness, nausea, cramps, diarrhea, and discomfort in the chest. Outward signs that someone has incurred poisoning include: sweating, myosis (contracted pupils), tearing, salivation, excessive respiratory tract secretions, vomiting, cyanosis (blue coloration), uncontrollable twitches, convulsions, coma, loss of reflexes and loss of sphincter control.

Repeated small doses seem to have a cumulative effect increasing risk with each additional dose. Large doses can be fatal. The toxicity information on the label indicates the amount of active ingredient needed to kill most of the pests. The higher the toxicity rating, the lower the dose needed to work on humans.

The rate of absorption through the skin is increased at higher temperatures and is especially quick in the presence of dermatitis. If you have a skin condition, you must exert extreme care in using these chemicals.

An antidote is available if symptoms of toxicity occur, but the victim must get to a doctor or hospital quickly. Take the pesticide container along.

Precautions

Now that you understand how the insecticides work, it may make more sense that you should always dispose of infested plants as quickly as possible to avoid the spread of insects. You must always mix insecticides in well-ventilated areas. You must protect yourself from touching the chemical or anything with which the chemical has come in contact. That means that you need to wear gloves and other protective clothing when you use an insecticide. Take care to wash yourself, your gloves, and your clothing promptly and thoroughly following the application. Keep it off your skin.

Avoid spraying around food areas, and keep pets and children away from treated plants. Don't eat, drink, or smoke while using pesticides.

Never reuse measuring tools or spray containers for anything except pesticide use.

Never store pesticides in anything except the original container, and do not share pesticides in improvised containers. It is unlawful to do so.

Mix up small amounts, and once pesticides are diluted, use immediately. They often lose effectiveness quickly after dilution anyway. Do not dispose of them in the sewage system. Do not pour them out on the soil in a concentrated area. If possible, only mix what can be used immediately.

Always read the label closely for special precautions, and keep the labeling with the container.

It's Your Responsibility

Insecticides are wonderful tools in the successful growing of African violets. It is certainly more pleasant to have beautiful, healthy blooming plants than it is to have violets besieged with an insect invasion. When it becomes necessary to use insecticides, you are taking on the responsibility of using them within the framework of the law. That, of course, is for your own good. We hope that your violets never become hosts to pests. But we also hope that when a pest comes to visit and brings his relatives (or makes babies) you will be able to control them or eradicate them safely.

Remember that good sanitation, isolation of new additions to your plant collection, and a watchful eye are the most desirable methods for preventing major outbreaks. Individuals with small collections might find that the garbage can is the most effective way to get rid of infestations. When the pests come, and they will, you will be armed with the proper attitude, safety measures, and the proper weapons to win the war.

20

Good Housekeeping

Despite the pleasure their great beauty gives us, African violets can be very time-consuming. It seems like there are always plants that need attention. It isn't unusual for an attentive violet grower with a large collection to spend one or two days a week working with plants. Most of that work is pure joy—working in soil, handling plants, and noting special qualities of certain varieties. Time flies. But one task is rarely fun—housekeeping.

It is easy to neglect housekeeping tasks in favor of the more delightful parts of African violet horticulture, but it isn't wise. Failure to keep a growing area clean now can result in disaster later. On top of that, visitors to your plant area may see the dirt and chaos before they take notice of your pride and joy. You've got a reputation to keep!

Every-Day Tasks

The secret to having perfect plants is to remove all imperfections. Any time you work with your violets, you should be removing any aging or yellowed leaves. Similarly, remove all dead blossoms as they fade and remove the entire stem when the final flower begins to go. (For more on this subject, see Chapter 17.)

Take time to keep the sides of pots wiped clean and the shelves free of spilled soil and other debris. Many of the nuisance pests (those that irritate but usually don't damage plants), like fungus gnats and springtails, depend on decaying organic matter for their food. This is also where they tend to lay eggs, especially in moist shaded areas beneath pots or below shelves. If your plant room doesn't get swept or vacuumed often or your windowsill is rarely wiped, you may be providing a nice breeding ground for these pests.

Keeping your growing area as clean as possible also helps to reduce the amount of dust in the air. African violets do need baths occasionally, but with cleaner air, those baths will be needed less frequently. Clean foliage is more capable of using sunlight, resulting in more efficient photosynthesis which will give you healthier, sturdier plants.

Clean up spills. Puddles of water can ruin surfaces. Replacing or refinishing surfaces could be a huge task, easily avoided by prompt wipe-ups. Spills may also promote certain insects and pests. Be especially careful in cleaning up messes involving chemical solutions like fungicides and insecticides. Some pesticide residues have long-lasting effects, so they need to be cleaned up carefully and thoroughly to protect yourself and others as well as your pets.

Empty the garbage. It is a bad habit to throw plant waste into the garbage and then allow it to remain in the plant room. Bacteria and fungi, as well as pests, thrive on this trash. If the garbage can is close to the plants, the trash that is left to stand can foster a serious outbreak of disease or insects. Wash the trashcan with a bleach solution or other disinfectant occasionally, especially when you are dealing with some disease problem. If you use a trashcan liner, close the bag before removing it from the can. Avoid bouncing the bag on the ground in the plant area to get more garbage in; this can force spores, insects, or whatever, into the air and create worse problems.

Keep yourself clean. If you have been gardening outside, wash thoroughly and change clothes before working with your violets. One of the easiest methods of transportation for tiny insects is hitchhiking on your hands and clothing. Your pets are also good carriers. If you have animals that spend part of their time outside, they should be kept away from your African violets as much as possible.

Be aware. A watchful eye for questionable changes in your plants should help you recognize if some problem is occurring. Treat your plants promptly with appropriate measures. Quick disposal of suspicious plant material may prevent the problem entirely.

Repotting Sanitation

Whenever violets are repotted, there will always be some degree of mess. It may even be part of the fun. Cleaning up at the end of a repotting day is usually a simple and obvious task. But it is important to use good sanitation methods throughout the day while you are doing the repotting.

Do not reuse pots or stakes unless they have been sanitized. Soaking used pots in a solution of bleach water overnight will make them safe to use again. Remove any crust, usually resulting from a buildup of fertilizer salts, which has accumulated on pot rims before reusing the pots.

Do not reuse potting mix. Discarded potting medium can be used to condition outside flowerbeds, but it should not be reused for other violets. Always use fresh potting mix from bags that have no holes torn in them. Be especially careful if your supplies have to be stored outside. Torn bags of soil can be contaminated by insects and diseases in these outdoor areas. It's a harsh world out there. A little caution here may prevent huge headaches later.

Keep tools clean and dry. A dirty tool can expose your plant to any pathogens that could be carried on that tool. If you suspect that you have a problem with fungus or bacteria, tools should be wiped or dipped with a solution of bleach, Lysol, or Physan 20. If you suspect you may have a virus present, our advisors recommend immersing tools in a solution of Physan 20 (one tablespoon to a gallon of water) for 10 to 15 minutes. Clean tools will not heal sick plants, but they will prevent the further spread of disease.

Separate newly acquired plants from older plants, preferably in a different room. Also, if you keep your potting area somewhat separate from your growing area, you will be able to work with new plants, while at the same time protecting older plants from exposure to unknown problems. Always be suspicious of new plants for a few months, regardless of the source.

Spring (Maybe Fall) Cleaning

At least once a year, it is wise to do a very thorough cleaning of your plant area. We find that our best time is in the summer because that is when we have the fewest plants on our shelves. It is the perfect time to clean. If your collection doesn't expand and contract like ours, you will simply need to choose a time that fits your life.

Shelves need to be emptied and scrubbed thoroughly, top and bottom, with a sanitizing solution. We usually use a bleach solution, but others prefer Physan 20 or Lysol. Wall and window surfaces near the shelves should also be wiped, as well as any fluorescent light fixtures.

At the same time, wash all plant trays, saucers or reservoirs. If you use a constant-water method, thoroughly clean all parts of that system. Be sure to use an algaecide that will prevent a rapid return of algae in the trays. Remove the mineral buildup that forms along the sides of trays.

Change air filters frequently and have your heating/cooling system checked to be sure that it is running efficiently with no gas leaks. You may wish to have air ducts cleaned to eliminate dust and pathogens, since clean air is healthier for both you and your plants.

Check fluorescent lights for aging tubes. Replace those that need it, and label new tubes with the current date. Be careful to replace only one tube in a unit at a time. Two new tubes can give off too much light, causing foliage to bleach (lose its deep green color).

Also, inspect your electric timers, which are especially notorious for wearing out without notice. We depend on them to keep lights turned on and off on schedule, but a stuck timer can bathe your violets in twenty-four-hour-a-day light, resulting in tight center growth and bleached foliage.

Dispose of chemicals that are no longer needed, that are now too old, or that have labels that are no longer readable. Be sure to follow the rules for proper disposal in your community.

Scrub floors, or clean carpets, with a disinfectant solution as well. This area is especially vulnerable to contamination.

After all that hard work is done (or before, if you prefer), clean the plants in your collection. Throw out any plants that look suspicious (or hopeless), or treat them for their problem before putting them back on the clean shelves. Throw away plants that are just taking up space or that don't really please you. Keep the ones you really enjoy. Leave plenty of air space between plants to allow them to grow without crowding.

Go through and update your records and make any notes that will be helpful to you as you continue to grow the cultivars on hand. If you've never kept any records, develop a system that works for you. When you go to buy new plants, you'll be less likely to overload on certain colors or to duplicate specific varieties. Make notes on what you'd like to find or purchase, and set some goals for your collection.

Also be sure that you've kept your membership dues paid for the African Violet Society of America or for your local club. You don't want to miss out on the magazine or newsletter.

Control Yourself

If all of these tasks sound overwhelming, it may be because your hobby has gotten larger than the time that you have to do it properly. If your growing area has one plant, it will be easy to keep up with all of the above tasks. If your growing area has one hundred plants or more, housekeeping will be a much larger job, and it will be much more important because of the risks of unsanitary conditions.

We cannot stress enough the importance of keeping your hobby manageable. Do not let it get out of control, and do not let it take control over you. It is really important to grow only as many African violets as you can take good care of. We all have to recognize our limits—some of us wish we had more space, and many of us wish we had more time. If you try to grow too many violets, you can easily become discouraged when you find you just can't keep up with them all. Small messes just become bigger ones.

Sometimes when faced with some sort of major disruption in your personal life, you might be better off to scale back your violet collection until you're back to smooth sailing again. How much better to have fewer plants that are truly beautiful, well-kept, and giving you pleasure than to have way too many plants that don't really look so good!

21

Keeping Cultural Practices in Balance

It is remarkable to us that African violets can survive very well in conditions quite different from what we recommend. We grow violets for competition and use the techniques that show-growers have found to produce the most perfect results. Those are the techniques that we pass along to you. Nonetheless, violets will survive and even thrive in different conditions if everything in those conditions is balanced as carefully as those we recommend.

A violet grower once showed us a violet that was in serious trouble. "I don't know what's wrong," she moaned. "Ever since I put them in the plastic pots, they have gone downhill." She had been growing her plants in clay pots previously. She had changed just one thing, but oh, what a difference it made!

Much of the art of growing African violets is in understanding how the pieces of the horticultural puzzle fit together. Change just one thing and you get a chain reaction. It is very easy to believe that you have a green thumb when everything is working. When it isn't working, it is very easy to believe that you are unable to grow violets. Success depends on understanding all of the elements that are affected by one modification.

Key Elements in Growing

There is not one "secret for success" in growing African violets. There are a number of key elements including temperature, humidity, water, air, soil, nutrients, containers, and light which work in combination. What any violet growers might describe as "perfect growing conditions" is actually the perfect balance of those conditions. The easiest method of growing for a violet beginner is to use a tried and true combination of these elements.

Here's a brief list of the balance of growing elements that we personally use and have success with:

Temperature: 70 to 75° F
Humidity: 50%
Water: unconditioned (not softened)
Water pH of 6.8 to 7
Self-watering system
Air: free of pollution
Potting Medium: mix of equal parts sphagnum peat moss, perlite and vermiculite
Nutrients: 15-30-15 fertilizer at a rate of one-fourth teaspoon per gallon in water reservoir
Containers: shallow plastic pots (one-third the plant diameter), with holes for drainage
Light: fluorescent light twelve hours a day, ten to twelve inches above leaves

What if you have all of these growing elements but one? Is that pretty good? It could be, but unfortunately, one variation could change everything!

Change the Temperature

Temperature is a crucial factor in plant growth. While violets will tolerate a range of temperatures from 60 to 85° F, they really do best at 70 to 75° F. Any change from this narrower range will affect African violets.

If the constant temperature is altered by five degrees cooler or warmer, a number of other elements may go out of balance; for example, humidity. Temperature controls the amount of moisture that the air can retain. The lower the temperature drops, the less moisture the air can hold, and relative humidity escalates. This may result in sweating (or condensation) on cool surfaces. This translates into a perfect environment for fungus. On the other hand, air tends to be drier at warmer temperatures, resulting in flowers that fade faster and water reservoirs that evaporate and go dry more quickly.

At constant cooler temperatures (65° to 70° F) plants will grow more slowly, leaves will closely overlap, and blossom colors will tend to be more intense. That sounds good. However, in the process, soil bacteria processes nutrients less actively and violets may be more prone to toxic levels of ammonium nitrates in the soil.

At higher constant temperatures (75° to 80° F), a plant's metabolism increases. This often results in more rapid growth, sometimes causing long petioles (stems of individual leaves) and more spaces between leaves as well as lighter shades in blossom colors. Higher temperatures increase transpiration, and violets will require more water. At these warmer temperatures, fertilizers are used more efficiently because soil bacteria are more active in breaking down nutrients.

Wide daily swings in temperature may result in disease problems. Humidity will fluctuate as temperatures change, making the control of fungus extremely difficult.

Changing just the temperature has a significant impact on your violets!

Change the Potting Mix

Using a potting mix different from our example can also upset the balance. Heavier, denser potting mixes will retain more water than the mix described above. This will result in a wetter medium with less air available to the delicate root structure. Heavier mixes (including organic dirt from the garden) might be used successfully by growers who tend to forget to water, or for those growing in clay pots. Lighter, fluffier mixes than our example above may not retain enough water, especially for those who live in regions with low relative humidity.

Some of the premixed violet potting mediums on the market may contain additives that surprise growers. Many contain wetting agents that cause the medium to absorb moisture more quickly for the first few months. As the wetting agent wears out, the potting mix absorbs water less easily, especially if it dries between watering.

Off-the-shelf potting mixes may also contain a charge of fertilizer. This information is commonly listed on the label. If fertilizer is added to the water after using this charged mix, violets may show symptoms of over-fertilization such as burned leaf edges, or orange "crud" in the center crown.

Even the way the potting mix is handled can make a difference if you pack it when repotting. Avoid the temptation to push down on the soil. Pushing on the soil presses air out, leaving less room for roots to grow. This can greatly slow the rate of growth above the soil.

Change the pH

When water and/or potting mix pH varies from the ideal neutral measure of 6.8 to 7.0, the soil environment around the root ball becomes more acidic (below 7) or more alkaline (above 7). This greatly alters a violet's ability to absorb nutrients in a usable form. When pH is not in the neutral zone, essential nutrients will not get into the plant no matter how much fertilizer is applied. Unfortunately, pH is not easy for a grower to control completely.

Soil pH can change as potting mix components age. Repotting at least yearly is wise to make the root environment fresh and return it to a more neutral pH.

Also, water pH has a great influence on the balance of pH achieved within a violet pot. This can be very difficult to monitor in areas where water supplies are constantly adjusted. Additives in the water can modify pH unpredictably. If many changes in pH are noted, it can help to add dolomite lime to the potting mix. Dolomite lime buffers pH so that it does not change so quickly.

When water pH is susceptible to change, a grower must pay attention! Fertilizers must be selected carefully. Urea-based fertilizers tend to cause more problems in acidic conditions. Soil conditioners can be applied to correct the problem, but these require constant monitoring. Many growers have found that the best solution is to change their water source. Some have found that rain water or reverse-osmosis water remains more consistent in regard to pH.

Change the Light Source

If you grow at the window instead of under fluorescent light, a number of the elements may be affected. The first thing you are likely to notice is that petioles often grow longer on the side of the plant that is away from the light source. As time passes this may result in a bend in the main stem of the plants. This may be improved by turning violets regularly.

Natural light may change the air temperature. During the day, direct sunlight produces heat. At night, however, temperatures can cool significantly. These fluctuations alter humidity as well as the growth rate. Window-grown violets may have a slightly coarse look because of this.

Window light may be too bright. Outside conditions, such as snow or reflective buildings, as well as seasonal changes, may cause foliage bleaching which occurs as chlorophyll is depleted.

Violets grown in windows are more likely to show seasonal variations. Those grown far north or south of the equator may suffer through the short days of winter, often not blooming well until days begin to lengthen. Similarly, in the long days of summer, they may have fewer blossoms because of heat stress.

It Goes On and On

We could play with this theme forever. You get the message. Change just one thing, and you will inadvertently alter other key elements. One little change can put your growing into imbalance, and your violets will suffer.

These reactions to your changes in culture may occur very slowly over a long period of time. That can confuse even the best of growers. It can be hard to remember when the problem you are observing today was not a problem. What was the moment when everything began to shift? Was it after the last repotting? Was it after you changed to a new fertilizer? Did it happen after a city announcement of a new water treatment program? The instigating change may have occurred months before a grower actually observes a difference in his African violets.

So what is our point? First, spend time thinking before acting. When your violets begin to change for the worse, it is easy to assume that disease or insects have invaded. Don't get out the chemicals until you are certain of that! Often, it is a simple change that occurred in your growing balance. If you can identify what changed, you may be able to correct the problem painlessly. More important, chemicals used to treat for pests can be hard on plants. An unnecessary application can aggravate the situation and make it even more difficult to diagnose or to recover.

Second, take notice of changes that are happening. You have to move to a new location. A product is no longer available. The city puts new additives in your water. Air becomes polluted. Things happen beyond your control. Just being aware that it can affect your violets will help you cope more effectively.

Third, be prudent. Sometimes you want to try something new. Try to proceed through the possible side-effects of your change sensibly. Remember that chain reactions can occur. You can contain that chain reaction by experimenting with one or two plants rather than your whole collection.

Finally, get advice from someone who is growing successfully in your area. The combination of elements that we listed above works well for us with the kind of heating and cooling system, water, and climate that we have in our area. You may have to use a different combination of elements in your situation. The easiest way to discover what works is to ask someone who has already succeeded.

Remember that Violet Grower who Changed Her Pots?

It was obvious to us why that grower we told you about had so much trouble after repotting her violets into plastic pots. She had been growing in clay pots and watering them twice a week. She had been using a very heavy soil, which can work in clay pots where moisture evaporates from the side of the pot. Once she changed to plastic, she needed to use a lighter soil that would allow air to circulate in the root system, and she didn't need to water as often. With these changes, the balance was restored and she was soon growing beautiful violets again.

22

Can This Violet Be Saved?

Saving an African violet from certain death is one of the most satisfying parts of growing. Recognizing which plants are worth saving is one of the most advanced skills.

Are you one of those people who likes to rescue abused violets that are in grocery and discount stores? Violets there are often in poor conditions. Plants may be crammed together on shelves with inadequate light. If they don't sell quickly, they mark them down and restock. These can be good bargains if you know how to save them!

Maybe your violet was stressed by the temporary help offered by friends while you were absent for a few weeks. Your major problem will most likely be that your plants suffered from uneven watering in your absence. These violets look sad but they can be saved, along with your friendship!

Ever come home with a plant and totally forgotten about it until weeks later? It happens! We've also heard several stories of people who have found violets left behind by neighbors who moved or had been confined in the hospital for long periods of time. It is surprising how often these plants can be saved.

The solution for saving any of these violets is to recognize their primary problem and then to apply emergency first aid. Once the immediate problem is under control, you need to provide a little follow-up support. The violets will soon be healthy and lovely.

Limp and Water-Logged

Violets that are found to have very wet soil and yet have limp leaves are probably victims of over-watering or perhaps under-watering followed by over-watering. In either case, the roots have ceased to take up the available water. This is an emergency situation!

The biggest danger here is the possibility (in fact, probability) of an invasion of pathogens like pythium or phytophthora that can cause crown rot in overwatered violets. You should transplant immediately, cutting off the roots, examining the main stem to cut above the rot, and rerooting the violets in fresh potting mix. (See Chapter Ten for more details on this subject.)

Did you note that violets that are limp and too wet are "probably" over-watered? There is also a possibility that they have an insect pest called soil mealy bug. To be safe, don't bring a sickly violet into your home that has these symptoms until you have read all the way to the end of this chapter and you know how to recognize the pest!

Too Dry

Many situations may lead to a violet becoming too dry. Since drought is not an uncommon occurrence in nature, violets have emergency systems that enable them to survive periods without water. Basically, all of the plant systems close down in an effort to conserve water and energy. While this sort of "hibernation" is going on, violets are also able to tolerate a much greater variation in temperature than usual. As long as the leaves maintain a green tone, and aren't becoming crispy-dry, there is a chance that they can be revived.

Water-deprived violets will be limp, just as over-watered violets were, but the soil will feel very dry and the pot will be extremely light when you pick it up. If you feel certain that the violets have only been deprived of water for a week or so, you can proceed to water them cautiously. The dehydrated violet must reactivate its systems gradually, and any efforts to hurry this process can be even more stressful to the plant.

Begin by watering very lightly and offering only a tiny amount of water the first day to moisten the soil. This will plump the roots up a bit and allow the water pressure inside and outside the roots to equalize.

On the second day, you should water from the top until water runs out the bottom of the pot. Allow the excess water to drain away. You may need to repeat this on the third day before you will see the leaves becoming firm again.

Usually the center leaves will be first to respond and stiffen. If the outside leaves revive, you should expect them to age and die within the next few weeks or months because of the stress. Any outside leaves that have not recovered in a week should be removed. Your violet will need to be transplanted at some point in order to bury the resulting neck, but there is rarely a need to hurry.

In extraordinarily dry conditions when your violet has been without water for weeks or months, the roots will have withered beyond recovery. You may need to use an intensive care method to rehydrate the plant so that it can regenerate roots.

First remove flowers and any leaves that are crispy dry. Then add enough water to the pot that it drains through. This creates an environment in which roots can grow. Next, increase the humidity surrounding the foliage. Lightly mist the leaves, and then place the violet inside a clear plastic bag or container. Seal it tightly closed. The moisture in the soil and on the leaves should provide enough humidity to cause droplets of moisture to form inside the container. The leaves will absorb some moisture directly from the air, allowing them to begin to function again. As they begin photosynthesis again, the plant will begin to make roots. The plant really needs to stay in this environment for at least two to four weeks. Once you begin to see growth in the center, or the formation of flower buds, you can be sure the plant is recovering from the stress. Older leaves that have not revived should be removed after a week or two in the closed environment to prevent fungus growth.

Tired Looking

If the violet isn't limp, but has that weary look of abandonment, it still needs some special care. The problem may be that the plant has been sitting in darkness. It might have been left in a box too long at the store, kept behind your drawn curtains while vacationing, or forgotten in some dark corner.

Violets left in the dark often have overly dark green leaves (because chlorophyll hasn't been used) and a lack of vigor (because photosynthesis hasn't been happening). Violet blossoms often have faded colors after periods of darkness.

The Society of American Florists recommends any African violet coming out of a dark environment should immediately be exposed to good bright light for at least ten hours. The bright light recommended would be about equal to the light generated twelve inches from a fluorescent in the very center of the tube. You could substitute a bright window, but be careful of the heat resulting from direct sunshine. It is amazing how much better light-deprived violets can look after just a few days of being treated with bright light.

What else can you do? It is very wise to clean dirt and debris off of tired-looking leaves. Blowing and light brushing are usually effective. A bath under a gently running faucet of tepid water followed by blotting with a soft towel or sponge will usually remove the grunge.

Finally, a really wise grower will remove all the flowers and all the bud stems as soon as the tired plant is home. Shocked plants need to spend their energy recovering rather than trying to bloom, and the mild injury of disbudding actually stimulates a higher level of photosynthesis.

Should you repot it immediately? No. Give your weary violet consistent care for at least a week or so. Once the plant has gotten comfortable, then you can surprise it with a transplant, if necessary. It will be stronger and more equipped to deal with the stresses that transplanting can cause.

Over-potted and in Horrible Soil

Repotting may be somewhat urgent if the troubled violet is severely over-potted or has been growing in a low quality potting mix. If the soil is very heavy and dense, it is wise to move it into the lighter porous soils that violet roots crave. If the plant is the same size as or even smaller than the pot, it is grossly over-potted. Sometimes these violets will grow into the pot, but often they do better if they are simply potted down into a smaller pot. (See Chapter Ten for more on this subject.)

Heat Damaged

There probably is no violet that looks more hopeless than one that got too hot. It happens so fast! The outer rows of leaves become completely watery, glassy-looking and limp in just a matter of hours.

The good news is that the newer center leaves in the crown are quite resilient and will tolerate more heat before they die. The outer leaves that are damaged by heat must be removed immediately. They are a favorite pathway for fungal infections. The crown will almost always survive and be fine. Once the crown appears vigorous again you should repot to bury the neck formed by the lost leaves.

True Trash—Infested or Diseased

There comes a time when a grower should not try to save a violet. Most of the time, we recommend that you do not accept or fight to save African violets that are victims of disease or insects. These are best controlled by disposal of the plants. This sounds harsh, but we cannot recommend that hobbyists with just a few violets spend the amount of money required to purchase chemicals for control. Nor can we recommend that hobbyists expose themselves to the hazards of using those chemicals. Even more, there is no reason to add a violet that would endanger your healthy plants. The disposal method is far and away the smartest, cheapest and safest course to follow.

If you are desperate to save the cultivar you may be able to do so by propagating a leaf that appears to be disease or insect free. To ensure that the problem doesn't continue into the next generation, you must practice good sanitation.

First, make a solution of chlorine bleach water (one-fourth cup bleach per gallon of water) or Physan 20 water (one tablespoon per gallon) and clean the knife (or any tools used to prepare the leaf) in the solution. This will help remove pathogens that could be passed on. After removing the leaf from the plant, submerge it in the solution for ten or fifteen minutes. This will help remove pathogens that are on the surface of the leaf. Finally, start the leaf in an impeccably clean container using fresh (never reused!) potting mix. Isolate the leaf in a clear, closed container. (For more on propagation, see Chapter Eight.)

How do you recognize a disease? Most fungus will produce rotting or some sort of fuzzy or powdery-looking growth. Some diseases cause stunting of the center or black desiccated patches on foliage. Virus-infected plants may have target-like spots on leaves or just generally look like they are not healthy.

How do you recognize insects? Once you see them move it's easy! Unfortunately many of the nastiest pests that are attracted to violets are very hard to spot. Be sure to look closely at flowers for spilled pollen and crawling thrips and at foliage for cottony webs that indicate foliar mealy bugs. Rolled-under leaf edges that are cracked or hard might indicate broad mites.

Cyclamen mite invades the center crown, sucking juices from the newest growth. Growers know they are present when a violet crown begins to grow very tight or foliage becomes usually stiff and glossy.

Soil mealy bug is larger than a mite but is very good at hiding in the soil. It is possible to find evidence of its presence rather quickly by lifting the violet out of its pot. Webbing around the roots in the soil and especially where the roots make contact with the pot is a good indication of infestation. The first above-ground symptom is usually outer leaves which sag unexpectedly even when the plant has been watered (very similar to the symptoms of over-watering and the onset of root rot).

Side Effects of Violet Stress

Sometimes violets that are recovering have some undesirable reactions to the stress of having been sick. It may happen that your troubled violet will go into a frantic suckering period, in which many new tiny crowns will develop. This is one of the emergency reactions that violets have to ensure the survival of the species. Allow the suckers to develop somewhat before removing them. Knocking these suckers out too soon may cause the plant to continue its emergency suckering. It will look like an awful mess, but as the plant stabilizes, it can be restored.

Sometimes, the recovering plant blooms differently or grows differently than it did previously. This is because stress seems to promote mutation. It is another of the emergency reactions that nature designed to guarantee that a species would survive.

Theoretically, a mutation may be more adapted to the new conditions and thus more able to grow. These mutations can be very frustrating to violet collectors who purchase unusual new varieties and then forget to take care of them!

Triage for Violets

Emergency medical personnel are trained to make decisions about which patients need immediate attention, which can wait for medical care, and, which are beyond saving. Violet growers can do the same thing. Plants that are in stress from poor culture can be saved! Patient, gentle treatment can bring violets back to their previously healthy condition. Working with plants that are contagious or fatally infected is dangerously futile.

What about the plants which need watering today? They'll probably wait while you handle the more serious problems. Don't put it off too long, though, or they'll be your next emergency.

23

Where Do Violets Come From?

If your nickname is African violets, where do you come from? This isn't a trick question! Africa, of course!

In the case of African violets, the locale separates them from the sweet violets that are commonly found in the northern hemisphere and are completely unrelated. African violets are more correctly called Saintpaulia by botanists.

It's a good question, though, to ask where it came from. Understanding the genus and the natural conditions in which it thrived provides a lot of information about the needs of a violet in your home.

What are the Species?

The species are the ones that grew in the wild, and should not be confused with the African violet hybrids generally grown in home collections. Species plants are correctly identified by the botanical title "Saintpaulia" with the name of the individual kind following and beginning with a lower-case letter. Saintpaulia is often simplified to an "S" when it is understood that African violets are the genus. So, the first violet discovered is often called S. ionantha.

Hybrid violets, on the other hand, are given names which are capitalized. The only thing that makes a hybrid special is that it is the result of cross-pollination. Since species are rarely available for sale except from private African violet collectors, it is fairly safe to say that all violets sold in regular retail outlets are hybrid cultivars.

The violet species tend to be a little less perfect than the hybrid cultivars. One grower astutely pointed out that hybrid violets grown for show are like animals which are domesticated and trained to perform for human beings. The species are more like animals allowed to run free and wild.

The Early History

Violets were found in eastern Africa near the equator in what is now Tanzania. A number of additional species have since been found in Tanzania and Kenya, but all were within this fairly small region in Africa that includes several mountain ranges that are just plain fun to say. The Usambara, Nguru, Ukaguru, and Uluguru Mountains were primary sites, with additional species found in the Teita and Shimba Hills.

In the late 1800s, specimens of African violets were found growing in the wild by several individuals. The first person to recognize the value of them was Baron Walter von Saint Paul-Illaire, a German officer for the Usambara district in East Africa, who had an interest in botany. In 1892, he collected samples of a plant he called the "violette Usambara."

Baron Walter sent plant material (probably both plants and seed pods) back to his father in Germany for further study. His father, Baron Ulrich von Saint Paul-Illaire, had a close relationship with the Royal Botanical Gardens in Hanover, Germany. Baron Ulrich shared the plant material with the director, Hermann Wendland, who was also a taxonomist. Wendland was the first to write the scientific description and to name them "Saintpaulia" after the Baron's family. He placed them into the Gesneriaceae family. (For more on the other gesneriads see Chapter 26.) Wendland named the species that he studied Saintpaulia ionantha, which in Greek means "with violet-like flowers."

Shortly after, a seed house owned by Ernst Benary in Erfurt, Germany, obtained the rights to the genus and began distributing hybrid seed. Saintpaulia rapidly caught the attention of a number of publications and additional new species were identified. For whatever reason, the name "African violet" was favored over the botanical name.

By 1926, a commercial operation in West Los Angeles, California, had obtained seed. Armacost and Royston chose ten of the best new hybrids and introduced them to the American public in the 1930s. Interest soared and by 1946 (just fifty-four years after Saintpaulia were discovered) there were enough avid growers and collectors that the African Violet Society of America was founded.

Currently, there are over twenty species identified. There are a number of the identified species that have clones which are very close to the species but vary in some significant way. Taxonomists are sometimes inclined to declare these variations as separate species and at other times tend to lump them together as one. The ability to test DNA is making it easier to determine which species are truly unique, but it is unlikely that scientists will ever agree on an exact final number of existing species.

Many of the known species are grown in the United States by hobbyists. A group of them, known as the Mather Collection, was kept at Iowa State University in Ames for years. A second major collection is maintained at the Upsala Biological Gardens in Sweden.

The Conditions in the Natural Setting

The natural environment in Tanzania was somewhat varied. Early notes said that samples of the genus Saintpaulia had been found at altitudes that were fairly close to sea level, as well as much higher in the mountains. Consistently, the plants were found in varying degrees of shade. While some species were found growing in earth, many were found growing in rocky mulch-filled crevices or on the mossy surface of rocks. Many were found near streams or waterfalls which provided high relative humidity.

The species often thrive on the vertical face of cliffs where they are out of reach from the wild goats that look on Saintpaulia as a treat. Violets in nature thrive in the absence of competition from other plants, as well as animals, often growing entirely alone.

Please note that the equator runs very near the region where violets were found. Some might jump to the conclusion that all African violets do well in heat, which is not necessarily true. Some violet cultivars will tolerate warm conditions, as did the species that were found near sea level. Most, however, were found at higher altitudes where temperatures could be much cooler.

The S. ionantha was discovered in the Tanga region of Tanzania which is quite near the eastern coast of Africa and at an altitude of only thirty to one-hundred-fifty feet above sea level. Because this species is the basis for much of the hybridizing that followed, its temperature needs are especially important to violet growers. The coolest temperatures there are around 18º Celsius (65º Fahrenheit), while the highest temperatures are about 31° C (not quite 90º F).

The location near the equator provides a very moderate variation of daytime and nighttime hours, so that wild violets received nearly equal periods of daylight to darkness every day year round. Even then, however, the seasons do vary from slightly warmer and longer days of summer in February and March to slightly cooler and shorter days of winter in July and August in the southern hemisphere.

Obviously, rain fell from the skies, but the moisture reached the plants by dripping through the high canopy of trees and plants overhead and by running across the rock surfaces and through the cracks. In the region of Tanga where S.

ionantha was found, the total yearly rainfall averages about 1337 millimeters, and rain falls one-hundred-twenty-three days a year. These numbers may be converted to show that, on average, one-half inch of rain falls every three days. Of course, nature is not so predictable. The rain tends to fall in the late summer, while the late winter months tend to be dry.

Good growers will quickly recognize how similar their indoor culture is to the one that nature provided outdoors.

Growing Species at Home

As it was stated before, the species are wild plants that do not grow as perfectly as most hybrid violets that are sold today. Anyone who chooses to grow them needs to allow for this untamed habit.

Species grown in home collections often do well in natural window light. They seem to be overwhelmed by artificial light, and often develop crinkled light-colored leaves when under fluorescent light tubes.

Many of the species will naturally develop "necks" or elongated main stems, especially of those that have a trailing, multi-crowned habit. The leaves of species often do not grow as tightly around the crown as do the leaves of hybrids. The species that are single-crowned can be repotted to bury necks, and generally the plants will look prettier when the necks are kept to a minimum.

While we recommend a one-to-three ratio of pot to leaf diameter for hybrids, the species aren't really suited to such rules. Instead, the pot should be in nice proportion to the plant, keeping a small pot but maintaining stability (so that the plant doesn't fall over!).

Much of the rest of the culture will be quite similar to that used for growing hybrids. They enjoy even moisture around their roots but with a porous potting mix that provides lots of air. Species may not respond to wick watering since some are rather easy to over-water. They benefit from fertilizer and even temperatures. And, like the hybrid cultivars, each species has some special preferences that a good grower will recognize over time.

Getting species violets to bloom may require some experimentation. Some are quite shy about blooming. If a species has not bloomed, it is often recommended that it be grown in a cooler area. S. goetzeana grew at a very high altitude and will not bloom except when subjected to very cool temperatures, and even then it will have only a flower or two.

Still Born Free

In just a little over a century, African violets have gone from being totally free and growing in the wild, to being one of the most popular plants in "captivity." Growers can learn a lot by adding some species to their hybrid collections. Just as the modern house cat has instincts that are rooted in its wilder relatives, so African violet hybrids have tendencies that are best explained by the needs of the Saintpaulia species. Preserving the original species is an important task that any one can do in a home setting. Just don't expect them to cooperate like a domesticated hybrid!

Registered Saintpaulia Species

From *AVSA's African Violet Master List of Species and Cultivars*—Listed by species' name, registration number, date of registration, name of individual describing it, and description of the plant's characteristics:

S. brevipilosa (S 10a) 1964 (B. Burtt) Single light purple/darker center; 1-4 per peduncle, very short lived. Light green, small, round, thin, glossy, soft, velvety, tightly bunched/pale back; randomly curved petioles. Usually single crown. Miniature to semiminiature to small standard.

S. confusa (S 16) 1958 (B. Burtt) Single dark purple, 2-6 per peduncle. Variable floriferousness. Medium green, thin, quilted, leathery, flexible, serrated/near-white back. Often multi-crowned. May develop sideways growth habit. Semiminiature to standard.

S. difficilis (S 15) 1958 (B. Burtt) Single medium to dark blue, 5-7 per peduncle. Chartreuse, longifolia, tends to spoon, thin, deep veining, crinkled, rough, long hairs. Long, bent petiole. Usually single crown, may sucker. Standard.

S. diplotricha Punter #0 (S 12c) 1947 (B. Burtt) Single pale lilac/bright yellow stamens; seven per peduncle. Dark green, pointed, thick, serrated. Single crown, may sucker. Small standard.

S. diplotricha Punter #6 (S 12a) 1947 (B. Burtt) Single pale lilac to light blue/bright yellow stamens; one per peduncle. Dark green, small, round, may spoon, lotus-type. Single crown, may sucker. Standard

S. diplotricha Punter #7 (S 12b) 1947 (B. Burtt) Single blue-gray to near white/bright yellow stamens. Dark olive green, plain, heart-shaped, pointed/light red back. Single crown, may sucker. Small standard.

S. goetzeana (S 10) 1900 (A. Engler) Single tiny pale lilac to near white/darker upper petals. Three or more per peduncle, rarely blooms. Dark green, small, round, thick, smooth edge/lighter back. Creeping, branched stems, multi-crowned. Miniature trailer.

S. grandifolia #237 (S 7) 1958 (B. Burtt) Single blue-violet, one or more per peduncle, floriferous. Light green, elliptical, very thin, long flexible petiole. Usually single crown. Large.

S. grandifolia #299 (S 7a) 1958 (B. Burtt) Single dark blue-violet, one or more per peduncle, very floriferous. Light to medium green, elliptical, very thin, crinkled, long flexible petiole. Usually single crown. Large.

S. grotei (S 17) 1921 (A. Engler) Single, light-medium blue/variable darker eye, 2-3 per peduncle. Flowers may hide under foliage. Pale-dark green, variable texture, round, serrated on most clones. Usually near-white back, occasionally red. Green or brown flexible petiole, variable internode length. Large trailer.

S. inconspicua (S 1) 1958 (B. Burtt) Single small blue-spotted white, atypical of other species, one or more per peduncle. Frail. Not known in collections. Miniature trailer.

S. intermedia (S 9) 1958 (B. Burtt) Single medium blue, 5-7 per peduncle, sparse. Olive green, small, round, tends to spoon, velvety, slightly serrated/purple-red back, prominent green veins. Single crown to trailing. Small standard or trailer.

S. ionantha (S 5) 1893 (H. Wendland) Single blue-violet, 4-5 per peduncle, very floriferous. Dark green, pointed, heart-shaped, tends to spoon, thick, quilted, glossy, slightly serrated, long red-brown petiole/red back. Large.

S. magungensis (S 19) 1950 (E. Roberts) Single small dark violet-blue/darker eye, 2-4 per peduncle, very floriferous. Round, cupped-down, pebbled, slightly serrated, brown petiole/green-white back, prominent midrib. Semiminiature trailer.

S. magungensis var. minima (S 19a) 1964 (B. Burtt) Single tiny light purple/darker eye, 1-2 per peduncle, rarely blooms. Medium, small, cupped-down, thin, hairy, serrated, red-brown petiole. Miniature trailer.

S. magungensis var. occidentalis (S 19b) 1964 (B. Burtt) Single medium violet-blue/darker eye, 2-5 per peduncle. Medium green, ovate, tends to fold and spoon, glossy. Bushy trailer.

S. nitida (S 13) 1958 (B. Burtt) Single dark blue-purple, 8-10 per peduncle, floriferous. Dark green, round, may spoon, smooth, glossy, slender brown petiole/red back. Open growth. Small or bushy trailer or multi-crowned standard.

S. orbicularis (S 14) 1947 (B. Burtt) Single small light lilac to almost white/darker eye, 5-8 per peduncle, floriferous but drops easily. Bright green, small, round to heart-shaped, thin, glossy. Single or multi-crowned. Small standard to standard.

S. orbicularis var. purpurea (S 14a) 1964 (B. Burtt) Single small dark purple, 5-8 per peduncle, very floriferous. Dark green, round to heart-shaped, thin, glossy/light back. Single or multiple crown. Standard.

S. pendula (S 8) 1958 (B. Burtt) Single pale-medium blue, one per peduncle, difficult to bloom. Pale to yellow-green, textured, slightly elongated to ovate, very hairy, serrated, variable internode length/pale back. Trailer.

S. pendula var. kizarae (S 8a) 1964 (B. Burtt) Single lavender, 2-4 per peduncle, floriferous. Light green, round, hairy, serrated. Trailer.

S. pusilla (S 2) 1900 (A. Engler) Single, tiny white/mauve top petals, one or more per peduncle. Leaves tiny, triangular/purple back. Not known in collections, but may exist in some mountain ranges in Tanzania. Miniature.

S. rupicola (S 10) 1964 (B. Burtt) Single light-medium blue, three or more per peduncle. Light-medium green, heart-shaped, soft, smooth, glossy, velvety/light back. Leaves sometimes thick. Multi-crowned standard or bushy trailer.

S. shumensis (S 3) 1955 (B. Burtt) Single pale blue to almost white/variable darker eye, usually four per peduncle, sparse bloom. Bright green, pebbled, glossy, slightly serrated, short petiole, leaf blade twisted in some clones. Single crown, but tends to sucker easily. Miniature to semiminiature.

S. teitensis (S 4) 1958 (B. Burtt) Single light blue-violet; 1-2 per peduncle, rare blooms hide under leaves. Dark, slightly pointed, may spoon; thick, rough, brittle, glossy/red, sometimes light green back. Usually grows upright. Standard.

S. tongwensis (S 6) 1947 (B. Burtt) Single pale blue, may show dark pinwheel marking when grown cool; 4-6 per peduncle, very floriferous. Dark green, pointed, narrow, very thick, hairy, slightly serrated/some red back. May appear variegated with mottled pattern over main veins. Usually upright single crown, rarely suckers. Standard.

S. velutina (S 11) 1958 (B. Burtt) Single small medium violet/darker eye, some white tips. Five per peduncle, floriferous. Black-green, round to heart-shaped, may cup up or down, thin, hairy, velvety, pronounced veining, serrated/red-purple back. Single crown, may sucker. Standard.

24

Beginner's Guide to Hybridizing

African violet hybridizing is the process by which new violets are conceived. The actual process of hybridization is actually rather dull, but making violet babies can get pretty exciting if you are patient enough to wait for seedlings to bloom. We're guessing that a lot of beginning hybridizers won't know where to start.

Blossom Physiology

Blossoms exist on plants because nature needs them for reproduction. Nature didn't have to make violet blossoms so beautiful (even ugly flowers make seeds), but that beauty certainly motivates some growers to get involved in the process.

All the plant parts needed for sexual reproduction are located within the blossom. The stamens, which are the "male" part of the flower, are tipped with anthers (the yellow pollen sacs). These normally occur in pairs but can sometimes be multiple pairs, particularly on double blossoms. When the blossom is first opening, the pollen sacs are immature. As the blossom ages, the pollen becomes powdery and the surface of the anther becomes thin, allowing the sac to be broken open, freeing the pollen to seek a sticky stigma.

The pistil, the "female" part of the flower, is often harder to see at a glance, particularly in double or semidouble blossoms. The pistil looks like a tiny syringe projecting out of the blossom next to the pollen sacs. At the tip of the pistil is the stigma, which is light in color and becomes sticky as the blossom matures. The fat part of the pistil at the very center of the blossom is the ovary, which swells and becomes the seed pod after fertilization.

Boy Meets Girl

When the blossom is mature, the pollen is easily released from its sac by some outside force. That could be an insect (who doesn't care what he's doing) or a hybridizer like you (who has carefully considered your goals). The pollen is then moved, or crossed, onto a stigma that is sticky at the peak of its maturity and ready to accept pollen. The grains of pollen will grow down into the ovary where the seeds are formed. A violet seed pod has one single chamber that contains as many as 200-300 tiny seeds, each with its own individual genetic code.

After a successful hybrid cross is made, the ovary will begin to swell, and the flower petals will begin to wilt and turn brown, usually within a week. The plant is "pregnant."

The violet seed pod now must mature. This process can take up to six months or more. During this time, the pod must remain on the plant with its faded blossom. For a while, it receives nutrition from the rest of the plant, but as the pod approaches maturity, the stem will gradually turn brown and dry up.

Once the seed pod is fully dry, it can be removed from the plant. We like to place it into an envelope, taking care to label it correctly with all pertinent information, and then set it aside for at least a week or two before planting. This allows the seed pod to mature fully and dry completely. The seeds will be extremely tiny and dust-like and can be easily blown away by the softest breath. Some pods are quite full of seeds and some have only a few. And occasionally, and very dishearteningly, some pods will contain no seeds at all. The size of the pod is not a good indicator of the contents.

To plant seeds, scatter them on a bed of moistened medium such as sphagnum moss or vermiculite both of which are naturally sterile. Lightly misting with warm water will help to bring the seed into firm contact with the surface of the medium. If the seed is viable, it will begin to grow, appearing as tiny green specks after two weeks or so. While the seed is first germinating, and then growing, it needs light, warmth, and humidity. When the baby plants grow to an inch or so, they should be removed from the seed bed and placed into tiny pots. These young plants will need about six months to grow before they are mature enough to bloom.

Unless the parents were the same species each of the baby plants is a new African violet cultivar; it will have a unique genetic code that is different from either of its parents or siblings. All babies are beautiful to their mothers, but many of the violets springing from one seed pod will be similar in appearance and unremarkable. Each could be given a name, however, because each is a new hybrid plant. Good hybridizers select out only the best of the best, if any, to keep and to name, however.

Please note that hybrid does not mean "high bred" or of high quality. It means only that the baby has two parents. Plants that originate from self-pollination are inbred and quite often are inferior, but they are still "hybrid" violets.

How to Pollinate

Even the dreaded thrips (who love to eat pollen) can make crosses and cause seed pods to develop. Pollinating is easy. We'd like to think that we humans could take this to a higher level doing something better than just making seed.

Good technique will increase your success in making a hybrid cross. A hybridizer should be sure that only one pollen parent is involved in the process. For this reason, one should always remove the existing pollen sacs of the seed-bearing parent's blossom leaving only the pistil. It is fairly easily to do this with tweezers.

Then, using clean tweezers pull the stamens off of the pollen parent's blossom so that the anthers and the pollen can be maneuvered directly to the seed-bearing parent's pistil, which as we said earlier, should be sticky and ready to accept the pollen. It may be necessary to flick the pollen sac to open it and release the pollen powder. Gently apply the pollen to the stigma making sure that it is well coated.

After the cross has been made, tag the flower stem with a label identifying the seed-bearing parent, the pollen parent, and the date of the cross. For example, "Tomahawk" X "Dance Time" would be the correct form for "Tomahawk" (the seed-bearing parent) crossed by "Dance Time" (the pollen parent). For beginning hybridizers, this will be interesting information to have a year later. For the master hybridizer (and you might become one), it is critical information as genetic lines are developed and offspring are used in further crosses. Knowing the seedling's parents will tell a hybridizer what to expect or hope for in the offspring for many generations. This information is also required if any seedling is to be registered officially.

Occasionally seed pods fail to develop. This can be because the blossoms were not mature enough when the cross was made, or they were past maturity and no longer fresh. Waiting for just the right few hours on both parents-to-be can sometimes be vital. Some plants seem to be sterile and refuse to set seed. Some set seed that is not viable. Cultural problems or poor growing conditions can also be the root of failure.

Some plants offer obstacles to successful crosses. Very double blossoms can often hide their sexual parts and be hard to work with, or those sexual parts may be joined to the petal rendering them sterile. We recommend removing center petals in the blossoms so you can see what you are doing. Plants with thrips are poor parents because of the possibility of self-pollination.

While the seed pod is developing, it is important to keep the seed-bearing mother plant in consistently good horticultural condition. Do not allow the plant to become too moist, as seed pods are vulnerable to fungus. In fact, slightly dry conditions may produce better results.

Most hybridizers have a favorite method of starting the seed. We often use a four-inch pot partially filled with light potting mix topped with a layer of vermiculite and moistened. We break the seed pod open onto a sheet of paper with a crease down the center and allow the seed to slide down the crease scattering the seed around the pot. We mist it lightly, then cover the pot with clear plastic wrap and secure it with a rubber band. The pot is labeled with the name of the seed parents, the date the cross was made, and the date the seed is sown. Alternatively, some hybridizers have indicated that the plastic salad containers from fast-food restaurants work well for germination.

Who is Mendel and Why is He Important?

Gregor Mendel was a well-known monk-turned-geneticist (by his study of garden peas) who first identified the model which would predict how offspring would look. He recognized that there were dominant traits for genes which were the most likely to occur, and recessive traits which would only occur if the dominant gene was not present. He chose to label a dominant gene with a capital letter and a recessive gene with a lower-case letter.

Every trait, in Mendel's model, is represented with two genes. They might both be dominant (XX) or both recessive (xx) or mixed (Xx). The trait prescribed by the dominant gene will appear. Any good encyclopedia will explain Mendel's laws and show the charts for predicting outcomes.

There are multiple sets of genetic traits which are influenced by a number of environmental conditions, all of which have an effect on the final appearance of the seedlings. It is very interesting, but complicated. As one begins to play with hybridizing, it becomes helpful to learn about these so that reasonable goals can be set and results can be understood. The African Violet Magazine includes a regular column on hybridizing which often includes information regarding dominant and recessive traits of violets.

What Violet Cultivars May be Used as Parents?

Any African violet can be used to hybridize. Patents limiting the propagation of violets pertain only to vegetative reproduction (putting down leaves or using suckers). The patent laws do not govern the pollen or sexual reproduction at this time.

Species may also be used. At this time, the majority of all African violets developed from the species ionantha. There is still a lot of experimenting to be done with the other saintpaulia species and many new characteristics may be found by those adventurous enough to try.

There is wisdom in choosing parents which exhibit the characteristics of the best African violets. Plants with poor blooming habits, weak foliage, or dull color will be likely to produce seedlings with similar characteristics. Unfortunately, with some experience you will probably find that even good parents can produce less-than-desirable offspring.

What Seedlings should be Named?

It is perhaps difficult to imagine throwing away seedlings. It is even harder to imagine keeping only two or three of the perhaps hundred seedlings that bloom from one seed pod. It must be done. Remember even a bug can pollinate. The ability to select only the best is the most important quality any breeder can have, and even a beginning hybridizer will be more respected if he is extremely choosy about what escapes a trip to the trash can.

After a seedling shows promise of outstanding performance, it should be grown under normal conditions, propagated through several generations, and watched. If the promise holds true, and the cultivar is indeed special, then it may deserve a name.

The hybridizer usually is the one to choose a name for the new cultivar. It can be almost anything. However, if you wish to register it with AVSA (the international registration authority for genus Saintpaulia and its cultivars), then it may not be more than three words, must be a traditional spelling, and must not violate trademarks. If another plant already has that name, then it may not be used in that form again.

If you have thought of a good name but have not decided which plant deserves it, you may reserve the name with the AVSA. The AVSA Registration Chairman is in charge of this and will send the necessary forms for registering a plant on request. Updates of newly registered plants and reserved names appear in the *African Violet Magazine.*

What Are the Chances?

The more crosses you make, the better your chances for finding the best violet. A studious approach improves the odds even more. However, there is every possibility that the casual hybridizer will hit the jackpot before the most earnest professional hybridizer.

Truly the violet world needs many people at work, learning the process of hybridizing and setting goals for new colors and combinations as well as improved strength and blooming. Recent years have shown a decline in the number of professionals in this field, so there is a lot of room for new faces.

Are you the hybridizer of the future? You'll never know until you try. It will give new meaning to your violet passion!

25

The Sporting World of African Violets

There's no perspiration involved here, and talent has nothing to do with it. Sporting is the curious habit of all plants, including African violets, to change without warning.

Defining "Sport"

The words "sport" and "mutant" actually mean the same thing—a sudden change or variation from the original. In the violet world, we do generally use the word 'sport' when referring to this phenomenon. It's a word that conjures up the idea of fun: football, baseball, and all that. On the other hand, there is something about the word "mutant" that conjures up thoughts of monsters in horror movies!

To quote the *AVSA Handbook for African Violet Growers, Exhibitors, and Judges*, a sport is an offspring which "shows a marked change from its parents due to changes within the chromosomes or genes. Sometimes when an African violet leaf is rooted, a plant which is radically different appears among the plants that are true to the parent plant."

This is not the same as when poor cultural conditions result in plants that grow and bloom somewhat differently. For example, blossoms with white edges may lose their edges during hot spells or those with normally deep blossom colors may begin to pale. Lack of fertilizer, inadequate light, or abnormal pH may cause foliage to lose vigor or color. These are not sports. Improved cultural conditions can quickly restore a sickly plant to its original appearance. Sports involve a genetic change, which is irreversible.

Any part of the plant may sport. Blossoms may change shape, form, color or color-pattern. Sports may also involve changes in foliage type, form, color or size. Myriad combinations of changes may occur as well.

Why Does It Happen?

With all the complexities involved in the genetic make-up of African violets, it is probably only natural that something goes haywire every now and then, and the unexpected comes about.

Most sports are simply a natural occurrence. Something in the genes breaks down or gets rearranged somehow, and the new plant displays characteristics unlike that of its parent. Perhaps some of these changes occur due to stress from environmental factors.

Some people have experimented with subjecting violets to various chemicals or to radiation in an effort to accelerate the occurrence of sports, and hopefully to come up with some radically new traits. Holtkamp Greenhouses in Nashville, Tennessee, actually launched seed into space via a NASA space shuttle. The seed orbited earth for six years before it was recovered and returned to earth. While in space it was subjected to forces and rays quite different from those found inside the atmosphere. The seed that germinated produced a number of interesting sports with characteristics that were quite unique. They have named the resulting series EverFloris.

Such deliberate efforts to achieve sports are rare. Most of the important sports that have added to the heritage and development of African violets have merely come along as surprises.

Importance in Violet History

Many sports are of negligible quality or uniqueness and should probably be discarded. However, on occasion, a sport can give rise to a lovely new cultivar which might be something completely different from anything ever seen before. In the 100 years since African violets were found growing in the wild, sports have played an important part in developing the wide range of violet types and colors available to us today.

The first white-blossomed violet was a sport. The first double-blossomed violet was a sport. Many of today's variegated African violets trace their ancestry back to a cultivar called "Tommy Lou," with green-and-white foliage, which sported from the green-leafed "White Pride." "Blue Boy," one of the earliest hybrids, sported from its smooth tailored foliage to a completely new curly type with a light mark at the base of the leaf. The sport was named "Blue Girl," and any plant with this leaf is now described as having "girl" foliage.

The complex genetics of African violets have indeed given rise to all sorts of mutations through the years, many of which have given us totally unexpected surprises.

Recently, there has been much interest in the chimeras, or pinwheels, with stripes of color running through the centers of the petals. Finally, there are the new yellows, which are reportedly due to the mutation of blossom pigments, giving us colors that were only dreamed of before and were often thought to be impossible.

Looking at the Pros and Cons

Sports usually pop up as a surprise. Some surprises are good, while others are not.

There are frustrations involved with propagating some of the more unstable types of violets. Oftentimes, violets with fantasy blossoms (those with streaks or speckles of color spread over another background color) will not bloom true to variety. A cultivar that should have pink blossoms with purple speckles may instead produce plants that bloom solid pink or solid purple. This is more or less to be expected with fantasies, unfortunately but it is most definitely not a desirable type of sport.

Similarly, other types of bicolor violets may occasionally revert to solid-color blossoms. This, too, is what would usually be described as an undesirable type of sport. Bicolor violets that are white-plus-another-color frequently sport to a solid color blossom. This is often accompanied by a change in the foliage color. Most bicolor blossoms with white are accompanied by light green foliage. When they sport to a solid color blossom, the foliage often develops dark reddish blotches on the underside of the new leaves in the crown. As time passes, the blotches seem to expand and the foliage becomes completely dark green in appearance.

Sporting may occur on a mature plant, but it may also happen during propagation. Fortunately, because of the different color of the foliage when bi-colors mutate, these sporting offspring often can be identified when quite young and be discarded before all the time and effort is put into growing them into mature blooming plants.

Just as foliage can change colors when sporting occurs, it can also change shape or form. Violets that should have smooth tailored foliage may suddenly appear with heavily ruffled, and sometimes unmanageable, foliage. Sometimes trailing violets which should have semiminiature foliage will suddenly have one part of the plant growing with standard-sized foliage resulting in an unattractive, ungainly look. Some foliage changes may be pretty and desirable, but most of the time they are not.

On the good side are some of the wonderful surprises that turn up. And some of these are very dramatic. A couple of years ago, we noticed a light-foliaged plant in a tray of otherwise dark green plants. It was identical in shape, form and foliage pattern, but it was a much different shade of green. This plant was set aside and watched with much anticipation since the original cultivar is a favorite. When the sport did finally bloom, it was a lovely full double white instead of the medium blue color that it should have been. That was a delight.

Other good things can happen. Favorite plants may suddenly sport to a new color or combination of colors, still exhibiting the growth habit and floriferousness that made the original variety such a joy to grow. Gorgeous chimeras may turn up where least expected. These may be the best of the sports, since they usually have the same desirable growth pattern as the original, but with the beautiful pinwheel blossoms.

If the change is pleasant, consider it a good sport. If the change is irritating, consider it a bad mutant.

Some Responsibility is Involved

This brings us to another point of consideration. What should you do when you have a violet sport? First of all, look at it with a very critical eye, determining whether it is indeed unique and attractive, and whether it should be kept or dumped.

If it is worth keeping, at least for a while, the plant needs to be properly labeled. Although some sports may seem deserving, do not give an original name to all the mutants that come along. Most of the time, it is probably best just to label a plant as "Sport of ____" or as "____ Sport." That's a completely honest way of labeling a plant as to what it really is. Just as hybridizers should name only the best of their seedlings, so also must all violet growers show some restraint in applying completely new names to the "oddballs" that crop up now and then.

Some varieties do have a propensity to throw the same sport from time to time for a lot of different growers. If each of these growers were to apply a different name to their sport, there could be great confusion in the violet world. If a sport worthy of being named turns up in your collection, it is always wise to contact the hybridizer in case the same sport has already occurred and has already been given a name.

The name game is especially important if the grower ever wishes to exhibit a particularly beautiful sport in an AVSA-judged show. It is a real temptation to give the mutant cultivar a name and enter it, but this is not the correct thing to do. Ideally, the plant should first be entered in a "new cultivar" or "sports and mutants" class. If it is awarded a blue ribbon, then it may deserve to be named.

There certainly are some frustrations in propagating African violets, hoping that they will come true and bloom the way they are supposed to, especially when dealing with some of the more genetically unstable bicolors and fantasies. This does put some responsibility on those who sell violets. Starter plants may not always bloom the way they are supposed to; and in our opinion, customers should be informed that this is a possibility, particularly with the bicolors and fantasies.

And yet, every now and then, as has happened so often through these one hundred years or so of African violet history, something truly revolutionary, unique and worthwhile will turn up when it is least expected—like a gift from above. Some are great milestones. Some are just small and simple joys. It is all a part of what makes the hobby of growing violets such "sporting" good fun.

26

Introducing the Relatives: The Gesneriad Family

In nearly all African violet shows there is a section for the "Other Gesneriads." Violets (or Saintpaulia) may be our favorite gesneriad, but there is a plethora of interesting cousins. Over 2,000 species of gesneriads are known throughout the world, but only a few are commonly available. Even some of the rarer genera of the family can be found in private collections with a little determined searching. The more gesneriads one has, the more one comes to respect this fuzzy family.

What Makes a Plant a Gesneriad?

In botanical terms, the family is known as Gesneriaceae, which is in Division 7 of the plant kingdom (seed plants). They are in Subdivision 2, which includes all flowering plants and, within that group, are labeled as Order No. 34.

Now, in simpler terms, all plants that are grouped as gesneriads (most pronounce it with a hard "g") have some characteristics in common. The reproductive parts of the gesneriad flower (the ovary and stigma) stand above the calyx (the base of the flower) and in most cases above the petals. Each gesneriad flower can form one single seedpod with many seeds inside. Gesneriads are not parasitic, and the leaf structure of each is simple (rather than compound, as for example, roses or parsley).

There are some interesting patterns in the family. The flowers of most gesneriads are joined at the base so that even if they seem to have flat blossoms (like violets) the petals are actually lobes of a tube. The flowers usually have four or five lobes which are commonly called "petals." Botanists describe the flower as zygomorphic because there is only one line of symmetry which will divide the blossom into two equal sections (or mirror images). In most cases, gesneriad flowers have two smaller top petals and three larger bottom petals.

The calyx, which is where the green part of the plant attaches to the flower, is always five-parted in any gesneriad, and in some cases the calyx is quite decorative. The Aeschynanthus, or lipstick vine, is a good example of this with two-inch flowers growing out of a long black tube-shaped calyx.

The leaves of the various gesneriads would seem to be radically different from one another, but all have oval or spatulate shapes. The surface texture, color patterns, and growing habits may distract you, though. The waxy surface of the trailing Nematanthus hybrids is far different from the multicolor-haired leaves of Episcia plants. But Nematanthus and Episcias are both popular members of the gesneriad family. And whether the hairs are obvious or not, botanists commonly distinguish new gesneriad discoveries in nature by the fuzzy surface on the foliage or stems.

The roots also vary significantly. There are three different root structures, which doesn't sound very interesting, except that it is how we divide the gesneriads into smaller groups. Many, like violets, have fibrous roots. A few, like Sinningias, have tuberous roots. Several others, like the Achimenes have scaly rhizomes, which go dormant for a season.

Joyfully, most members of the family can be propagated easily and many can be cultivated into bloom in home situations.

How Did They Get Their Name?

Long before anyone seriously attempted to describe the family of gesneriads, a man named Konrad Gesner studied botany as a source of medicines. He was born in Switzerland in 1516 and was educated as a result of a scholarship provided by Ulrich Zwingli, a famous theologian. He was well respected, and his works were reprinted and studied for over 200 years. When the gesneriad family was described in 1693, a French botanist suggested that Gesner be honored by naming the plant family after him, although Gesner personally had not studied them.

Let's Meet a Few of the Relatives

Episcias are one of the more commonly available "other" gesneriads. Sometimes, inexperienced growers will call these plants "Chocolate Soldier" which is the name of one of the older popular hybrid cultivars of this genus.

All of the Episcias have gorgeous foliage and are often exhibited without flowers for their ornamental quality. They do bloom easily, most with red or orange flowers. You may have seen Episcia "Cleopatra" with its large and delicate pink, mint green and white leaves at African violet shows. It usually requires a terrarium-type container to thrive. Sturdier varieties like Episcia "KeeWee," with darker reddish tones thrive with minimal care.

Episcias make beautiful hanging displays and love warm sunny locations. One caution: they are very sensitive to cold and perish at temperatures below 50°F.

Another very popular plant is Columnea, which has a very striking blossom, usually red or yellow, that suggests the shape of a flying fish. For this reason, it is often called the "goldfish plant." These can grow in a limp trailing style, with small fuzzy leaves, or in a more upright woody form with large coarse hairy leaves. It is not uncommon for these to carry over one-hundred blossoms at once, and the care is very similar to African violets.

Achimenes, one of the gesneriads with scaly-rhizomed root structure, seems to thrive as a hanging porch plant, especially in the warmer areas of the country. The tube-shaped blossoms can be as large as three inches across. The flowers flare into wide dramatic trumpets that often feature interesting veining and color variations. They are messy inside the house and will quickly go dormant if allowed to dry out even briefly.

Gloxinias are also in this family. The gloxinia that your florist sells is actually not a Gloxinia in scientific terms; however, it is a gesneriad and actually a large showy member of the genus Sinningia. The true Gloxinia has blue bell-shaped flowers on wild sprawling stems and has a scaly-rhizome root structure, causing it to go dormant occasionally.

Sinningias are probably the gesneriad second in popularity to violets because of the mislabeled florist's gloxinia. The other members of the Sinningia family may not be quite as grand, but they provide some of the most beautiful and varied flowers to be found among gesneriads. The tiniest of Sinningias could grow inside a baby food jar (not an attractive picture, but it shows how tiny they are), and, of course, the florist's gloxinias can easily grow two feet or more in diameter. All Sinningias also may experience a period of dormancy at the end of the bloom cycle and will grow again from the tuberous root when the time is right. They also grow easily from seed. Care again is rather similar to African violets, although some of the larger types may need more intense light.

Another gesneriad with fabulous blossoms is the Streptocarpus. There are many variations of growth habits in this group; some are annuals and some are perennials. The feature that draws them altogether is the seed pod, which has a twisted look. Streps (as they are affectionately known) have foliage that is quite different from any other gesneriads; the leaves are often very long and strap-shaped with a frail, thin texture and striking veins. In recent years, however, breeders have been working on compact hybrids causing Streptocarpus to soar in popularity. Most of the blossoms have a tube shape that flares into open graceful lobes with rich color, especially down the throat of the flower. These plants seem to favor slightly cooler conditions (55º to 75°F) and are vulnerable to fungus when kept too damp.

In recent years there also has been a surge of interest in Chiritas and Petrocosmeas each of which have lovely foliage, interesting flowers, and neat growing habits. Both are fibrous rooted and fit into African violet collections quite comfortably.

There are many more gesneriads. And, we're sure that many experienced growers who read this will think of others that we should have mentioned. There is great fun in trying some of these and watching for others that can be grown alongside our African violets.

Common Horticultural Needs of the Family

Nearly all of the gesneriads need care remarkably similar to violets. Good bright light, usually a fluorescent light, will guarantee better blooming. They generally need porous airy soils, regular fertilization, and good humidity. Most prefer even moisture except for dormant periods. They are somewhat sensitive to fungal diseases and those with soft hairy foliages are quite vulnerable to rot if they are grown in wet conditions. The greatest variation of culture between the different genera is probably in temperature preferences. Since gesneriads are found worldwide in many climates, the grower must be especially aware of the temperature needs when selecting new types to grow.

The Correct Way to Write a Gesneriad Name

This may seem overly fussy to some, but there is a correct form for writing the name of plants. If the genus name is known (because you are discussing Episcias, for example) you may from then on write the names as E. reptans (using the lower case for the name when it is a species) or E. "Chocolate Soldier" (using the upper case when it is a hybrid cultivar).

Similarly, the African violet's scientific name is Saintpaulia, and so one of the Saintpaulia species would be written as S. ionantha, while a hybrid cultivar is most correctly written S. "Tomahawk".

Where to Find Gesneriads

Those who are members of the African Violet Society of America and receive the magazine will find that many advertising vendors offer a selection of some other gesneriads. Gesneriads are also frequently offered for sale at African violet shows. A few areas of the country have gesneriad clubs which are affiliated with The Gesneriad Society, an international group which is devoted to the study of all gesneriads. It can be found on the internet at www.aggs.org. This site will also direct visitors to vendors who sell gesneriads of all types.

The *African Violet Magazine* also features a regular column on the other gesneriads which can guide you into the more specific needs of certain species in the family.

Invite Some Home

There's an old joke that fish and relatives stink after three days, but you'll probably want to enjoy African violet relatives for a long time. At least try an Episcia or one of the others that seems to match your conditions. You'll soon be hearing comments from friends, who "never saw anything like that before!" It's a pretty nice family to know.

27

Using Violets in Design

It seems to be a natural step from growing violets well to trying to make them even more beautiful in designs or at least placing them in pretty containers. Unfortunately some "green thumb" growers feel "all thumbs" when it comes to arranging flowers. But it goes the other way, too; some very average growers are true artists in design. If you've never tried, we'll try to give you an explanation of what it is all about.

Official AVSA shows have a special division for designs using violets with a variety of other plant material. The division includes sections for container gardens, designs using an entire violet plant, and designs using just African violet blossoms with other materials.

The reason for designing with violets is simply because it is fun. African violets are not the perfect cut flower for doing floral designs, but their colors and textures are very special. It can be quite satisfying to place violet blossoms or whole plants into an arrangement; their beauty seems new and refreshing when exhibited in a different way.

Can violets be grown in design-like settings? Not usually. A violet plant really grows best in a pot of its own, with plenty of space for the leaves and bright even light. Most designs do not provide these. If you wish to play around with violets in design, think of it as a temporary situation, not as a permanent, decorative fixture.

Violet shows offer three design sections for exhibitors: container gardens, arrangements using whole violet plants, and arrangements using violet blossoms.

Container Gardens

Container gardens come in several types, but the most familiar are dish gardens. These are open shallow dishes of plants including at least one blooming violet. Violet shows do not permit designers to use dishes that are divided into separate sections, because the goal is to create a miniature landscape, maybe of a meadow or a formal garden. Ideally, a dish garden lets us peek into a different world and imagine ourselves down among the plants. The plants are required to be growing in common soil so that roots might grow together as they would in nature. They should be types of plants that would commonly be found together in nature. Cacti and violets are not naturally found in combination, so they are not to be planted together.

As you might expect, the plants are supposed to look as if they have been growing in the dish for some time, but in reality, the violets will not usually thrive in this environment indefinitely. Miniature or semiminiature violets work best because their size remains in better scale with other plants. Very masterful designers may find unusual plants that can grow in this limited environment which do not quickly overwhelm the scene; but most of us are limited to whatever we are able to find and must enjoy it for brief time periods. Even show growers add the violet plants just days or hours before going to show so that they are to be in bloom for judging.

The creation of a landscape that is truly in a little world of its own happens in another container garden called a terrarium. This is a planting in a transparent container with a lid that permits a closed atmosphere and theoretically waters itself. Small rocks and bits of wood add interesting detail. Mosses and some petite green plants like ivy work well because they prefer to grow in the high humidity. It does require much knowledgeable searching at plant stores as well as in nature to find the perfect plants. Growers find that many plants soon outgrow the space or need fresh air. Terrariums were a rage in the 1970s, but high failure rates have caused most of the public to abandon this type of container. They can work beautifully for short periods of time with violets, if you are willing to work at it. If you do try, be sure to build in a natural drainage system, using sand or loose material at the bottom of the container, where excess water can collect.

Even more difficult is a bottle garden. Like building a ship in a bottle, the challenge is to present a scene that appears impossible to create. The bottle must have an opening that is too small for a hand to enter. These are planted with sticks and long handled tools. Bottle gardens are rarely seen because they are so difficult, and because the plants often do not survive.

One last container garden style is the natural garden, which uses a piece of driftwood, lava rock, or other natural material as a container for growing plants. These may have several pockets or growing areas. Natural gardens are challenging in the long run, because the plants may not have much space for root growth or have proper drainage conditions. It is also often difficult to water the plants without dripping. In the case of driftwood, the wood may begin to rot away. These are beautiful, however, in the hands of skillful designers who use trailing plants like ivy or miniature trailing ficus to crawl across the surface with upright plants and violets to add visual interest and color.

For a grower who does not plan to enter a show, it can be fun to try one of these container garden styles to use as a table centerpiece or as a conversation starter when company is coming. The most successful gardens imitate nature and do not have plants packed together, but more likely have some open spaces. At home you have the luxury of breaking the rules that the show exhibitors must follow!

Arranging with a Whole Plant

In a violet show, this would be called an "interpretive plant arrangement." These designs often get quite large, but they allow the designer to put an African violet into a setting that may be quite unlike anything in nature. In African violet shows these are put together only to last for the length of the show. The rules of AVSA require that plants used in design be removed from the pot. The roots are wrapped in a material that protects them and then are fit invisibly into the design.

Novice exhibitors often make the mistake of using the soil around the plant to stick other design elements into, which is contrary to AVSA rules. In a show, this would eliminate the design from being considered for any award. Even without such rules, it is not good for any plant to have foreign materials shoved through its root systems.

If a beginner were to try placing a plant in an arrangement for a home decoration, the violet could be left in its pot. This way, it can easily be returned to its normal growing space when the design is disassembled. It is usually wise to use a low container or a pile of rocks, wood, or plant material to hide the soil or pot beneath the violet's leaves. Other plant material should be secured into a traditional base of florist foam or a kenzan (sometimes called a needlepoint holder or "frog".)

Good design should always try to look like it won't fall over or fall apart. Ideally, a design should cause your eye to want to move and examine various sections of the design. Using distinct lines, harmonious colors and contrasting textures will make the design more satisfying. It is also wise to consider proportions. If you are having a party and want to bring out a theme with some accessory item, consider that accessory's size as you make the design. Also, remember the most basic of details: plants and containers should be clean.

The real fun here is that the designer does not have to try to duplicate nature the way one must when planting container gardens. Any plants and any ideas may be combined to give an original view. In a show, each class usually has a theme which the designer is supposed to interpret. At home, a designer can just have fun using whatever is available to make a satisfying arrangement. As a hint: It seems that the less one fusses, the more successful the design will be.

Arranging with Violet Flowers

"Interpretive flower arrangements," as they are called in AVSA shows, are designs in which violet blossoms are removed from the plant and used in combination with other elements including cut plant material. These may seem very difficult at first, but many designers love the freedom of not messing with a root system. There are a number of unusual design types that can be done when just using the blossoms.

Traditional floral arrangements are usually designed in florist foam or on kenzan using assorted fresh cut flowers and greenery. Violet designers use these too, but they have to improvise a bit to get violet blossoms worked into an arrangement since they have such short stems! If violet blossoms are to appear on a high branch in a design, a small water tube might have to be cleverly placed with glue and camouflaged with moss. Some designs are done with blossoms out of water and expected to stay fresh for only a few hours. Sometimes moistened cotton balls are tucked behind blossoms. We have a set of long glass piping, such as might be used by a chemist, which has been used several times to place flowers higher in a design. Necessity is the mother of invention!

Violet shows often feature both large and small arrangements of cut violet blossoms. The small designs are often done with one or two flowers plus a bit of other plant material to create a line. Tiny little vases and pots, or even lids from medicine bottles make good containers for a bit of florist foam or just a supply of water.

Large interpretive flower arrangements usually require a well established line using branches, greenery, or manmade items with violet blossoms placed strategically. The addition of a small figure, a rock, or other item often finishes the arrangement. The entire design is placed on a mat or in front of a colored background to set it apart from its surroundings. Designers experiment with this most basic form to give it a distinctive look.

An intriguing design form is one that is seen underwater in a clear glass bowl. These designs are usually very simple with a few blossoms and a bit of greenery that are secured and weighted, perhaps by using hot glue to attach materials to a kenzan. The design is then set down into the container, and water is gently poured in until the bowl is full. The water and curve of the glass magnifies the design and the color dramatically. Very simple designs can be done in small glass containers using only one blossom with a fishing weight secured to the back.

Some of the most imaginative styles of designs can be done using violet blossoms. Mobiles, which are suspended in air, designs with moving parts, and free form art styles are all possible.

Probably the most challenging part of designing for a beginner is deciding to remove a blossom stem from a blooming plant. This isn't really difficult, but some growers are reluctant to take any flowers off of their plants. The best choice for design are blossom stems that have two or three flowers open and several buds left to go. Hold the stem between two fingers and move it back and forth as it is gently pulled loose. The flower stem should be cut at an angle with a sharp knife and placed in clear lukewarm water until it is ready to be used.

Using Violets Decoratively

Most growers now and then like to "dress up" an African violet by placing the plant into something pretty, particularly for holidays or special occasions. In a violet show, the plant would actually be potted into an "unusual container" to enter in that class. At home, it is really better to set the plant in its pot into a basket, a piece of china or pottery or perhaps a beautiful brass or crystal container. The plant will grow better in a regular pot that provides good drainage and the correct amount of space for the roots. As a finishing touch, the violet in its pretty container can be set on a mat or piece of fabric in a color that will complement the plant.

Large broad baskets can hold several violets, each in their own pots, using Spanish moss, excelsior, or even cellophane around them to hide empty spaces. Touches of ribbon or accessories can make this into a spectacular centerpiece.

Plants can stay in the decorative containers for fairly long periods of time providing that there is plenty of available bright light and that regular watering is maintained. The most common failures occur when plants are left standing in water for days because the fancy containers conceal the need to pour away the excess. We'd be rich if we got a dime for every violet that met its death this way!

You may not have the gift of creating magnificent designs that inspire the world, but most violet growers can occasionally use their plants in an artistic way that will please friends and family.

There is a fair amount of help available for persons who want to learn more about design. The library is one source. Your local florist will usually help you obtain necessary materials or suggest ways that you might accomplish an idea. Garden clubs offer opportunities to see the work of veteran advanced designers in their shows. To learn more specifically about African violet design, read the *AVSA Handbook for Growers Exhibitors, and Judges* which is offered for sale through the AVSA office.

It's hard to believe that violets could be even more beautiful, but we keep trying!

28

Good Investments—Buying Violets by Mail Order

It is always fun to settle in with the *African Violet Magazine* ads and mail order lists from commercial growers of African violets, or to search online vendors. It's great to dream about what purchases to make next. But how can anyone tell whether the plants listed are going to be really good or even what is expected? How do you choose? How do you avoid wasting money?

Some growers give up and just order everything. If you have the space and money, this can be great fun! Some growers give up and buy nothing until they see it growing in someone else's collection. That is safe, but there is a certain excitement in waiting for the first blossoms to form on new varieties that have been ordered sight unseen.

Smart growers learn how to read between the lines of printed descriptions and choose what they believe will be the best choices for their own particular collections. This is a fun challenge, and it doesn't have to require much money, especially if you are patient enough to grow your new plants from leaf cuttings.

Understanding the Language

There are a number of terms that African violet growers routinely use which probably make no sense at all to a beginner. The following are some common terms with their definitions:

Variegated—This describes foliage that has white, pink or creamy (sometimes more golden in tone) markings on the surface of the leaves. "Tommie Lou" is frequently used to describe the pattern of variegation that edges the perimeter of the leaf. "Lillian Jarrett" is a variegation pattern that runs from the center spine of the leaf toward the edges. "Champion" variegation is less distinct and appears as a mottling of light and dark greens across the leaf. This is also known as crown variegation because it usually is most pronounced on the center leaves of a plant, with the outer, more mature leaves developing a more even green coloring.

Fantasy—This describes a blossom color pattern of flecks, spots, or streaks of one color across a different underlying color. The "fantasy" hybrids tend to be a little less stable than solid color blossoms; that is, they sometimes bloom without the markings or sometimes only half of the plant will show the pattern of markings. Leaf cuttings will occasionally produce plants that do not bloom true, or in the same pattern as the parent plant. Why is it called "fantasy?" Because the first cultivar that exhibited color flecks was named "Fantasy!"

Red—This is a real misnomer. For years, hybridizers have been trying to achieve fire-engine red. When the plum-magenta shades were first developed, they were called "red." Later on, the newer burgundy and maroon shades were also called "red." Today, there are a few hybrids with a deep reddish coral tone that are called "red" too. If a variety is a fairly new release, "red" probably means a burgundy or a near-red shade. If it is an older variety, it may be a reddish-purple or deep fuchsia.

Geneva edge—This is recognized as the distinct white outlining the blossom's primary color. If the outlining color is not white, the blossom will be described as "edged in" a color. This trait is so named because the first cultivar that exhibited the edge was named "Geneva."

Chimera—This is a rare form of plant that is characterized by a double set of genes. There are two distinct sets of genes within a single plant. African violet chimeras bloom with a pinwheel pattern; that is, each petal is striped with a distinctive second color. Chimeras do not come true from leaf cuttings, and plantlets therefore tend to be more expensive. This uniqueness can be well worth the extra cost.

Single, double, semidouble—This describes the number of petal layers on the blossom. Have you seen triple layers? So have we, but the description usually stops at double. Semidouble blossoms do not have a full second row of petals, but have a tufted petal in the center of the blossom. Many long-time growers equate the description "single" with the tendency of the single violet blossoms to drop off their stem while still fresh. Most of the newer singles being released, however, are "stick tights" that do not drop.

Miniature, semiminiature, standard—This refers to the overall mature size of the plant. Minis should grow no larger than six inches across, while semiminis may grow to a diameter of eight inches. Microminiatures have recently been developed, but no specific size is guaranteed at this time. They are expected to grow and bloom at a smaller size than miniatures. Standard plants grow larger than eight inches. They may be "compact" and not grow larger than about twelve inches in diameter. They may be "large" and grow easily to twenty or more inches.

Matching the Description to Your Collection

Not all growers are seeking the same type of violet. Not all violets are produced for the same purpose. Matching the type of violet to your interest level is important.

Persons who exhibit African violets in competition seek plants that develop perfect symmetry of leaf pattern, bloom heavily, travel well to shows, and fit into specific color classes in a show. Those cultivars that do not really perform well as youngsters, waiting until they are very large and mature before demonstrating their excellence, might be quite desirable for a show grower.

Retailers, like grocers and discounters, want plants that grow quickly (and thus economically) and have sturdy blossoms that don't wilt in tough conditions. Often they want varieties that will put up a good head of bloom on plants that are not really large. They also like a variety of color and type that will attract buyers.

Hobbyists who collect violets for their own pleasure want a variety of plants that have interesting blossoms and foliage and that bloom frequently. Even when variety is the goal, collectors value violets that grow easily.

Advertisers in the *African Violet Magazine,* as well as vendors on the internet often are trying to appeal to all of these buyers. While they are trying to market all of the varieties they list, they do try to give clues that will help you sort through the descriptions for what you are seeking. They try to use the word "show" when describing plants that will be most suitable for exhibitors. That "show" word can also indicate that the plant grows a bit larger than average standard-sized plants.

Fortunately, there are a limited number of African violet cultivars that do fit the needs all types of growers. These are plants that propagate easily, grow symmetrically, bloom fairly heavily when reasonably young, and yet can be grown into large, spectacular specimens for shows. Vendors will often describe these plants as "effortless," "easy," or say it "grows itself." Those are good hints of the quality of the violet.

Some Pitfalls

Novelty-blossoming varieties—those that have either unpredictable or unusual color pattern—are often attractive to collectors, especially those who are searching on the internet. They can be disappointing, however, because the cultivars may not be as sturdy, free blooming, or as apt to propagate true as the less-novel types.

Spectacular photos can make a specific cultivar seem quite appealing. These may be wonderful plants, but there are no automatic guarantees. Remember that phenomenally unusual color marking may be quite unstable, meaning that your plant may not bloom true.

The annual listing of the Best Varieties or the Honor Roll in the *African Violet Magazine* may also guide you in choosing good varieties. The Best Varieties lists results of the annual vote for the favorite plants of AVSA members across the country. Another list that is published annually, the Honor Roll, recognizes varieties that have won awards in shows. This is a great help for persons who wish to exhibit, but it may be less helpful for collectors.

A Possible Solution

Since there is obviously no simple way to find the perfect plants for your own pleasure, you must be ready to make a few mistakes. Do try ordering plants from one or two companies. If you are satisfied, order from them again. You may wish to trust the company to make one or two choices for you in addition to the other plants you order. Often the grower will send you a real gem that would otherwise have gone unnoticed.

Remember that some violet cultivars do better in specific climates. If you live in a hot climate, you may need to be cautious about plants hybridized in cooler climates, and vice versa. It is wise to note the name of the hybridizer and order only a few of his/her plants at first. If those plants do well, then look for more varieties from the same hybridizer.

Finally, when trying out a new plant, give it some time. Don't decide too quickly that it is "great" or "no good." It takes time to develop a friendship, and some plants are not as likeable when immature as they will be later. Some colors or growth patterns may not be desirable until seasonal temperatures change. Sometimes an ugly duckling grows into a beautiful swan.

Try new varieties. You will have fun.

29

Survival Techniques for Violets When the Owner must be Away

Have you ever taken a vacation away from home and asked a friend or relative to take care of your plants while you were gone? Have you ever had to go to the hospital or care for a family emergency only to discover upon your return that your violets had an emergency of their own? If you have, you've probably already learned that no one cares for your plants as well as you do. In fact, the best way to care for violets when you're away is to get the violets to take care of themselves.

There are, of course, various considerations to be taken into account when you're going to be leaving your violets home alone. How long will you be gone? Do you have an occasion coming up in the near future so that plants need to be kept in tip-top condition, or do you just want to keep them alive? And is there someone that you really trust to take care of your violets as you would?

The main things to be concerned about are the basics of temperature, light, and water—things that you need to watch even when you are home. With some minor adjustments, you can leave home with confidence that your violets will be in reasonably good condition upon your return.

Keep Temperatures Comfortable

When leaving home for a while, it is very tempting to turn off all temperature controls and save some money. However, replacing your violets will not be cheap if you have serious heat or cold damage!

If the weather is at all likely to be hot while you are gone, do adjust the air conditioning to prevent extreme overheating inside your home, perhaps setting the thermostat somewhere around 85° to 90° F. While violets do not like to be above 85°, they can tolerate it for brief periods of time. Whether or not air conditioning is available, it would be wise to find a naturally cooler place in the house for them during this time. Perhaps in a basement (if light is available to them there), or at least a little nearer the floor, since warm air rises.

If, on the other hand, the outside temperatures could turn quite cold, adjust your thermostat so that the heat will come on to prevent a drop below 55° F. This temperature can cause damage to the roots, but it will not usually kill the plant. Of course, a few degrees warmer than that would be more desirable. Again, look for places where the temperature may stay more moderate, perhaps on a high shelf or away from drafty windows and cold floors.

It is also wise to ask the trusty friend or relative to check in on the house to make sure that the temperature controls are functioning.

Light Needs

Plants do need some light to continue to live. When you are gone, you may wish to provide the same light the plants are used to getting. This is best only if you are using fluorescent lights which are on a timer to go on and off automatically. In order to take advantage of temperature controls described above, you may wish to set the timer to run the lights at night rather than in the daytime. The lights add heat to the growing area, which can be helpful at night during cold periods. Night operation can prevent further injury during hot spells since the lights will not add even more heat to the already warm daytime hours.

If the plants are grown in natural light, it may be beneficial for you to move the plants away from the windows where temperatures fluctuate more. It is permissible to close drapes to help even out the temperature changes, but do allow some light to enter the room. Reduced light will not promote beautiful growth, but the plants will tolerate it for several weeks. Cutting back on light will slow growth somewhat and consequently also will reduce the water needs of your plants.

To Water or Not to Water

Now that we've discussed adjustments you may need to make with regard to the temperature and light needs of your African violets, we need to address the biggest question: How are you going to keep them watered during your absence?

We've heard so many stories from people whose violets were hopelessly overwatered by temporary caregivers. We'd like to offer some suggestions about watering, along with a perhaps surprising suggestion that you simply let your plants go dry.

Many veteran growers use constant watering systems to keep their plants healthy with a minimum of attention. This enables them to grow a larger number of plants than they might otherwise be able to handle. Using one of these watering methods and a little common sense can make it simpler to be absent up to a month without having your violets show signs of serious neglect.

Wick watering, "Texas style" potting and capillary matting are three of the most common systems used. There are variations of these, including attractive self-contained pots. (See Chapter Three for more information on special watering systems.)

We do not recommend switching over an entire collection of violets to a new watering method solely for vacation purposes. Fine-tuning is needed with these methods, and you cannot do that if you are not there. You might wish to experiment with just a few plants just to see what happens.

Surprisingly, it may be better to let your plants go dry. African violets are amazingly resilient and can be successfully brought back after a long dry spell. They are actually rather succulent in nature.

There are two methods. The first is simply to deny the violets water in your absence, which is safe if you are only gone for about two weeks. If you use this method, revive the plants slowly when you return by giving each pot a small amount of water the first day and then water normally on the second day. This allows roots to revive gradually and avoids shock.

A second method for letting violets go dry is to put them into hibernation. It is especially effective when you must be absent for longer periods. It requires a small amount of preparation. First remove outside leaves so that only a few center leaves remain. Water each plant lightly, but be sure all excess water is drained away. Put them inside clear containers and seal them tightly inside so that there is no air movement or moisture loss. Depending on the seal, violets can wait for months or even years in such a container. Photosynthesis will cease when there is inadequate moisture (thus stopping growth), but the cells will not die until there is no moisture at all. If you can maintain your violets at a point that is between inadequate and zero moisture, violets will remain alive in hibernation for a very long time.

Whichever watering method is used, it is always best to remove all buds and blossoms before leaving. While the plants are blooming, they are consuming more water. Since you will not be there to see those blossoms, and since the plants need to conserve water, we recommend that before leaving, you either snip, pinch, or pull out all flower stems. The extra advantage to this is that there will be no unsightly dead blossoms to remove when returning, and often your plants will begin to set new flower stems during your absence.

Do take a good close look at your plants when you get home. Without your watchful eye, it is quite possible to have had an outbreak of a fungal problem—like powdery mildew—or a bug problem, such as mites or thrips. Apply remedies as needed.

Upon your return, there may be necessary grooming to do—removing dead or faded leaves and/or blossoms—and there may well be repotting to be done, but at least your African violets will have survived!

Section Four—Just For Fun

30

Violet Quirks

Have you ever had a violet do something really weird? Ever call a violet friend to come over and see the freak in your collection? Maybe even taken a picture of the oddity? African violets are alive. They grow sometimes in normal predictable patterns and sometimes in unexpected ways. It's the unexpected, the quirks, of violet growing that we want to ponder.

Deformity

Violets, like all living things, are subject to distortions and deformities. DNA may have tiny flaws which can affect cell division in many different ways.

One example of this would be two leaves that share a common petiole (stem). The effect may be two fully formed leaves at the end of one petiole, or it may be a leaf with two tips. Sometimes the leaf just has a lumpy look. Usually the petiole will be thicker than usual and exhibit a rib where the two leaves should have separated. This type of leaf deformity may appear only occasionally in a particular plant and be a small problem resolved by removal of the odd leaf. We have seen plants, however, that persistently grow with this deformity through many generations. There is no cure for this except to dispose of the plant.

Occasionally a leaf may grow out with a twisted stem which refuses to lay flat. This is extremely irritating to growers who wish to exhibit the plants in competition. It is the result of an uneven growth rate, either in the size or the number of cells on opposite sides of the leaf stem. Some plants may consistently show this irregular growth and will never grow in the perfect rosettes that characterize championship plants. Those same plants may have blossoms that cause us to forgive the sins of their foliage. Most violets don't have to go to show.

Blossoms can also share a common pedicel (the branching stem that connects the individual blossom to the main trunk of the peduncle or flower stem). That results in two blossoms which are back to back and held in an uncomfortable looking position. It is not usually a persistent condition on any plant, but some cultivars do this infrequently.

Occasionally, blossoms may open with indistinct shapes. Violet blossoms are commonly either star-shaped or pansy-shaped. It is possible for one blossom to take on a more peculiar shape (or just the other shape) as a result of a "genetic blip" in its growth pattern. In that case, one flower looks odd, but all the others are normal.

Sometimes the distortion is the result of a cultivar which has a faulty genetic code. A good example is the rare and most annoying distortion of blossoms which form with no flower petals! This reportedly was a problem for Nolan Blansit who developed the yellow hybrids. His problems resulted from inbreeding which was required to isolate the unique color gene. Inbreeding may be a valuable hybridizing tool, but it also tends to allow the expression of faulty genetic traits.

Instability

Some African violets come from unstable genetic strains; that is, the plants will not consistently pass their characteristics on to the next generation through propagation of leaf cuttings. Some of the offspring will look like the parent, but some may bloom with an entirely different color. This change is referred to as a "sport." While many violets will occasionally sport, the unstable strains sport on a regular and almost predictable basis. Varieties with fantasy or bicolor blossoms commonly fall into this category. Their instability is passed along to plantlets propagated from leaf cuttings and to hybrid seedlings in which the unstable plant was used as a parent.

Violets with fantasy blossoms, those that show speckles or streaks of a contrasting color to the background are apparently all somewhat unstable. The fantasy hybrids that we have worked with will frequently produce sports which have some or all solid color blossoms. We have seen a violet sport on which one-fourth of the plant bloomed true (pink with blue streaks), one-fourth bloomed with a pink and blue chimera (striped) pattern, one-fourth bloomed blue, and one-fourth bloomed pink. These plants may also have a blossom which is partly fantasy and partly a solid color. Although this is interesting, it is not desirable. Good growers learn to dispose of varieties that are sporting too often.

Another group of violets that tend to be unstable are those with at least two different color areas on each blossom. Plants which exhibit irregular color patterns or splotches and smears of color on a white background are often the most unstable. These varieties will often signal that they are sporting to a solid color with a change in the green coloration of the foliage. A dark patch on lighter green leaves is a good indication that some or all of the blossoms are sporting to a different and undesirable pattern.

Weird Things

Sometimes a violet plant will do something truly weird and unlike any other plant in a collection. Why? Perhaps it has a tendency inherited from long-ago ancestors. Perhaps the plant gets confused. The weird things are really fun.

A good example is the occurrence of what is often called a "basket". This is a small plant with a distinct crown of four or more leaves which forms on a blossom stem (rather than the more common sucker at the base of a leaf). It hangs up in the air like a flag and can be removed and placed in soil to root. These are quite different from the small wing leaves which are often found on blossom stems.

Similar to this, tiny suckers can grow from almost any cell on the plant. Sometimes, a tiny plant will begin to form on the top or underside surface of a leaf or on the edge of the leaf. This is most likely to show up where there has been damage to plant tissue like a crack or nick in the foliage. More distressing is when the crown (or center of the plant) itself begins to produce suckers, causing the plant to have multiple crowns. Injury from disease or insects can provoke this behavior, but sometimes it is spontaneous.

Another oddity occurs when a flower suddenly shoots a second blossom stem from its center so that the two blossoms almost look like a shish-kebab. They can be quite close together and look like an extra-thick double blossom or be spaced farther apart.

Rare Violet Types

Diverse as they might be in coloration of foliage and blossoms, most African violets today have a fairly similar overall appearance because hybridizers have found certain violet types perform better in shows or are easier to sell in the marketplace. Thus, most violets today have fairly tailored flat foliage with occasional varieties that are ruffled or quilted and either pansy- or star-shaped blossoms. But there remain some interesting oddities that are not often seen. One unique group is wasp blossoms, which are, as you might expect, shaped like a wasp with very narrow lobes on the petals. These frequently occur with unusual compound leaves that have one large and two smaller lobes. These leaves may be bustle-backed with a ruffle of leaf tissue on the underside near the leaf stem or even piggybacked with a leaf atop a leaf.

Another unusual blossom type, most frequently found in the miniature varieties today is the bell. The blossom is single and the petal cups to form a bell-like shape.

Less commonly seen foliages include "longifolia" leaves which are strap-like and narrow, spooned foliage which cups into a concave shape at the base of the leaf, and supreme foliage which is very thick and hairy with strong pencil-like petioles. Another interesting one is the "Clackamas" foliage in which the veins of the leaf follow the contour of the leaf in a parallel pattern and meet at the tip in a pattern similar to the leaves of lily-of-the-valley.

Weird violets are interesting to see and to share with others. Because the oddities are sometimes less perfect than the more familiar plants, they are in danger becoming extinct. Perhaps you are protecting one of them now or would be interested in obtaining some.

AVSA maintains a list of Vintage Violets based on voluntarily-shared inventories of cultivars grown in private collections throughout the membership. Interested growers send in lists of plants in their collection, while others may ask if a certain hybrid is listed. The chairman acts as a liaison between the growers so that the older hybrids can continue to be available.

Diversity is Lovable

It is easy to be attracted to the normal, well-behaved and lovely violet. But if we were all normal, well-behaved and lovely, the world would be a dull place. The violet kingdom has a few quirky relatives, a few naughty children, and a few ugly ducklings, but they add a lot of interest to our world.

The best part about really unusual behavior in our violets is that it requires a close eye for us to spot it. Keeping our eyes on our violets is the most enjoyable part of the hobby!

31

African Violets Myths and the Real Truth

Almost everyone you meet knows something about African violets. That may sound like a good thing, except that most of them have heard the myths and not the truth. Maybe it's because so many of us grew up in homes that nurtured (or killed) a violet. In any case, some of these myths have become so prevalent that some people are reluctant to try growing African violets. That is a dreadful shame! So let's review a few of the myths, speculate on why they developed and, most of all, let's look for the truth

"African Violets are Easy to Kill"

If you have gotten far enough into the hobby to be reading a book, especially the end of the book, you already know that this is not really true. Violets are actually quite durable, most of the time. There are, however, several good ways to kill an African violet. Note that we are talking about absolute death here, not just a sickly appearance or lack of bloom.

Probably the most common cause of death in African violets is overwatering. Violets are quite vulnerable to crown rot, a fungus which commonly reaches the plant through water or soggy soil. Any violet in heavily saturated soil is vulnerable.

Extreme heat or cold can also kill violets fast. When violets are kept between 65°and 80° F they will not die. When temperatures are 15° either hotter or colder, damage or death is more likely.

Once any grower has the watering and temperature under control, the violets are likely to survive. They may not be perfect, but they won't be dead.

"Violets Do Best in a North Window"

Finding the right window in which to place those first few plants is always a challenge. Growers in the mid-twentieth century and earlier probably did have the best luck with a north window, because there was no air conditioning to cool the area when it got hot. Plants in brighter windows would cook during warm summer months.

Assuming that you are able to cool the inside temperature during very hot spells, the violets will often thrive and bloom better in brighter windows than north-facing ones. In many locations, the best light is found at an east- or south-facing window. Even with air conditioning, west windows seem to get too warm for violets to thrive.

If the north window (we're talking northern hemisphere here) is the only choice, be sure to place the plant quite close to the glass. It helps if the window is large and not shaded by drapes, roof overhangs, or trees.

Advanced growers have found that the best light is usually artificially produced by fluorescent light tubes. This does not need to be expensive or fancy. It does need to be within about twelve inches of the plant and on about twelve hours a day.

"Don't Touch the Leaves or They'll Die"

Sorry, Grandma, but this myth is probably your fault. Violet leaves are turgid (or stiff) when the plant has been recently watered. A leaf is more likely to snap away from the plant at this time. Many early African violets were especially brittle. Our best guess is that Grandma did not want to lose any leaves to careless fingers of children and sternly warned all comers not to touch!

Losing a leaf will not kill the plant, although it can spoil the perfect beauty of a symmetrical "wheel" of leaves. Touching the surface of the leaf will usually not cause any damage either.

The leaf surface is covered with tiny hairs, which have a nap. They all tend to grow toward the outside edge of the plant. If you need to brush debris off the leaf surface (or if you just enjoy petting your plant), stroke the leaf from the stem part of the leaf to the tip. This will follow the nap of the hairs. Stroking opposite the nap will break the hairs off and can leave minor cosmetic damage.

Bruises caused by pressing or bumping the leaves are actually damaged cells, and this will eventually lead to dead patches in the leaf tissue. Damage can occur when plants are shipped or transported, when violets are dropped, or when naughty children get involved. These injuries are usually not fatal to the entire plant so long as the very center of the plant is not destroyed.

"Don't Get Water on the Leaves"

We're picking on Grandma. She probably started this myth because she didn't want anybody pouring water onto the crown of the plant in an effort to help her out, and because wet leaves sitting in the sunshine seemed to develop spots or even holes. She was half right and pretty observant, but when it comes to washing foliage, getting the leaves wet is the only way to do the job.

It is never wise to allow water to stand in the crown of the violet. When watering the plant from the top, the water should be applied directly to the soil and not to the leaves. The leaf hairs will suspend droplets of water very neatly in the crown and provide favorable conditions for any fungus spores in the area. Serious damage can result.

Violets with wet leaves (or just with droplets of water on the leaves) can be damaged when set directly in bright light. The light (and heat) are magnified by the water, resulting in spots and sometimes dead tissue or holes in the leaf. Minerals in the water can also cause spotting on the foliage. This is not fatal, but it isn't attractive. When the leaves are wet, blot them and allow the remaining moisture to evaporate in the shade before returning them to their brighter home.

On the other hand, when plants are dirty from dust, smoke, cat hair, or whatever, they enjoy a good bath. Begin by putting a drop of mild dishwashing detergent in a misting bottle with very warm water. Then mist the dirty leaf surfaces, avoiding the crown as much as possible. Allow this to stand for a few minutes. Next, adjust the water faucet to a very tepid temperature and a gentle flow. Hold the plant at an angle under the flow, allowing the water to run toward the outside of the plant, again avoiding getting water in the crown. Blot the leaves with tissue or a soft, natural sponge to remove excess water droplets. Set the plant away from bright light until the foliage surface has dried. You'll be amazed at how fresh the plant looks. They also seem to grow better and really thrive when clean.

"Clay Pots are Best"

Clay pots, because they are a natural material, may seem preferable to plastic. It is an individual choice depending on growing conditions. For some people, clay pots actually are best. But this is not true for everyone.

Clay pots are often best for those who grow in very hot conditions. The evaporation from the clay works as a natural form of cooling for the violet.

If you are currently using clay pots and decide to try plastic, you may find that the plants die from overwatering. Clay pots simply allow the excess moisture to evaporate more quickly; plastic does not. If you decide to change to a different type of pot, you will probably need to adjust your soil mix and watering habits.

There are a few problems with clay pots, especially the cost and weight. Clay pots do tend to absorb salt over time and violet leaves that touch a salt-saturated rim will often be damaged. The majority of advanced growers now prefer plastic.

"Good Violets are Hybrids ... the Rest Come from the Grocery Store"

To understand why this is a misleading statement, you have to understand what a "hybrid" is. A hybrid cultivar is the result of cross-breeding. If it is not a hybrid cultivar, it is a species, which have their origin in nature. Species are fairly rare and cannot be described as hybrids. However, virtually all other violets cultivated today are hybrids. Some are good, and some are not. Most violet hybrids purchased at grocery stores (or wherever) have the potential to become beautiful plants under the right growing conditions.

"Coffee (or Eggshells or Whatever) is Good for Violets"

There are lots of home-remedy types of treatments for African violets. As proof of the durability of the plant, most of these things don't kill them. That doesn't mean it is better for them! Fertilizers and the proper potting mix will provide everything that violets really need. The extra ingredient may not hurt, but it really isn't needed. Home remedies may supply one or two nutrients naturally, but these are rarely really complete enough to meet all of a violet's needs. If you like to do it and it hasn't caused any harm, go ahead, but we personally much prefer the more tested cultural practices.

"My Violet Does Better When Sitting Next to my Mother's Picture"

Yes, we actually heard that. It's not true—probably. You can figure out why. Statements like this do make it fun to talk with other violet growers, however.

There's not all that much mystery to growing African violets. If good light, adequate water, even temperatures, porous soil, and a regular fertilizing program are maintained, violets will not only grow, they will bloom.

32

What Kind of Grower Are You?

Does that question sound too personal? We're not talking about being a good or a bad grower. Rather, we're talking about your purpose for growing violets. Growers can be pretty different in viewpoint. The reasons and goals for growing African violets, among other things, can affect the methods and the equipment that are needed. While every grower is a little unique, here are some fictitious growers with different viewpoints and the techniques that work best for them. So, what kind of grower are you?

Beulah Buy-and-Throw

Beulah likes to go to the store or the violet show and choose a beautiful blooming violet. She takes it home to set in a prominent spot on her coffee table and enjoys having the color in her room. When the flowers are gone, she throws it away and buys another.

Advice to Beulah:

Light: Use whatever is available.

Watering method: Water once every five to seven days, either into the top of the pot or by filling the saucer below. With either method, the saucer should be emptied within a half an hour.

Pot: Use whatever it comes in. Beulah might enjoy choosing a pretty piece of pottery or brass that she can use to hide her unpretentious store pot.

Fertilizer: Any balanced fertilizer, used according to package directions, is good idea but not really necessary.

Grooming: Pick off the dead flowers as they fade.

Transplanting: Won't happen. Toss tired plants and buy new ones, perhaps three or four times a year.

Wendy Windowsill

Wendy wants to keep a violet on her windowsill. It was a gift, and she feels responsible for keeping it alive for as long as it is possible. She likes to see it in bloom. She probably won't buy another.

Advice to Wendy:

Light: Place next to a bright window where the air temperature is almost always near 70°F.

Watering method: Same as Beulah, or use a constant water method, such as wicking, to avoid forgetting.

Pot: Could be a clay pot to get that natural look, but then Wendy needs to water twice a week. Could be an inexpensive plastic pot or a decorative pot (with a hole for drainage), or even a pot that will self-water.

Fertilizer: Use a balanced, water-soluble African violet fertilizer that is added with each watering.

Grooming: Remove spent flowers and whole flower stalks when no buds are left. Remove dead leaves as they fade.

Transplanting: If a clay pot is used, most commercial potting mixes will be acceptable. In other pots, use a fairly light mix using half commercial all-purpose potting mix and half vermiculite or perlite. Repot once a year to bury the neck that is under the leaves.

Olivia Office

Olivia is a lot like Wendy. She bought one violet to keep at work to brighten her space. She never really knows what is happening to it when she goes home. When she has questions about how her violet is doing she uses her computer to go to www.avsa.org for an answer.

Advice to Olivia:

Light: Place near a bright window that doesn't get too warm. Better yet, set it on top of a file cabinet and near a ceiling fluorescent fixture. Even better, find a spot in her cubicle under a fluorescent desk light that is plugged into a timer set to go on automatically for twelve hours each day. That way, an eight hour workday will not shortchange the violet's need for light.

Watering method: Olivia could use the same method Beulah uses, but using a constant water method (in a specially designed pot) would be better if the office air is dry.

Pot: Same as Wendy, but stability is important, especially if a constant water method is used (the boss hates when the computer gets wet!)

Fertilizer: Similar to Wendy.

Grooming: Similar to Wendy.

Transplanting: Once a year, but it is best done at home during vacation time. After transplanting, place the plant into a clear plastic bag and set it in a bright spot out of direct sunlight. No water is needed while it is in the bag. When the vacation is done (or shortly thereafter), the violet will be ready to return to the office, and no one there will have to apologize for forgetting to water it.

Betty "I-Have-a-Lot, Probably-Six-or-Seven"

Betty doesn't have a huge collection by many standards, but she really enjoys having violets around the house. She expects to have some in bloom most of the time. She's a little more sophisticated in her growing techniques than Wendy or Olivia. She might subscribe to the *African Violet Magazine*.

Advice to Betty:

Light: Similar to Wendy. More plants require a larger window, and one that faces east and/or south works well. Better, place a few plants under a small fluorescent light fixture (under a cupboard or on a table) so that the violets still get good light when the daylight hours are short. Betty has enough violets and likes her plants enough to invest in a timer to regulate the amount of light her collection gets under those fluorescents.

Watering method: Similar to Wendy, either hand watering or using a constant watering system like wicking.

Pot: With only six or seven, any affordable pot can be used, but all of the violets should be in the same type pot so that watering schedules and care remain the same for each plant.

Fertilizer: Same as Wendy.

Grooming: Similar to Wendy. Watch for insects and fungus. Multiple plants share problems and a watchful eye will solve problems before they are out of control.

Transplanting: Once a year repot all of the violets in the same session. By then, her violets will have a neck below the lowest row of leaves, because of old leaves that have been removed. Scrape the neck with the dull side of a knife to remove dried brown scab tissue. Lift the plant out of the pot and cut away enough soil from the bottom of the root ball to equal the length of the neck. Set the violet back into the pot, add fresh potting mix (same type as recommended for Wendy) to the top of the pot to bury the neck.

Sally "I-Don't-Have-Many, Just-Fifty-or-So"

Sally really loves African violets, and she hopes to get more. She belongs to the African Violet Society of America, and reads the magazine as soon as it comes. She has ordered violets to be shipped to her. She belongs to a local violet club. She sells a few at the annual club sale, but she usually buys more.

Advice to Sally:

Light: Sally may want to keep a few in windows, but a collection this large really needs to be under fluorescent lights to do well. She would be wise to build or invest in a lighted stand. The lights should be set about ten to twelve inches above the foliage and turned on for ten to twelve hours each day. A timer would be a good investment.

Watering: It is possible to water each plant individually, but in a busy week, Sally might be tempted to postpone the job too long. Constant water methods will make life easier. Each plant could be placed above its own reservoir with a wick dangling below the pot into the water. The reservoirs need to be refilled before they empty, but may last for several weeks before needing attention. A second choice would be to place a number of violets with wicks above a large tray of water that has a grating across it. Adding water to the tray once a week ensures constant water, but it can be done more quickly. A third choice would be to use capillary matting in the large trays. Potted violets with wicks are set directly onto wet matting and water needs to be added weekly to be sure the matting stays fairly moist.

Pot: Decorative pots are probably too expensive for Sally's large collection. Plastic pots will be the best choice if a constant watering method is used so that pots do not go dry too quickly. Sally should look for pots that 1) are squatty, to accommodate a shallow root system, 2) have a rolled or smooth edge to protect leaves against sharp edges, and 3) are about one-half to one-third the diameter of the violet. If she uses capillary matting, she will want a pot that is flat on the bottom for better contact. Sally may also want to choose a pot that can be written on, so that the hybrid name will stay with the violet that is in the pot.

Fertilizer: Sally should use a good water-soluble fertilizer just like Wendy, but she might find that her club members recommend a specific brand or type that works best in her climate and with the chemistry of her water. She might get more flowers by using a formulation that has a higher percentage of phosphorus (the middle number).

Grooming: Sally should set aside a little time each week to look closely at her plants. Since they are watering themselves, it would be easy for insects or diseases to invade without being noticed. Dead flowers and spent bud stems should be removed and disposed of outside the growing room. Leaves that are fading in color or that are smaller than the leaves above should be removed. Side shoots (called suckers) need to be removed before they have more than five or six leaves. She should adjust the distance between plants to keep leaves from touching. Sally might also find that she doesn't mind throwing away violets that aren't performing as well as she expects to make room for better varieties.

Transplanting: Sally should be watching for exposed necks under the lowest row of leaves on each of her violets, and transplanting regularly to bury that neck. She will want to use a potting mix that is formulated especially for violet hobbyists (her club may sell a mix that works well in their climate). She may want to mix her own recipe using one part milled Canadian sphagnum peat moss, one part coarse vermiculite, and one part coarse perlite, with dolomite lime to buffer the pH. She should also watch how fast her small plants are growing and transplant them into slightly broader pots as they grow bigger than three times the diameter of their current pot. She will also want to take leaf cuttings to start new plants of her favorite varieties to sell at club sales or to share with friends.

Gary Greenhouse

Gary wants to grow a fairly large number of violets inexpensively by taking advantage of natural sunlight. He may have lots of other kinds of plants in his greenhouse, too. He knows how to control air temperatures that soar during the daylight and cool significantly in the evening. He pays attention to publications about greenhouse growing, especially articles on pest and disease control. Like Sally, he has an interest in associating with other African violet growers.

Advice to Gary:

Light: Gary depends on available light but he should watch out for bleached foliage on the violets. This would indicate that he needs to increase the amount of shading on the glass to protect them from too much light. If he chooses to grow violets underneath benches filled with other types of plants, he might wish to add fluorescent light fixtures to supplement light during winter months.

Watering: Gary probably should have a specialized system for watering all of his plants. He might choose drip irrigation or an ebb-and-flow system that adds fertilizer automatically. He should not use a hose to spray water across the surface of violet leaves or spots will result.

Pot: If Gary lives in a warm climate, he might be wise to choose clay pots, because they provide natural cooling to the soil on hot days. If he chooses clay, he must be careful that the pots are squatty and similar in diameter to those recommended for Sally. He may need to protect lower leaves from damage caused by the salts that accumulate in the walls of the pot. If heat is not such a problem, plastic pots will work well following the same guidelines as Sally. If he uses drip irrigation or ebb-and-flow watering, he may need a pot that has an uneven bottom to allow air-flow underneath.

Fertilizer: Similar to Sally. If Gary injects one fertilizer into his automatic system to water all different types of plants, he should probably choose a balanced 20-20-20 formula. Gary should be monitoring his pH and salt levels fairly carefully.

Grooming: Gary should watch his plants closely for insects and disease, especially if the greenhouse is ventilated with fresh air. While his grooming should be similar to Sally's regime, he needs to be especially careful to avoid bad habits of tossing dead leaves and flowers onto the floor.

Transplanting: Same as Sally, but could use a somewhat heavier mix (with a greater percentage of peat) if potting into clay pots.

Katie Commercial

Katie is in business to sell African violets. She grows many varieties of mature plants to exhibit and to use for propagating plants to sell. She has customers visiting her growing room, and she advertises plants to sell in the *African Violet Magazine*. She has hybridized several new varieties that she named and introduced. She has no idea how many violet plants she has at any one time, but it is probably thousands.

Advice for Katie:

Light: Katie could choose either the greenhouse setting (following the advice for Gary) or choose to use many fluorescent lights on shelf units in her place of business. If she chooses the latter, she will need to watch the air temperature closely because so many light units produce more heat.

Watering: If Katie uses the greenhouse, her method should be similar to Gary. If she grows inside a building, her methods will be like Sally's. Katie might want to hire a helper to be responsible for the watering so that Katie is freed to do more technical work.

Pot: Katie wants to make a profit, so choosing inexpensive pots is best. If she will be shipping violets through the mail or carrying many plants to sales, she will want the pots to be lightweight as well. Katie will probably choose plastic pots, purchased in case lots, in several sizes to fit all of the different stages in which she sells plants. Keeping track of the variety names will be especially important for Katie, so she should have a good labeling system for her pots.

Fertilizer: Similar to Sally. Katie might want to offer her favorite fertilizer for sale to her customers.

Grooming: Similar to Sally, but must be done daily to keep good order. She would be wise to make this part of her routine.

Transplanting: This should be a regular weekly task for Katie. She should be thinking ahead to when plants need to be ready for sales and setting a schedule for when to put down leaves, separate clumps, and move small plants up into the mature size pot.

Priscilla Prizewinner

Priscilla grows African violets to show in competition. She wants to perfect her growing and exhibition skills so that she can win big prizes. Her collection is easily as large as Sally's, but she chooses her violets by how symmetrically they grow, how easily they bloom, and for specific size and color classes in show competitions. She tries lots of different varieties and throws away (or sells) the ones which do not perform for her. She is a member of at least one club so that she can compete in shows, and she even takes plants to the national AVSA convention when it is close to her.

Advice to Priscilla:

Light: Similar to Sally, but Priscilla should watch plants very closely to see how they react to the fluorescent light. She should move plants that are reaching upward into the brightest light at the center of the light unit and move plants whose leaves are bleaching (even a little bit) closer to the edges of shelves. As show dates approach, Sally should be increasing the amount of light each week up to fifteen hours a day in the last two weeks. She should keep track of how old her fluorescent tubes are and replace them yearly. She may want to invest in more expensive tubes designed to maximize growth.

Watering: Similar to Sally. Priscilla will be very careful not to splash water on leaves when she refills trays. She knows the judges will deduct points for water spots.

Pot: Similar to Sally. Priscilla should choose pots that are the color that show schedules require, usually white and/or green. She might watch for especially pretty or novel containers to grow a violet for an Unusual Container class. She would be wise to add a leaf support ring to each pot to hold leaves in a horizontal position (and not hanging down) for more perfect growth patterns. She must keep track of the variety names carefully so that she enters plants that are correctly identified. She should adhere closely to the rule of keeping the pot one-third the diameter of the leaf span as the plants grow.

Fertilizer: Priscilla should make her fertilizer decisions very carefully. She does not want to over-fertilize and cause burning on the edges of leaves (she will lose points in competition), but she must fertilize enough to get rich green foliage, extreme vigor, and a full head of bloom. She will probably choose a balanced fertilizer (or one with somewhat higher phosphorus) for the six months that she disbuds, and then switch to one with extra phosphorus in the last ten to fifteen weeks. She should be watching closely to see how her plants are reacting and making adjustments in the measurements accordingly. Priscilla should leach her show plants with clear water every month or so to be sure that excess fertilizer salts are being removed.

Grooming: Similar to Sally, but Priscilla will do this with religious fervor. Priscilla should disbud all violets (remove all flowers and buds) she intends to show for about six months before the show. She should then stop disbudding and allow buds to develop about six to eight weeks before the show date. Three weeks before the show, she should remove any open individual flowers so that new buds will keep developing at a rapid rate. She should wash the leaves of her violets two or three weeks before the show by holding the plants at an angle under a gently running stream of tepid water, after which she should blot the foliage dry. She should also remove outside leaves (especially ones that are smaller or have imperfections) to achieve a nearly-perfect, round pattern. In the final hours before entry, she should brush away any particles of dust, remove any blossoms that are spent or becoming transparent, and carefully remove any remaining stubs of leaves or flower stems.

Transplanting: Priscilla should transplant at least twice per year, keeping her plants in fresh and very light potting mix (as recommended to Sally). She should not disturb roots as she pots her rapidly growing violets into larger pots, and she must never ever pack the soil. She should pot her plants slightly deeper into the pot, so that, if leaves are removed just before the show, the resulting neck can be buried by adding a little potting mix to the top of the pot. She should always pre-moisten her mix to avoid dust and debris on leaves.

Did You Find Yourself?

Violets can be grown in so many ways using many different methods. It would be biased to suggest that any one was more or less important than the other. Growers simply have different aspirations. Hopefully, you found one grower who is most like you and some good tips to improve your growing style. As time passes, and you master your technique, you may find that you want to try a new or different way of approaching the hobby. We hope you grow in lots of ways!

33

Test Your Violet I.Q.

Just for fun take the following test and record the answer that most accurately reflects your growing habits. Then compare your answer with the section following and find your score!

1. I water my violets ...
A. When I think of it or when the plants seem really dry.
B. Once a week, on the same day each week.
C. Constantly, using a self-watering system designed for violets.
D. Water?

2. When I water ...
A. I let the violets stand in water for however long it takes to soak up the water.
B. I water a little bit into the top of the pot, but never enough to run out the bottom.
C. I use a self-watering system and occasionally water from the top to leach the soil.
D. I water thoroughly either from the top or bottom and empty the saucer soon after.

3. The following best describes the light my violets get:
A. Fluorescent light 12 inches above the foliage for twelve hours a day.
B. Bright window light with plants sitting nearby.
C. Some light from windows with plants sitting in center of room.
D. Fluorescent light 2 to 4 feet above the foliage for 16 to 20 hours a day.

4. The following best describes my fertilizing habits:
A. Once or twice a year, if I think of it.
B. Once a month, following package directions

C. Once a week or constantly (if using self-watering system) at a slightly weaker-than-recommended rate.
D. Once a week using a little more than is recommended.

5. The following best describes the soil in which my violets are growing:
A. Good firm garden dirt.
B. Potting mix that is fairly dense and packs down well.
C. Very loose porous potting mix that is not packed down at all.
D. The soil mix that my violets came in when I got them.

6. The temperature in my growing space is …
A. Usually around 72° F during the day and a little cooler at night.
B. Variable, sometimes over 80° during the day and much cooler at other times.
C. Usually below 70° all the time.
D. Usually warmer than 80° all the time.

7. My violets are growing in pots that are …
A. Made of plastic or non-porous materials.
B. Clay.
C. Mixture of both clay and plastic or non-porous materials.

8. Measure your violet's leaf span (the diameter across), then measure the diameter of the pot in which it is growing. The ratio of the leaf span to the pot is:
A. 1 to 2 (plant is half the diameter of the pot).
B. 1 to 1 (plant is the same size as the pot).
C. 2 to 1 (plant is twice the size of the pot).
D. 3 to 1 (plant is three times the size of the pot).

9. I repot my violets …
A. I don't.
B. At least once every year.
C. Whenever I see a neck developing underneath the leaves.
D. Whenever they start to look sick.

10. If I saw a side-shoot forming between the leaves of my violet, I would …
A. Poke it out immediately.
B. Remove it carefully when it was big enough to be planted in its own pot.
C. Let it grow.

ANSWERS (Give yourself the points awarded for your answer)

1. A = 0 points, B = 1 point, C = 2 points, and D = subtract 1 point.
This question is about how often to water. Constant self-watering is the ideal way to provide consistent moisture to violets and to maximize blooming and growing. Once-a-week water will still result in nice plants, but this method is vulnerable to changes in your schedule as well as abnormally low or high humidity (which will change how much water your violets demand). Watering only when plants appear dry, or when you think about it, will result in small, tired-looking leaves and few flowers. Forget to water entirely and your hobby is at risk.

2. A = subtract 1 point, B = 0 points, C = 2 points, and D = 1 point
Although this question also addresses watering, the issue here is how much. Again the self-watering method wins out. It provides enough water (unlike choice B) without the risks of root rot that choice A has. Notice the addition to self-watering however! Once in a while, a good grower will water violets from the top of the pot so that the water runs through leaching out fertilizer salts that inevitably build up. If you self-water but don't leach, subtract one point. Choice D is a very satisfactory method for watering violets, particularly when water is occasionally added at the top of the pot.

3. A = 2 points, B = 1 point, C = 0 points, D = 1 point
Violets require fairly bright light in order to produce flowers and a flat leaf pattern. Ideally, they should be grown under fluorescent lights as described in A. The length of day and the distance from the leaves may vary slightly from grower to grower, however. Subtract one point if these lights are left on day and night, 24 hours. Since artificial light isn't always a possible choice, growing your plants in a location very close to a bright window is a good substitute. Give yourself a bonus of one point if you turn your plants at least once a week to even out the amount of light to all sides. In many office situations, the option of placing violets near a ceiling fluorescent fixture that is lit for long hours each day works well. Subtract one point if the ceiling lights are on for less than twelve hours a day. Are your violets sitting far away from adequate light? You may notice that the leaves seem to be growing upward and that your violets don't bloom well because of this.

4. A = 0 points, B = 1 point, C = two points, and D = subtract one point.
It may surprise you to find that it is wise to use a conservative approach to fertilizing. A regular and frequent diet of weak fertilizer will produce better results for most growers than the other methods, especially if it is added to the constant-water reservoir. Too much fertilizer can result in a build-up of salts in the soil which cause leaves to burn. It is actually more dangerous to overuse fertilizer than to forget it entirely! On the other hand, violets do need their nutrients, and proper fertilizing will improve blooming and growing patterns.

5. A = subtract one point, B = 0 points, C = 2 points, and D = 0 points
Neither garden dirt, nor the average potting mix that is available in stores will provide your violet roots with the amount of air and space that they need for optimum growth. Only a very loose mix that is not packed down at all will allow those fine fibrous roots to thrive! Often, the soil that your violet came in will also be too heavy (greenhouses tend to use one mix for all types of plants). Try this test: poke your finger into the soil in which your violet is potted and push it all the way to the bottom of the pot. If this is impossible or very difficult, the soil is too heavy and needs to have a "soil lightener" added such as perlite or vermiculite. This airy mix is also best for constant-water methods of growing.

6. A = 2 points, B = subtract one point, C = 0 points, and D = 0 points
Temperature is surprisingly important in determining the overall health of violets. Temperatures which are in the mid or low 70s are ideal. The more consistent the temperature, the more consistent the growth of the leaves will be. But when the temperature is consistently too warm, the leaves will grow with invariably long stems resulting in a lanky look. When the temperature is regularly too cool, the leaves grow with stems that are habitually too short which may be so tight that blossom stems can't get through. Too cool temperatures can cause flowers to be deeper in color and to last longer (not an awful problem), while warm temperatures will have the opposite effect of fading colors and shortening the life of flowers. Either of those choices remains better than widely varying temperatures during the day. Aside from the resulting problems of uneven growth, these temperature differences allow fungus to thrive.

7. A = 2 points, B = 1 point, and C = 0
Non-porous pots (plastic is the least expensive) are really best for growing violets. Plastic pots work well with constant-water methods of growing, do not accumulate salts on the rim, are lightweight, and easy to clean for reuse. None of that is

true for clay pots. It is also difficult to find clay pots in the squatty smaller size that violets prefer. Using a combination of different types of pots requires you to use different watering patterns (even if you don't constant water), according to the pot type, since clay pots will dry out sooner and watering must be done more often. This is not easy to track, and eventually some plants will be over- or underwatered.

8. A = subtract one point, B = 0 points, C = 1 point, D = 2 points
Violets like to be in small pots! Nature planted them in the crevices between rocks, and they have never thrived in big spaces since. Violet leaves should always cover the entire pot and hang over the edges. This allows the roots to fill the entire pot, maximizing their use of available water, and encouraging the violet to direct its energies toward flowering.

9. A = subtract one point, B = 2 points, C = 2 points, and D = 0
It is important to repot violets frequently—not into a bigger pot but into fresh soil that buries any exposed neck. Regular repotting is not as stressful as desperation repotting (when your violet is no longer thriving). In fact, violets that are repotted yearly may live for forty years or more! You may use either the calendar (once a year) or your eyes (see a neck and repot that violet) as a successful guide. Subtract two points if you forget to look.

10. A = 2 points, B = 2 points, and C = 0 points
Side-shoots on violets are called "suckers." Growers have a choice of eliminating them immediately or using them for propagation purposes sometime later. Suckers with four to six leaves should be removed, either for propagation or the garbage. Some growers prefer to poke them out when they have four leaves or less, but do be careful that it really is a sucker and not a flower stem! Allowing suckers to grow to full size will put them in competition with the mother plant. Eventually, it will have a bushy form, and often flowers are reduced in size or number. It won't kill the plant to leave it, but good growers know better.

Scoring:
15 to 20 points—You are a top-notch grower and really ought to be exhibiting your perfect violets at an AVSA show!
10 to 15 points—You do pretty well with violets, but there is still room for improvement.

5 to 10 points—Your violets are probably just getting by. Why not try a few of the tips and see how much better they can look?

5 points or less—There are no lost causes and no brown thumbs—only those who haven't learned how! It's time for you to find more information on this wonderful hobby so that you can really enjoy it!

Index

African Violet Magazine xiii, xiv, 45, 117, 161, 162, 175, 180, 182, 183, 201, 204
African Violet Master List (AVML) xiii, 110
AVSA Handbook for Growers, Exhibitors and Judges 23, 44, 59, 74, 164, 179
Air movement 10, 41, 42, 47, 116, 120, 121
Airborne problems 43, 116, 135, 143
Air (soil aeration) 28, 42, 143, 153
Algae 17
Ammonium toxicity 37–39

Bacterial disease 121–122
    Erwinia 121
    Impatiens Necrotic Spot Virus (INSV) 122
    Virus disease 122
Basket 62, 193
Beneficial microorganisms 35
Blossom(s)
    Chimera xvi, 51, 62, 64, 166, 167, 181
    Fantasy 52, 58, 166, 181, 192
    Geneva edge 181
    Solid color blossoms 181
Blossoms
    Color of 110
    Deformed 191
    Grooming 112
    Quantity of 108
    Size and type 109
Blooming 76–81
Blooming schedule 81–85
Botrytis 19, 43, 79, 113, 116, 117
Broad mites 126, 148

Calcium carbonate 30

Carbon dioxide 40, 55
Charcoal 30
Chemicals (See pesticides)
Chimera xvi, 51, 62, 64, 166, 167, 181
Chlorine 18, 47, 117, 119, 120, 148
Chlorophyll 11, 36, 40, 46, 89, 96–99, 115, 142, 146
Chlorosis 36, 38
Cleanliness 134–138
Climate 45, 46, 143, 183, 202–203
Container gardens 174, 177
Copyright law 51
Crown 11, 59–65, 73, 92, 106, 113, 118
    Multiple crown (See suckers, trailers)
Crowns, problems 18, 37, 60, 65, 73, 117–118, 122, 126, 127, 144, 147, 148, 197
Crown rot 67, 116, 117, 119, 144, 195
Crown variegation 96, 181
Cultural conditions 36–39, 69, 81, 101, 122, 139–143, 164
Cultivars 3, 192
Cultural perfection 107
Cyclamen mites 44, 60, 79, 126, 148

Deformities 191–194
Design 174–179
    Container gardens 174, 177
    Interpretive plant arrangements 176
    Interpretive flower arrangements 177
Diatomaceous earth 130
Disbudding 65, 80, 83, 85, 89, 109
Dolomite lime 19, 29, 30, 91, 142, 203

Erwinia 121

Fantasy blossoms 52, 58, 166, 181, 192
Fertilizer, Fertilizing 27, 30, 32, 34–39, 78, 89, 124, 130, 210
    Ammoniacal nitrogen 35, 38
    Ammonium phosphate 35
    Blood meal 30
    Constant fertilizer method 14
    Cottonseed meal 30
    Fertilizer burn 17, 18
    Fertilizer salts 17, 37, 135, 206, 209
    Fish emulsion 37, 38, 57, 58, 89, 99
    Foliar feeding 37, 57, 89, 99, 100
    Inorganic fertilizer 32, 38, 124, 130
    Macronutrients 18
    Micronutrients 18, 37
    Nitrogen 18, 31, 35–37, 57, 89, 97–99, 121
    Nitrate-based fertilizer 35
    Organic fertilizer 30, 34, 37 (See fish emulsion)
    Over-fertilizing 36–38, 91
    Phosphorus 18, 35, 37, 78, 83, 202, 206
    Potassium 18, 35
    Slow-release fertilizer 30, 35
    Trace elements 35, 37
    Urea-based fertilizer 29, 35, 37, 38, 142
Fertilizer problems, deficiency 36
First Class xiii, 110
Fish emulsion 37, 38, 57, 58, 89, 99
Fluorescent Light (See Lighting)
Foliage
    Rosette foliage 56, 59, 92, 94, 106
    Variegated (See variegation)
Foliar feeding 37, 57, 89, 99, 100
Foliar mealy bugs 127, 148
Fungicides 31, 117–121, 135
Fungus gnats 20, 119, 127, 134
Fungus, fungi 19, 115–121, 148
    Botrytis 19, 43, 79, 113, 116, 117
    Crown rot 67, 116, 119, 144, 195

Phytophthora 116, 117, 118, 144
Powdery mildew xv, 19, 43, 47, 79, 116, 119, 120, 121, 187
Pythium 32, 116, 117, 118, 144
Root rot 28, 32, 88, 117, 118, 148, 209

Genetic differences 3, 4
Genetic trait 11, 75, 79, 161, 192
Geneva edge 181
Gesneriads 169–173
Greenhouse 28, 31, 40, 46, 125, 129, 203, 204
Growing conditions (See Cultural conditions)
Grooming xv, 12, 65, 94, 112–114, 187, 199, 200–206

Humidity 17, 19, 41, 47, 77, 92, 115, 119–121, 140, 146, 152, 159, 209
Hybrids xiv, 11, 51, 59, 60, 95, 96, 99, 150, 165, 170, 181, 192, 198
Hybridizing xiv, xv, xvi, 152, 158, 161, 162, 192
Hibernation 145, 186

Impatiens Necrotic Spot Virus (INSV) 122
Insecticides (See Pesticides)
Insects (See Pests)
Interpretive flower arrangements 177
Interpretive plant arrangements 176

Judging 104–111

Latitude 45
Leaching 14, 17, 37
Leaf bleaching 11, 77, 142
Leaf cuttings (See Propagation)
Leaf stems 3, 21, 46, 117
Leaves, myths 196, 197
Light/Lighting 3–12, 45, 145, 185
    Artificial light 4, 5, 84, 92, 153, 209
    Color spectrum 5

Cool white tubes 9
Electricity costs, 8
Fluorescent lighting 4–6
Fluorescent light units 6
Fluorescent tubes 7–9, 107, 205
Gro-lux tubes 9
Growing under lights 7
Incandescent light 5
Infrared 5
Kilowatt hours (KWH) 8
Light spectrum 5
Light waves 5
Natural light 4, 9, 12, 48, 94, 142, 153, 184
Phosphors 5
Ultraviolet light tubes 6
Wide spectrum tubes 9
Light requirements 3, 76, 82, 185, 209

Macronutrients 18
Magnesium carbonate 30
Mail order 180–183
Master Variety List (See AVML)
Micronutrients 18, 37
Mildew (See fungus, powdery mildew)
Miniatures 74, 87, 92, 175
Mites
    Broad mites 126, 148
    Cyclamen mites 44, 60, 79, 126, 148
Mold 116
Mutant, Mutation 149, 164, 167 (See sports)

Neck 68–71, 108, 114, 201 (See repotting)
Nematodes 27, 32
Nitrogen 18, 31, 35–37, 57, 89, 97–99, 121 (See fertilizer)

Orange crust 60

Pathogens 31, 32, 43, 68, 115–117, 136, 144, 148
Pasteurization (soil) 32

Peat moss 27–29 (See potting mix)
Peduncles 46
Perlite 16, 18, 22, 27–32, 42, 54, 72, 91, 127, 140, 200, 203, 210 (See potting mix)
Pesticides 31, 24, 125, 124–132
Pests 17, 79, 124–133, 147
    Broad mites 126, 148
    Cyclamen mites 44, 60, 79, 126, 148
    Foliar mealy bugs 127, 148
    Fungus gnats 20, 119, 127, 135
    Incidental chewing insects 128
    Nematodes 27, 32
    Soil mealy bugs 79, 127, 148
    Springtails 128, 1134
    Thrips xv, 43, 59, 79, 122, 125, 130, 148, 160, 187
Petioles 3, 5, 21, 46, 69, 76, 106, 141, 14, 194
pH 18, 19, 29, 32, 36, 39, 47, 67, 72, 78, 91, 98, 140, 141, 142
Photosynthesis 11, 34, 40, 42, 80, 97, 135, 146, 186
Phosphorus (See fertilizer)
Phytophthora 116, 117, 118, 144
Pistil 158, 160
Plant light requirements 3, 76, 82, 185, 209
Plant metabolism 37
Plant size
    Standard single crowned 92, 93
    Large standards 75, 85, 86–90,
    Miniatures 74, 87, 92, 175
    Semiminiatures 74, 97, 92–93, 175
Pollen sacs 43, 79, 125, 158, 160
Pollination 160
Pollution 43
Potassium 18, 35
Pot size 23, 74, 85, 88, 108, 211
Pots 21–25, 27, 143, 210
    Clay pots 21–25, 139, 141, 143, 197, 198, 203, 204, 211
    Novelty pots 24, 202
    Plastic pots 21–27, 139–142, 202, 204, 210
Potting 73–75, 88 (See repotting)

Over-sized pots 78
Over-potting 147
Potting mix 26–33, 67, 72, 78, 141, 210
    Commercial soil mixes 26, 48, 141
    Organic soil 27, 32, 33
    Porosity 28, 88
    Soilless potting medium 27
Potting mix ingredients 26–31
    Coconut coir 31
    Dolomite lime 29, 30
    Horticultural charcoal 30
    Peat moss 27–29
    Perlite (See perlite)
    Rock wool 31
    Styrofoam beads 31
    Vermiculite (See vermiculite)
Powdery mildew 43, 47, 79, 116, 119–121, 187
Propagation, propagating 51–58, 92
    Blossom stem 551, 552, 62,
    Leaf cuttings 47, 51–58, 62, 64, 92, 100, 116, 122, 180, 181, 192, 203
    Suckers (See suckers)
Pythium 32, 116, 117, 118, 144

Repotting 12, 66–75, 82, 203
Root ball 23, 27, 42, 67, 71, 72, 75, 77, 84, 141, 201
Root rot 28, 32, 88, 117, 118, 148, 209
Root system 23, 27, 42, 47, 56, 60, 67, 72, 88, 143
Rooting hormones 55, 75
Roots
    Fibrous 28, 31, 42, 54, 67, 98, 179, 172
    Scaly rhizomes 170
    Tuberous 179–171

Rosette foliage 56, 59, 92, 94, 106

Saintpaulia xiii, 10, 151–154, 162, 169, 172

Sanitation 134
Scale of points 105, 111
Secondary crowns 61–63, 67, 113
Seedlings 158, 161, 162, 167, 192
Seedpod 162
Self-pollination 159, 160
Semiminiatures 74, 97, 92–93, 175
Soil bacteria 26, 35, 39, 98, 140, 141
Soil mealy bugs 79, 127, 148 (See pests)
Soil pH 18, 19, 32, 36, 39, 78, 141, 142
Spagnum peat moss 28–29 (See potting mix)
Species xiii, xv, xvi, 10, 12, 21–23, 53, 61, 64, 80, 91, 94–95, 117, 121, 148–155, 157, 159, 161, 162, 169, 172, 173, 198
Springtails 128, 134
Sports, sporting 52, 164–168 (See mutation)
Starter plants 74
Stunting 60
Suckers 51, 59–67, 84, 92, 93, 110, 111, 113, 148, 154–155, 157, 161, 193, 203, 211
Surfactant 30
Systemic pesticide 130
Symmetry 3, 5, 61, 62, 64, 92, 105–108, 169, 182

Temperature 5, 40–46, 78, 88, 98, 140, 184, 172, 210
Terrarium 47, 57, 60, 171
Texas-Style Potting 16, 77
Thrips xv, 43, 59, 79, 122, 125, 130, 148, 160, 187 (See pests)
Toxicity 29, 37, 38, 39, 131, 132
Trace elements 35, 37
Trailers/trailing varieties 12, 93, 94
Transplanting (See repotting)
Transpiration 41, 42, 141

Urea-based fertilizer 29, 35, 37, 38, 142

Variegation/variegated foliage xv, 7, 35, 36, 41, 46, 52, 57, 84, 96–100, 157, 165, 180

Vermiculite 27, 29, 31, 42, 54, 90, 140, 159, 161, 200, 203, 210 (See potting mix)
Vintage Violets 194
Virus disease 148

Water/water quality 13–20, 47, 77
    Chloramines 18
    Chlorine 18, 47, 117, 119, 120, 140
    Distilled water 19
    Mineral content 18
    Nitrate levels 18
    Rain water 19
    Reverse osmosis 19
    Water pH 18–19, 47, 140, 142
Watering methods 77, 87, 144–145, 185–186
    Capillary action 14, 15
    Capillary matting 15, 17
    Constant water methods 14, 34, 77 202
    Self-watering pots 16, 87, 91, 209
    Texas-style potting/watering 16
    Top-watering 13, 14
    Wick-watering 14, 15, 91, 153, 186
Watering problems
    Over-watering 145, 195
    Water-deprived 67, 145
Weather 5
Wetting agent 30
Window Growing 5, 9–12, 45, 94, 95, 142, 196

978-0-595-44344-4
0-595-44344-3

Made in the USA